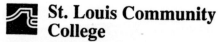

Count Dracula Goes to the Movies

Count Dracula Goes to the Movies

Stoker's Novel Adapted, 1922–1995

by

Lyndon W. Joslin

McFarland & Company, Inc., Publishers
Jefferson, North Carolina, and London

Library of Congress Cataloguing-in-Publication Data

Joslin, Lyndon W., 1956–
    Count Dracula goes to the movies : Stoker's novel adapted,
1922–1995 / by Lyndon W. Joslin.
      p.   cm.
    Includes bibliographical references and index.
    ISBN 0-7864-0698-4 (illus. case binding : 50# alk. paper) ∞
    1. Stoker, Bram, 1847–1912. Dracula.   2. Stoker, Bram,
1847–1912—Film and video adaptations.   3. Horror tales,
English—Film and video adaptations.   4. Dracula, Count
(Fictitious character)   5. Dracula films—History and criticism.
6. Vampire films—History and criticism.   I. Title.
PR6037.T617D784   1999
791.43'6—dc21   99-16978
                                                                CIP

British Library Cataloguing-in-Publication data are available

Manufactured in the United States of America

McFarland & Company, Inc., Publishers
  Box 611, Jefferson, North Carolina 28640
   www.mcfarlandpub.com

For Emily.
Also for Mom, who was afraid
these movies would warp me.
(She was right.)

Acknowledgments

Thanks to Mr. Jeffrey "Perfect Pitch" Ragsdale for the information about the musical selections. What I know about music would almost fill a small thimble.

Thanks to Mr. Christopher Lee, the last of the greats, for years and years of entertainment. Because of him and Peter Cushing, I couldn't pass Hammer Funeral Home, in the Louisiana town where I grew up, without a shudder at the thought of what must be going on in the back room. When Mr. Cushing died, I joined some friends for a Peter Cushing Memorial Video Fest. May such a tribute to Mr. Lee be years away.

Thanks to Mr. John Wesley Downey, my agent, of Good Karma Management, for his belief and enthusiasm. (Thanks also to John for pointing out the correct spelling of "Jonathan." To get *that* wrong would have been embarrassing.)

Thanks to Mr. Ron Borst of Hollywood Movie Posters, and to Howard Mandelbaum of Photofest, for the stills illustrating this book. The captions are all quotes from Stoker, even if the context sometimes suffers.

Thanks to everyone involved in any way with the creation of the films reviewed in this book, even the ones I don't particularly like. Hard work is hard work.

Sleep well, Soledad.

Table of Contents

Introduction:
The Novel as Basis for Film

In my college years, the professor under whom I studied world literature later taught a course about novels and their film adaptations. Having fulfilled my English requirements, and having a full slate of other studies to pursue, I didn't take this particular course, interesting though it sounded.

Late in the quarter, I stopped by the professor's office for a visit, as I occasionally did; we were on friendly terms, her world lit course having been a pleasant experience. I asked her how the film course had gone, and she sank deep into her chair. She confessed that it had left her depressed and frustrated, and had led her to the conclusion that novels simply cannot be filmed.

Much has been said about the differences between literary works (such as novels) and temporal works (such as plays and movies). Much debate has been carried on as to whether, in fact, any literary work, whether a novel, a short story, or even a play intended for the stage, can be adapted to the screen.

One of my earliest experiences with the difference between a movie and a novel from which it was adapted was the H.G. Wells work *The War of the Worlds* (1953). In the pre–VCR days of my childhood, I caught every TV screening I could of the movie, which had come out a few years before I was born. (I didn't see it on the big screen until a 25th anniversary re-release in 1978.) I must have read the book when I was nine or ten, an illustrated, school-kid-oriented, unabridged copy I still own.

Having seen the movie first, I was initially baffled by the book. The movie is set primarily in California, though with scenes from around the world, as a solidly American cast battles the goons from deep space. Yet the book opens in England before the turn of the century! I didn't get it then, but I soon forgot the time-space discrepancy and found myself absorbed in Wells' gripping tale.

Years later, after I'd become familiar with certain pragmatic realities of filmmaking, the reasons for the update and the relocation of Wells' story became clear to me. For one thing, "period pieces" are always more expensive to make than contemporary stories. For another, the movie was made by an American studio primarily for American audiences, and since Americans are famously provincial (probably even more then than now), the setting was changed to America. Finally, budget considerations most likely played a large part in changing the Martian war machines from walking tripods (which could have been done, expensively, with stop-motion animation) to death-dealing, wire-hung boomerangs.

That said, what remains in the transition from page to screen? A few narrative crumbs survive more-or-less intact, and in the end, germs save the day. While differing widely in detail, the screen and page stories are essentially similar; thus, the spirit, the kernel, the "gist" of the novel survived.

The primary criterion, then, as to whether or not a filmed adaptation of a novel is successful is whether the novel's spirit is preserved in the transition. The adapters can merge or even delete characters, telescope events, rearrange chronology all they want, as long as what the story is really about is preserved. Conversely, the adapters can include minute details and reams of dialogue from the novel ... yet still miss the point. An example is the 1974 version of F. Scott Fitzgerald's *The Great Gatsby*, which—by attempting to include every detail, every incident, and every word of dialogue from the novel—turns a slim little volume into an almost two-and-a-half-hour talkathon that wallows in exactly the sort of "appalling sentimentality" that the novel's narrator, Nick Carraway, deplores.

Of course, there are degrees of both success and failure. An adaptation that preserves the novel's spirit may do so by the skin of its teeth. For example, *Charly* (1968), adapted from *Flowers for Algernon* by Daniel Keyes, features an Oscar-winning performance by Cliff Robertson in the title role of a retarded man turned into a genius by an experimental operation. The film successfully captures the novel's poignancy concerning the unexpected consequences of such an experiment. But in addition to making use of badly-dated 1960s film gimmicks (multiple-screen images, *2001*-esque color distortions, etc.), it disappoints by rushing to its conclusion: the incident which gives the novel its title isn't even in the movie!

Then, too, a successful adaptation can still be, in other respects, a poorly-made movie. *The Last Man on Earth* (1964), the first screen version of Richard Matheson's *I Am Legend*, is a reasonably faithful adaptation, but it is desperately low-budget, and looks it; even Vincent Price, miscast in the title role, seems to be slumming. (Its next version, 1971's *The Omega Man*, with Charlton Heston, is a slick, big-budget affair that goes completely off the rails.)

An adaptation that fails to preserve the "gist," which can range from barely missing the mark to being astonishingly wrong-headed, may be a delight in other ways. *2001* (1968) and *The Shining* (1980) are two prime examples of the striking differences that can arise between a picture-taker (Stanley Kubrick) and a storyteller (Arthur C. Clarke and Stephen King, respectively, both of whom were disgruntled by the adaptations). Yet while *2001* is widely regarded as one of the greatest films ever made, *The Shining* was so unsatisfactory, to both King and his readers, that it was remade as a TV miniseries in 1997.

Comes now *Dracula*, written by Bram (Abraham) Stoker (1848–1912), published in 1897 and never out of print since. In 1997, we saw not only the hundredth anniversary of the novel's publication, but the 75th anniversary of its first (or, at any rate, earliest surviving) film adaptation in 1922 (also the year, incidentally, of the birth of Christopher Lee, an actor much associated with the film role of the Count). Much has been said and written about Stoker himself, and of the research, background, and inspiration that went into writing the novel. These considerations, other than some delving into historical and folkloric aspects that influenced both the novel and its film versions, are beyond the scope of this book. So, too, here at the end of the first century of *Dracula*, is the extent to which the Count has become so very much a part of pop culture, turning up in every medium from TV series to cartoons to comic books. The primary focus here is a comparison of the film adaptations (including made-for-TV movies) of Stoker's original story that have been produced between 1922 and 1995. Of these adaptations, there are almost a dozen.

I omit the following productions: a 1956 or 1957 NBC-TV version starring the late John Carradine, who had played the Count on stage and screen before; a 1965 British TV production with a wildly miscast Denholm Elliott; and a 1973 Canadian TV version. Copies of these offerings, if they exist at all, are as rare as hens' teeth. If anyone can provide information as to where a copy of any of these adaptations can be found, I would be greatly indebted. Also apparently lost are two unauthorized 1920 versions, one Russian, one Hungarian, and a 1952 Turkish opus, *Drakula Istanbul'da*, supposed to have been based on both the Stoker novel and the life of Prince Vlad the Impaler—with the Ottoman spin on it, one presumes. There reportedly is a 1997 Irish television version that relocates Dracula's destination to County Sligo in northern Ireland!

With so many adaptations missing in action, whenever I state that this or that version is the first or the only version to include a particular feature of the novel, I refer necessarily to the versions under consideration. I've read, for example, that in *Drakula Istanbul'da*, the Count climbs down the outer wall of his castle. If true, then this version is the first one in which he does so, long before the 1977 BBC-TV adaptation with Louis Jourdan. Not having seen the Turkish film, however (as apparently almost no one in the U.S. has, and not many people in Turkey), I must give this nod to the newer version.

After the examination of each pure adaptation in its turn, two additional sections will provide an overview of the Dracula series by Universal Studios and Hammer Films, these being the only two major studios to make a regular "franchise" out of Dracula movies (along with other Gothics, including Frankenstein). Emphasis will be on the development (or lack thereof) of Stoker's character through these two very different series. A final section will take a brief, non-exhaustive look at what can be called "Shadows of Stoker": the novel's ongoing influence on films that, while not adaptations, clearly borrow elements of *Dracula*—characters, dialogue, even entire scenes.

Dracula is certainly one of the most-filmed characters in all fiction—maybe *the* most. Films that include him (however briefly) number more than two hundred by some tallies. Figures differ, since some enumerators may include films that despite their titles (e.g., *Blood of Dracula* or *Countess Dracula*) have nothing to do with Dracula at all. Other difficulties present themselves. For example, in *The Magic Christian* (1969), Christopher Lee, star of the Hammer Dracula series, has a cameo as a vampire on board a luxury liner. Is he Dracula? If so, does his fleeting appearance make *The Magic Christian* a "Dracula movie"? A book attempting to catalog every *bona fide* Dracula movie, with or without including sightings such as that in *The Magic Christian*, would run the risk of bogging down in quibbling over trivia. I prefer, therefore, to stick to a comparative discussion of the adaptations themselves, and of the series of sequels spawned by two of them. Of most other movies about, or featuring, Dracula—the various spin-offs, knock-offs, rip-offs, and the encounters with space aliens, bikini girls, and Billy the Kid—the less said, the better.

Prolific authors Raymond T. McNally and Radu Florescu, experts on all things Dracula (who have, if anything, made a few too many trips to the well), wrote a 1989 biography of Vlad the Impaler (their second) titled *Dracula: Prince of Many Faces.* That title serves us well here, since, even in the relative handful of films under consideration, the Count comes to us in many guises: as a gaunt, rat-faced, pestilential presence; as a suave, tuxedoed Continental gentleman; as a fierce aristocrat almost (but not quite) devoid of any trace of humanity; as a hard-nosed old (*old*) soldier; as a venomous seducer; as a pseudo-Byronic lover-boy wannabe; as a spidery, love-starved old creep; as a romantic fop blubbering over his lost love; and, most recently, as a clown. He comes to us speaking German, English, Spanish, even a smattering of his native Romanian. He comes sometimes in forms Bram Stoker would have recognized, but more often would not have. For as Professor Van Helsing points out, Dracula is a shapeshifter.

The surrounding story, too, is never quite the same twice; like the same story told by different eyewitnesses, the tale, from one telling to the next, sometimes varies in a few details, sometimes changes almost beyond recognition. And its characters shift and blur, merge and reemerge, vanish and reappear, take on each other's names and identities, depending on the telling.

Sometimes the spirit of Stoker's novel travels with them. Sometimes it, too, is distorted, or is lost entirely. Let's go to the movies. Count Dracula, in one form or another, is waiting there in the dark.

I. Stoker's Novel Adapted

For comparison purposes, we begin this section with an episodic synopsis of the novel, which will emphasize only the more visual (and, rarely, aural) aspects of the novel, including characters, action, and some minor details, since these are what end up on the screen in the various film adaptations.

Our consideration of each film version will likewise begin with a synopsis, with the novel's synopsis serving as both model and yardstick. Whenever possible, similar or identical language is used to describe parallel incidents in novel and film which, at first look, may seem quite different, in order to underscore the similarity between them. "A violent confrontation ensues," for instance, covers everything from fistfights to running gun battles. This descriptive broadness also serves to illustrate that different films have parallels between scenes, even when those scenes are not found in the novel. To give one very non-Stoker example: The synopses of *Horror of Dracula* (1958) and the TV movie *Dracula* (1973) both feature the following sentence: "Jonathan, now a vampire, must be killed with a stake." True enough in both films (just one of a number of parallels between these two particular versions, as will be seen), although a viewing of the two of them would reveal very different circumstances.

Since some of the film versions use reams of the novel's dialogue, to list every incidence of a Stoker line onscreen would be cumbersome. Thus, only a few key lines will be featured within each synopsis (one of which, perhaps surprisingly, is *not* from Stoker at all, but is an invention of the movies, and a perennial favorite. You'll know it when you see it.)

Commentary follows each synopsis, concluding with consideration of the question of how well each version, in its turn, captures the spirit of Stoker's novel. After each review is a brief discussion of the musical score of the movie in question, with emphasis on the main title theme—its style, structure, and instrumentation—and an indication of whether a commercially released recording of the music is available.

A Synopsis of Stoker's Novel

The year is not given, but is sometime in the late 19th century. On behalf of his employer, Mr. Hawkins, Jonathan Harker travels to Transylvania to close a real estate transaction with Count Dracula.

Jonathan keeps a written daily journal. He receives a letter from Dracula.

En route, Jonathan meets fearful, superstitious people at an inn and on a coach. They are frightened at the mention of Dracula's name, and because it is the eve of St. George's Day, when the forces of evil take command at midnight, a woman gives him a crucifix, which she says is "for your mother's sake." One of the other passengers says "the dead travel fast."

On the coach to Bukovina, drawn by four horses harnessed abreast, another passenger explains to Jonathan that a gesture he saw directed toward him by peasants at the inn is a charm to ward off the evil eye.

The coach only takes him as far as the Borgo Pass, where Dracula's own carriage picks him up. The Count himself, in disguise, drives the carriage. He offers Jonathan a cloak and a flask.

En route to the castle, the carriage is pursued by wolves. The Count dismounts from the driver's seat and sends them away. Jonathan sees mysterious blue flames flickering all along the roadside.

At the castle, Jonathan is greeted by Dracula, who is tall, thin, white-haired, and very pale. The Count carries a lamp and is dressed totally in black. He has a white mustache, noticeably sharp teeth, pointed fingernails, hair in the center of his palms, and pointed ears.

Dracula helps Jonathan with his bags and shows him to his room, making excuses as to the absence of his servants.

Jonathan enjoys a supper in which the Count does not join him. The table settings are of solid gold. Wolves howl outside, and the Count remarks, "Listen to them—the children of the night! What music they make!"

Jonathan notices that there are no mirrors in the castle.

Later, Jonathan discovers the library.

Jonathan and Dracula discuss the sale of the old house in London, which is called Carfax.

Jonathan cuts himself shaving. In his shaving mirror, he notices that the Count has no reflection. The sight of blood excites the Count, but he is repulsed by the crucifix. Dracula breaks Jonathan's mirror by dropping it out the window.

Jonathan realizes he is a prisoner in the castle.

Dracula tells Jonathan about Transylvanian history. He then tells Jonathan he must stay at the castle for a month, in order to help the Count perfect his English. He instructs Jonathan to write false letters home, saying he has already left Transylvania.

Looking out a window, Jonathan sees Dracula climb head-first down an outer wall on two separate occasions.

Jonathan is attacked by three vampire women, two brunettes and a blonde. The attack is stopped by the Count, who gives them a baby to feed on. Jonathan awakes later in his room.

Jonathan tries to mail a shorthand letter to Mina Murray, his fiancée, by tossing it to some workers outside the castle with a gold piece. But they give the letter to the Count, who burns it as Jonathan watches.

A woman comes to the castle pleading for the return of her child. Wolves kill her.

Jonathan confronts Dracula about his being detained. The Count tells him he is free to leave whenever he pleases, but when he tries, wolves bar his way.

In desperation, Jonathan climbs out his window and down an outer wall. He finds a vault in which the Count reposes in a coffin-like box. He is in a death-like trance, with blood on his mouth, and he appears to be younger. Jonathan also finds, in a similar state, the three women. Jonathan tries to kill the Count with a shovel, but fails, whereupon he flees in terror.

Jonathan waits helplessly as Dracula's final travel preparations are made. Dracula departs, leaving Jonathan at the castle, at the mercy of the three women. Jonathan makes a desperate leap to escape, not to be heard from again for many weeks.

Back in England, Lucy Westenra becomes engaged to Arthur Holmwood, a young nobleman, having also been courted by Dr. John Seward and by Quincey P. Morris, a Texan.

Dr. Seward keeps a phonograph journal.

Renfield is a patient in an insane asylum run by Dr. Seward. He catches and eats insects and birds in the belief that he can thereby absorb their souls and prolong his own life. Renfield asks Dr. Seward for a kitten.

Mina, Lucy's best friend and Jonathan's fiancée, also keeps a diary.

Mina and Lucy go to Whitby for the summer.

Along with fifty boxes of earth, Dracula travels, first by cart, then by river boat, and finally by ship, to England. En route, he terrorizes and kills the crew of the ship, the *Demeter*. The crew's fate is ultimately learned from the ship's log and a note found in the captain's pocket.

The ship weathers a storm and drifts into port at Whitby. A "large dog", evidently Dracula incognito, leaps from the ship and runs away. The ship's captain is found dead and lashed to the wheel, a crucifix in his hand. The rest of the crew are missing. A newspaper account tells the story.

The paper also reports that Mr. Swales, a colorful local seaman who used to visit Mina and Lucy during their walks in a seaside cemetery, is found dead shortly after the ship's arrival.

Lucy walks in her sleep. Mina follows her to the cemetery and sees her being preyed upon by Dracula, who disappears. Mina pins a shawl around Lucy's shoulders and walks her back to her room.

Lucy suffers from a mysterious illness that leaves her pale and weak. She also has two tiny wounds on her throat. Mina thinks the wounds were caused by the pin she used to fasten the shawl.

Dracula's boxes are moved to Carfax by a moving company.

Jonathan is nursed back to health in a convent hospital in Europe. Mina goes abroad to bring him home.

Renfield becomes excited and briefly escapes when Dracula moves into Carfax, which is next door to Dr. Seward's asylum. Renfield is linked to the Count because his particular pathology makes him vulnerable to the Count's influence.

Dr. Seward, upset over having his proposal to Lucy rejected, considers taking chloral to help him sleep.

Jonathan and Mina are married abroad.

Returning with her mother to their London estate of Hillingham, Lucy is placed in the care of Dr. Seward. Lucy's illness baffles Dr. Seward, so he sends for Professor Abraham Van Helsing, his former professor, to come from Amsterdam to have a look at her.

Despite transfusions from Arthur, Dr. Seward, Van Helsing, and Quincey, Lucy continues to waste away because of nightly visits from Dracula.

Van Helsing places garlic in Lucy's room and prepares a wreath of it for her to wear in her sleep. But her mother removes it, with disastrous results.

Renfield attacks Dr. Seward, cutting his wrist and lapping up the blood from the floor. "The blood is the life!" he cries.

In order to get to Lucy, Dracula drugs all the servants in her home with laudanum.

The window to Lucy's room is broken by a wolf which, under the Count's control, has escaped from a nearby zoo. Lucy's mother, who is in the room at the time, dies of a heart attack.

Lucy's teeth seem to be longer and sharper.

Jonathan and Mina return from Europe.

A number of the Count's boxes are removed from Carfax, which greatly disturbs Renfield.

The wounds completely disappear from Lucy's throat overnight. On her deathbed, Lucy speaks with strange seductiveness to Arthur. Van Helsing prevents him from kissing her.

Shortly afterward, Lucy dies and is buried.

Jonathan is shocked to see Dracula in the streets of London, looking younger still.

Lucy, now a vampire, victimizes children, who claim to have been with a "bloofer [beautiful] lady." These attacks are described in a newspaper clipping.

Mina and Van Helsing read Jonathan's diary to learn what they can of Dracula.

Van Helsing reveals that the wounds in the children's throats were not made in the same way as Lucy's wounds, but were made *by* Lucy.

Van Helsing leads Dr. Seward to the graveyard. Inside the tomb, Lucy's coffin is empty. Afterwards, they find nearby a child who is unharmed.

The next day, Van Helsing and Dr. Seward return to the graveyard. They discover that Lucy has returned to her grave.

That night, Van Helsing returns to the graveyard with Arthur, Dr. Seward, and Quincey. Again, Lucy's coffin is empty. Soon, Lucy returns to the tomb, carrying a child, whom she carelessly drops when she is confronted by Van Helsing and the others. After trying to sweet-talk Arthur, she retreats from a crucifix and re-enters the tomb.

Van Helsing and the others return to the tomb the next day. Arthur stakes Lucy, whereupon the peace of true death is seen on her face. Van Helsing then decapitates her and fills her mouth with garlic.

After everyone compares notes, it is discovered that the Count's home at Carfax is right next door to Dr. Seward's asylum.

Mina takes a room in the residential wing of the asylum, where Jonathan will soon join her.

Jonathan, meanwhile, has traveled to Whitby, where he learns that all of the Count's boxes were transferred to Carfax by the firm of Carter Paterson.

Mina pays Renfield a visit.

Van Helsing, Jonathan, Mina, Dr. Seward, Arthur, and Quincey agree to join forces against Dracula. Van Helsing tells the others of his suspicions regarding Dracula: the Count is centuries old; he can transform himself into a wolf, a bat, or a mist; he casts neither shadow nor reflection. But the Count has his limitations: he can't enter a building unless he's invited; he rests by day in his box of earth, and although his powers cease by day, he can and does come out in daylight if he must; he is repelled by garlic and crucifixes; he can be killed with a stake through the heart or by decapitation. Van Helsing identifies the Count as "that Voivode Dracula."

Quincey takes a shot at a large bat flitting around outside. The bat is not harmed.

Van Helsing decides it would be best to exclude Mina, a mere woman, from the group effort to hunt down Dracula.

Renfield pleads with Dr. Seward to release him at once.

Van Helsing, Jonathan, Arthur, Quincey, and Dr. Seward infiltrate Carfax and count the boxes, determining some to be missing. At Carfax, they encounter a horrid smell and are attacked by rats.

Dracula turns his attention to Mina, entering her room as a mist while the men are at Carfax. Mina has a vivid nightmare about his visit.

Mina visits Renfield a second time. He can tell Dracula has been able to get to her.

Two nights later, Dracula deals Renfield a fatal injury. As he dies, Renfield reveals to Dr. Seward and Van Helsing that the Count has been entering the asylum through the window of his cell. Renfield reveals he invited Dracula into the asylum, thereby enabling him to get to Mina, because the Count promised him countless rats and other red-blooded animals as a means of prolonging his life. Dracula kills Renfield when Renfield tries to keep him from once again passing through his cell to attack Mina.

In order to get to Mina, Dracula casts a trance over Jonathan. Dracula forces Mina to drink some of his blood from a cut on his chest. Drinking his blood will create a psychic link between him and Mina so that he can compel her to obey him. Van Helsing and the other men burst in upon this scene. Jonathan's hair turns white when he wakes and sees what has happened.

It is decided that henceforth Mina should be included in the group's procedures.

Mina's "taint" is shown by a scar on her forehead, made by a communion wafer.

Van Helsing and the others seek out the rest of Dracula's boxes, in several other houses he has bought, and sterilize them all, including those still at Carfax, with communion wafers. After confronting them as they sterilize the last of the boxes, Dracula flees, leaping out a window.

Van Helsing must rely on Mina's psychic link to Dracula to learn where he is. Dracula is aboard the *Czarina Catherine*, a ship bound for the Black Sea port of Varna.

Mina shows increasing signs of becoming a vampire.

Van Helsing and the others travel by rail to Varna to await the arrival of the *Czarina Catherine*. But the Count, who can use Mina to learn of their whereabouts, outwits them, and the ship sails on to Galatz. Van Helsing and the others pursue Dracula to Transylvania.

The pursuers split up: Van Helsing and Mina travel by carriage, the others separately.

Near Dracula's castle, the three vampire women approach Van Helsing and Mina. Van Helsing encloses Mina in a circle of crumbled communion wafers, a barrier which neither she nor the women can cross. He holds the women at bay until they leave. The horses die of fright.

The next day, Van Helsing goes alone into the castle and kills the women, staking and beheading them. There is a tomb in the castle inscribed with the single word: DRACULA.

Just before sunset, Dracula approaches the castle. He is in a box on a wagon driven and guarded by Gypsies. A violent confrontation ensues, in which Quincey is mortally wounded.

Dracula is killed when Quincey stabs him in the heart with his Bowie knife and Jonathan decapitates him with his kukri. As Dracula dies, a look of peace is seen on his face. After his death, his body crumbles to dust, the scar fades from Mina's forehead, and Quincey dies.

◆

Nosferatu, eine Sinfonie des Grauens

(U.S. title: *Nosferatu, a Symphony of Horror*)

Prana Films (1922)
Directed by F. W. Murnau
Screenplay by Henrik Galeen
Running time: 1 hour 24 minutes.
(Beware cut version running 1 hour 3 minutes)
Available on video

Cast (names in parentheses as listed at the time of the film's original release):

COUNT DRACULA (GRAF ORLOK) . . . . .Max Schreck
RENFIELD (KNOCK) . . . . Alexander Granach
JONATHAN HARKER (THOMAS HUTTER) . . . . Gustav von Wangerheim
NINA (ELLEN) . . . . Greta Schroeder
WESTENRA (HARDING) . . . . G. H. Schell
LUCY (RUTH) . . . . Ruth Landshoff
THE PROFESSOR* (PROF. BULWER) . . . . .John Gottowt
THE TOWN DOCTOR (PROF. SIEVERS) . . . . .Gustav Botz
SHIP CAPTAIN . . . . Max Nemetz
FIRST MATE . . . . Wolfgang Heinz

*Pre-"restored" video versions list "the professor" in the credits, yet refer to him as "Professor Van Helsing" in the dialogue cards.

Synopsis

(Information in parentheses appears as it is featured in "restored" video editions, presumably meaning restored to the way it was when the film was first released): The year is 1838 (1843). On behalf of his employer, Mr. Renfield, Jonathan Harker travels to Transylvania to close a real estate deal with Count Dracula. The house he plans to sell the Count is in Bremen (Wisburg), across the street from the house where Jonathan lives with his wife, Nina. Jonathan leaves Nina in the care of his friend Westenra and his wife (sister), Lucy.

En route, Jonathan meets fearful, superstitious people at an inn. They are frightened at the mention of Dracula's name, and because they believe the forces of evil will take command after dark.

That night, Jonathan reads a book about vampires. Part of what he reads seems to indicate that the Count is centuries old. (No such indication originally.)

Next day, he catches a coach which only takes him as far as a certain point, and then he must walk. Later, Dracula's own carriage, driven by the Count himself in disguise, picks Jonathan up.

At the castle, Jonathan is greeted by Count Dracula. The Count is tall, thin, and very pale, and dresses totally in black. He is completely bald and has noticeably sharp teeth, pointed fingernails, and pointed ears.

The Count makes excuses as to the absence of his servants. He serves Jonathan a supper, but does not join him in eating it. Jonathan cuts himself on the thumb while slicing bread. The sight of blood excites the Count.

Jonathan awakes the next morning and learns that he's been bitten. In a letter he writes to Nina, he says he thinks they're

"... one of the men ... came to my cabin, and in an awestruck way confided to me that he
thought there was a strange man aboard the ship."—Log of the *Demeter*

Max Schreck as the vampire menaces the ship's captain in *Nosferatu* (1922)
(courtesy Ronald V. Borst of Hollywood Movie Posters)

bug bites of some sort. He mails the letter to Nina via a passerby on horseback.

Dracula sees and asks about a picture of Nina as he and Jonathan discuss the sale of the old house.

Jonathan is attacked by the Count. Meanwhile, back in Bremen, Nina walks in her sleep. The Count's attack is stopped by a psychic cry from Nina.

Jonathan realizes he is a prisoner in the castle. Looking for a way out, he finds a vault in which the Count reposes in a sarcophagus in a death-like trance. Jonathan flees in terror.

Later, Jonathan watches helplessly as Dracula makes his final travel prepara-

tions. Dracula departs, leaving Jonathan at the castle alone. Jonathan makes a desperate leap to escape, not to be heard from again for several weeks.

Along with six boxes of earth, Dracula travels first by cart, then by river boat, and finally by ship, to Germany.

Jonathan, meanwhile, is nursed back to health in a convent hospital.

Back in Bremen, Renfield (Knock), who seems to have become involved with the Count by unknown means before Jonathan's trip to Transylvania, has been institutionalized in an insane asylum. For unknown reasons, he eats insects. "Blood [is life]! Blood [is life]!" he cries.

Also in Bremen, Professor Van Helsing teaches his students about vampire-like creatures of nature, the Venus flytrap and the hydra. Jonathan, fully recovered, heads for home.

En route to Germany, Dracula terrorizes and kills the crew of the ship, the *Demeter*. (Originally unnamed.)

Meanwhile, in Bremen, Nina sleepwalks again.

The ship drifts into port in Bremen. When Dracula arrives in port, Renfield becomes excited, attacks one of the asylum attendants, and escapes.

Jonathan arrives in Bremen the same day as Dracula.

Dracula moves his boxes to his new home himself. (As a vampire, he draws his strength from the unholy soil they contain.)

The ship's captain is found dead and lashed to the wheel with two wounds on his throat. The rest of the crew are missing. The crew's fate is ultimately learned from the ship's log.

Panic breaks out when it is learned that the ship, swarming with rats, has brought the plague to town.

Against her husband's wishes, Nina reads the same book about vampires that Jonathan read.

Meanwhile, Lucy succumbs to the plague. Westenra goes to fetch the professor (Sievers).

Based on what she reads, Nina concludes the only way to kill the Count and rid her town of the plague is to sacrifice herself: she must entice the Count to come to her by night, then keep him at her side until daybreak.

(The frightened townsfolk believe Knock to be, not just an escaped lunatic, but the vampire and the source of the epidemic.)

As the time approaches, Nina sends Jonathan to fetch the professor (Bulwer).

Dracula is killed when he stays too long at Nina's side. The sun rises, vaporizing him. After Dracula's death, Renfield, who has been recaptured, mourns, and Nina dies, Jonathan and Van Helsing having arrived too late to save her. Like a miracle, the plague ends.

Commentary

One of the well-known ironies surrounding the original *Nosferatu* is that, although it was the first widely-known film version of *Dracula* (as opposed to the two earlier versions, one Russian and one Hungarian, which seem no longer to exist), it was an unofficial, plagiarized adaptation. The novel was still under copyright at the time, and although Bram Stoker himself had been dead since 1912, his widow, Florence, successfully sued Prana Films for copyright infringement. Part of the court's judgment was that all copies of the film were to be rounded up and destroyed.

This development brings us to another well-known irony: far from being snuffed out, *Nosferatu* is today F. W. Murnau's best-known film, rivaled only by his 1927 film *Sunrise* (which is archly referred to near the end of the 1994 film version of *Interview with the Vampire*).

Yet another irony: Plagiarized or not, *Nosferatu* is, for much of its running time, debatably the closest, most brilliantly-realized evocation of Stoker's original vision ever filmed. Certainly the vampire count is depicted much as Stoker describes him, here in Jonathan Harker's words: "... a tall old man ... clad in black from head to foot, without a single speck of colour about him anywhere.... His face was a strong—a very strong—aquiline, with high bridge of the thin nose ... with lofty domed forehead.... His eyebrows were very massive.... The mouth ... was fixed and rather cruel-looking, with peculiarly sharp white teeth; these protruded over

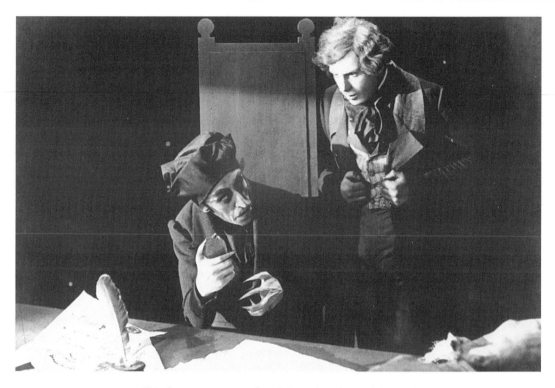

*"I had now an opportunity of observing him, and found him
of a marked physiognomy."*—Jonathan Harker

**Max Schreck as the Count and Gustav von Wangerheim as Jonathan Harker
in *Nosferatu* (1922) (courtesy Ronald V. Borst of Hollywood Movie Posters)**

the lips ... his ears were pale, and at the tops extremely pointed.... The general effect was one of extraordinary pallor. ... the [finger]nails were long and fine, and cut to a sharp point." The only significant difference between Stoker's description and the film's interpretation is that the Count, in the novel, has white hair (at first) and a full mustache, while in the film, he is totally bald. Together with his pallor and his skeletal thinness, the baldness of his "lofty domed forehead" creates a skull-like appearance.

The actor behind this ghastly face was named Max Schreck, long thought to be a pseudonym, since "schreck" is German for "terror." That this was his real name doesn't keep some people from making a film-hipster's joke out of it: in *Batman Returns* (1992), Christopher

Walken plays a character named Max Schreck.

As indicated above, when the film was first produced, the names of the characters were all changed in an unsuccessful attempt to mask the plagiarism. (Attentive film viewers will recognize the name "Orlok" as the inspiration for the name of the autobiographical character, Byron Orlok, played by Boris Karloff in Peter Bogdanovich's excellent and unsettling 1968 film *Targets*, as well as catching an echo in the name of the vampire Count von Krolock in Roman Polanski's 1967 film *The Fearless Vampire Killers*.) Over the years, the pretense was dropped, so that by the time *Nosferatu* first came out on video, the characters' names were changed back, for the most part, to what Stoker had written. An exception lies in the Seward character, Professor Sievers, who simply became "the town doctor." The names "Westenra" and "Lucy" were given to characters to whom they did not apply, about which more later.

In more recent years, the "restored" video version has not only returned the names created by scriptwriter Henrik Galeen, but has also restored some twenty minutes of scenes that had gradually been pruned from the film over time, as well as the atmospheric tinting of the various scenes, and different (presumably more accurately translated) action and dialogue cards. (It should also be noted that, in the opening credits, the "restored" version admits, as the pre-"restored" version does, that the screenplay is based on Stoker's novel.) For the sake of consistency with the discussion of other versions, Stoker's names will be used.

Already we see a confusion, which will continue through most adaptations of *Dracula*, as to what, exactly, to make of Renfield. How to "explain" his involvement with Dracula? This version, which sees him as Jonathan's boss, who sends him to Transylvania no doubt knowing full well what will happen to him there, gives Renfield something more to do, plot-wise, than eat bugs and rant in an asylum cell. But that doesn't explain the mystery of Renfield's relationship with the Count; if anything, it only deepens it.

En route to the castle, Jonathan's ride in Dracula's carriage gives us a glimpse of the vampire's alternate universe. As evidenced by the speeding-up of the film, which sometimes makes modern audiences laugh (though usually not for long), the vampire experiences time and space differently from the way the living do. The scene lapses into the use of negative imagery: in the vampire's nocturnal existence, day is night, and dark is light, and vice versa.

Except for the absence of the three vampire women, Jonathan's experiences in Dracula's castle are much as Stoker describes them. Instead of the women, Jonathan is attacked by the Count himself. Nina, sleepwalking in Bremen, sends up a psychic cry which, the corresponding title cards tell us, warns Jonathan of the danger. Yet we can see what really happens: it is the Count, chillingly enough, who is on Nina's "wavelength" and hears the call.

Much has been made, in film commentary over the years, of the disturbing dichotomy between Nina's two "husbands," Jonathan and the Count. In addition to the Count's hearing her psychic alarm, Nina, in another somnambulant trance, also says ambiguously, "He is coming. I must go to him!"—as both Jonathan and Dracula separately approach Bremen. They both arrive in town the same day. The closest Stoker comes to explicitly "mirroring" Jonathan and Dracula is insofar as the Count's hair starts out white and later turns dark, while Jonathan's does just the opposite.

Even in this very first version, we already see the introduction of a non-Stoker plot device that has been enduringly popular in various adaptations of *Dracula*: a scene in which the Count asks Jonathan about a picture of, in this case, his wife. Other than an odd compliment about the loveliness of her throat, Dracula does nothing about the picture this time, which, as will be seen, is not always the case in other adaptations.

Dracula loads six boxes onto a cart and sets out for Bremen. (Since these six are the only ones we see, that is given as the total count in the synopsis above.) Being a complete loner—remember, he even drives his own carriage, albeit in disguise—the Count loads this cart unassisted, then climbs into a box which closes itself, via primitive stop-motion photography. The cart then takes off, driverless.

Discovered in his box in the cargo hold of the ship, the Count hinges upward from the heels in a horrifyingly impossible manner. Though this movement itself is not from the novel, it demonstrates the vampire's tendency to move unlike a normal, living human being as effectively as does Stoker's description of the Count climbing head-first down a wall (an image which would not be filmed until more than fifty years after *Nosferatu*). This spring-heeled jack-in-the-box gesture was later revived in *Bram Stoker's Dracula* and spoofed in *Dracula: Dead and Loving It*, as well as "borrowed" by the peculiar kung-fu vampire film *The Legend of the Seven Golden Vampires* (1974), and by the movie-movie *Fright Night* (1985).

Dracula's ship arrives in Bremen; ever the loner, he moves his boxes into his new home unaided, not even making use of the escaped Renfield. While the film does not grant him the power of transformation into a bat or wolf, Dracula can and does have the ability, as per Stoker, to walk through walls.

Next day, the captain of the otherwise unmanned ship is found dead; the ship's log reveals the terror and panic of the crew's last days....

And there, just over an hour into the film's running time (and less than fifty minutes into the "unrestored" version), the adaptation of Stoker comes to an end. What short time remains of the story is purely the invention of screenwriter Galeen.

In this reinvention, the long agony of Lucy Westenra, so central to the novel, does not take place at all. The woman traditionally identified as Lucy Westenra in *Nosferatu* is, in the film's original *dramatis personae*, Ruth, the sister (not the wife) of Harding, a friend of Jonathan's (i.e., Hutter's) with whom he leaves Nina (Ellen) when he departs from Bremen. The closest Ruth Harding comes to undergoing

anything like Lucy's slow death is when she succumbs to the plague. Her husband Westenra (or brother Harding) goes to fetch "the professor" (Sievers, originally), and that's that: this scene is unresolved even in the "restored" version.

While the plague Dracula brings to Bremen is, like most of the latter part of the film, a non-Stoker development, it's not devoid of a Stoker underpinning. The rats that spread the plague bring to mind Renfield's vision of the gift the Count offers him: "'Rats, rats, rats! Hundreds, thousands, millions of them ...' and I could see that there were thousands of rats with their eyes blazing red—like His, only smaller."

Then, too, the association of plague, or of lethal epidemics generally, with vampirism is valid from an anthropological/mythological standpoint as well. Paul Barber, in *Vampires, Burial, and Death*, points out the connections between vampirism and the plague, connections such as contagion and foul smells, which led to the early belief that vampires *caused* epidemics. This belief was itself a corollary of a much earlier belief, that death is caused by the dead, as jealous revenge against the living.

Similarly, the Rev. Montague Summers, in his encyclopedic study *The Vampire in Europe*, observes, "In his chronicle under the year 1343 Sebastian Moelers relates that during a terrible visitation of the Black Death cases of vampirism were numerous in the Tyrol...." The date is suspect, since the first European outbreak of what came to be known as the Black Death struck Sicily in 1347, not reaching Tyrol until sometime the following year. Summers continues, "At Danzig in 1855 [nearly contemporary with *Nosferatu*] there was a fearful outbreak of cholera, and it was bruited about the whole province that the dead returned as Vampires to fetch the living." Quoting from the historian William of Newburgh, Summers relates a case of a 12th-century vampire in Berwick, Scotland, in which people feared that "owing to the fact that black decomposition of this foul body horribly infected the air with poisonous pollution as it rushed to and fro, the plague or another fatal disease might break out and sweep many away, a disaster which had not infrequently been known to happen in circumstances similar to this."

Interestingly, Summers' book was published in 1929, well after the making of *Nosferatu*. Galeen and Murnau may have drawn on other sources of folkloric knowledge as their basis for the plague in their film; one hesitates to believe that such an appropriate inclusion is the result of nothing more than a lucky guess. Historical sources, too, may have lent inspiration: In *The Black Death*, Philip Ziegler writes, "Scandinavia was attacked by way of England. … [the plague] was carried by one of the wool ships which sailed from London in May, 1349. A member of the crew must have caught the plague just before sailing. … within a few days all the crew were dead. The vessel drifted helplessly until at last it ran aground somewhere near Bergen. The perplexed Norwegians ventured aboard and discovered, too late, what sort of cargo their visitors had brought." A strong parallel with the film is evident. Then, too, the plague first arrived in Sicily by ship. As carefully as Stoker researched his novel, one can only wonder why Dracula, arriving by ship, and with such a potent disease vector as an army of rats under his command, *doesn't* bring plague to London.

As the plague rages, Professor Bulwer, later renamed Van Helsing, plays no part in the discovery and destruction of the vampire in Bremen. He only enters the story towards the very end, when Nina sends Jonathan to fetch him … apparently to get Jonathan out of the house so she can keep her mutually fatal tryst with Dracula.

Shadowless in Stoker, Dracula here casts a menacing shadow that seems to precede him, almost to detach from him, to take on a "life" of its own. This tendency is most marked when, near the film's end, he stalks Nina: the shadow of his long-taloned hand flows across her and closes over her heart in such a way as to seize it … and she clearly feels its grasp. This use of a nearly or completely disembodied and strangely tangible shadow was a possible influence on Carl Dreyer's 1932 masterpiece, *Vampyr*, and was no doubt the cue for the Count's footloose shadow in *Bram Stoker's Dracula*.

As often happens to Dracula and other vampires in the movies, here he is done in by sunlight. Stoker's Dracula can and does come out in broad daylight; he does so in the novel three or four times. Nor does he come out only on cloudy or gloomy days: "It was a hot day for autumn," Mina writes in her journal of the day she and Jonathan encounter Dracula in Hyde Park, and so they find "a comfortable seat in a shady place." Not until *Bram Stoker's Dracula* do we find a Count who can so rub elbows with the diurnal populace.

It would seem, though, that Dracula's daytime appearances are not without risk. "His power ceases," Stoker has Van Helsing say, "as does that of all evil things, at the coming of the day…. Until [the sun] sets to-night, that monster … is confined within the limitations of his earthly envelope. He cannot melt into thin air nor disappear through cracks or chinks or crannies. If he go through a doorway, he must open the door like a mortal." In the novel, a sailor aboard the *Demeter* creeps up on Dracula by night and tries to stab him, "but the knife went through It, empty as air"; this incorporeality compares with a chilling scene in *Nosferatu* in which the

Count makes a spectral, translucent appearance on board the ship. By contrast, later in the novel, when the Count confronts Van Helsing's party as they sterilize the last of his boxes, Jonathan takes a swing at him with his kukri: "A second less and the trenchant blade had shorn through his heart. As it was, the point just cut the cloth of his coat, making a wide gap...." So being afoot in the daytime, per Stoker, evidently robs the Count of some of his nighttime invincibility. But at the time of Jonathan's attack, the 1:30 p.m. sun does the Count no harm at all.

Folkloric vampires, too, can shrug off the sun's rays. Summers, again quoting from William of Newburgh, tells of another 12th-century vampire who, after "he had harried people during the night alone, ... began to wander abroad in plain daylight, dreaded by all...." He further notes that, per a treatise by Allacci, the vampiric *vrykolakas* of the Greek archipelago "is so destructive to men that sometimes he appears in full daylight, even at noon." In his 1928 book *The Vampire: His Kith and Kin*, Summers writes that "vampires may wander abroad during the day, and that the vampire truly is *daemonium meridianum* (the noonday devil)."

What a startling revelation (I believe the trendy term is "paradigm shift") many people find this to be! They're usually as startled as is Van Helsing surrogate Professor T. Eliot Stokes (how's that for a pseudo-literary name?) upon seeing Barnabas Collins in broad daylight in *House of Dark Shadows* (1970). Vampires in daylight? The very idea yanks the rug out from under decades of vampire movies, many of them quite good. (One of the few other vampire-by-daylight movies that leap to mind is 1958's *Curse of the Undead*, a Gothic western about a vampire gunslinger which is therefore a tad difficult to take seriously. Another is 1974's *Captain Kronos: Vampire Hunter*, a late Hammer

Films effort which is in a category of its own.) The "noonday devil" also undermines the wildly overpraised writings of Anne Rice, as well as knocking the struts out from under legions of Goth-punk vampire poseurs who mouth such inanities as, "Well, I know I'm a vampire 'cause I, like, blister in the sun after just a few minutes. Oh, and I'm descended from Vlod [*sic*] the Impaler, too."

So whence comes this cinematic conceit, this bit of what I call "Hollywood folklore" (which also includes such false notions as "you become a werewolf if you're bitten by one"), that a vampire is killed, even vaporized, by sunlight? For more than seventy years now, movie vampires (Dracula included), when exposed to sunlight, have faded, withered, melted, crumbled to dust, burst into flames, even exploded ... all with no basis in folklore. (Or in classic literature: J. Sheridan Le Fanu's often-filmed vampiress, Carmilla, was even more of a daytimer than Dracula.) Why?

Part of the confusion may arise from the folkloric tradition, referred to by Summers, that the vampire is *more likely* to be abroad at night. This is hardly surprising, since vampire "attacks" upon their sleeping victims were, in fact, nightmares. Haunts of all types tend to go "bump" especially at night; even the ghost of Hamlet's father vanishes with the cock's crow. From this tendency apparently there arose an assumption that it *had* to be so; and that a vampire, not merely an apparition but a physical presence, would suffer physical harm from sunlight.

Other factors leading to the characteristic heliophobia of movie vampires would seem to be the simple (if not simplistic) good-evil/darkness-light dichotomy; the ease of using the sunrise deadline as a suspenseful plot device; and, of course, the opportunity such a scenario offers to devise ever more sophisticated

"His power ceases, as does that of all evil things, at the coming of the day."—Van Helsing

Max Schreck in *Nosferatu* (1922) (Photofest)

special effects to depict the daylight demise of a vampire. Compare, for example, the sudden fade-out of the Count at the end of *Nosferatu* with his agonizing dissolution at the climax of *Horror of Dracula*, as will be seen; then compare either of these with the pyrotechnic solar destruction of the vampire in *Fright Night*, and it is evident that the law of heightened expectations is at work. In the final analysis, if there were such things as vampires, then the movies promulgating the baseless notion that you're safe from them by daylight would have to be placed on a par with the old Civil Defense films of the 1950s that tried to convince you that radiation was no big deal: they could get you killed.

As for the image used in *Nosferatu*, of the vampire vanishing in a puff of smoke,

it may have found its inspiration in the films of French stage magician Georges Méliès, who flourished around the turn of the century. As a filmmaker, Méliès was still at heart a stage illusionist, inventing most of the basic special-effects techniques he needed to bring new and different illusions to the screen. Most of his films dealt with fantastic or supernatural subject matter, including appearances by the Devil. In one of these, a gigantic devil (Méliès himself), exposed to a cross, disappears with a puff of smoke.

Nosferatu ends with the death, not only of Dracula, but of Nina. The novel ends with Quincey's death, which, while less "sacrificial-lamb" in nature than Nina's, is nonetheless a selfless act, incurred in the effort to destroy the vampire. So even after Stoker's narrative leaves off, elements of the novel's spirit linger to the end of *Nosferatu*. Murnau's artistry, and that of the film's art director, Albin Grau, make this adaptation still one of the very best, if not always the most literally faithful to Stoker.

Musical Notes

Nosferatu, though a silent movie, originally had an orchestral score by Hans Erdmann accompanying it. This score is another aspect of the film (along with tinting and considerable running time) that gradually fell by the wayside over the years. Video copies, such as the ones I used for research purposes, usually have music added, which may or may not be appropriate. (Lately there is a video edition whose musical accompaniment is provided by a CD from a "Gothic" band called Type O Negative.) Similarly, cable showings and repertory screenings—the latter less common since the advent of cable and video—often add musical accompaniment, with greater or lesser effective success.

Back in the '70s, for example, there was a screening at the Rice University Media Center which was "scored" by a recording of randomly-chosen keyboard works by Bach. The Count's first appearance was ridiculously accompanied by the third ("Presto") movement of the Italian Concerto in F Major, a cheerful, "sunny" piece. The natural result was a wave of snickers and groans through the audience.

Amazingly, after more than seventy-five years, a new score has been composed for *Nosferatu*. Available from Silva Screen Records (SSD 1084), the music was composed by James Bernard, the veteran film composer who scored much of the Hammer Films horror series, including *Horror of Dracula*. On the CD, an orchestra of more than seventy pieces is conducted by Nic Raine. Bernard, in the notes accompanying the CD, comments, "[Orlok's] theme is unrelenting and is mostly played by a brass section of four trombones, four trumpets and a tuba. I took the title, *Nosferatu*, to make the theme, as I have done in many of my other scores, such as [*Horror of*] *Dracula*." Which is to say, the main title theme has a four-note motif that echoes the four syllables of the film's title.

The main theme, titled "Overture—Omens of Nosferatu", is in 4/4 time, and is primarily in E minor; its emphasis is on that key, though it has a variety of tonal centers. Played by a full orchestra, it places special emphasis on the winds and percussion, with the strings playing an important secondary role almost co-equal to the other sections.

Naturally, this CD presents itself as the obvious choice for accompaniment of a video viewing of *Nosferatu*. At 63 minutes in length, it is exactly as long as the shorter, "unrestored" version of the film; even so, strange to say, the scenes of the video, and the music evidently meant to accompany them, are not in synch with each other. It takes some fussing with the remotes to coordinate them, but the results are impressive and worth the effort.

Dracula

Universal Pictures (1931)
Directed by Tod Browning
Screenplay by Garrett Fort
Adapted from the stage play by Hamilton Deane
and John L. Balderston
Running time: 1 hour 15 minutes
Available on video

Cast

COUNT DRACULA . . . . Bela Lugosi
MINA Helen . . . . Helen Chandler
JOHN HARKER . . . . David Manners
RENFIELD . . . . Dwight Frye
PROFESSOR VAN HELSING . . . . Edward Van Sloan
DR. SEWARD . . . . Frances Dade
MAID . . . . Joan Standing
MARTIN . . . . Charles Gerrard
DRACULA'S WIVES (unbilled) . . . . Jeraldine Dvorak
Dorothy Tree
unknown

Synopsis

The year is not given, but seems to be in the 1920s. Renfield travels to Transylvania to close a real estate deal with Count Dracula. As we ultimately learn, he has traveled in secret; no one knows of his expedition.

En route, Renfield meets fearful, superstitious people on a coach, who are frightened because it is Walpurgis Night. Later, he encounters people at an inn who are frightened at the mention of Dracula's name. A woman gives him a crucifix, which she says is "for your mother's sake."

The coach continues on its way, taking Renfield as far as the Borgo Pass, where Dracula's own carriage picks him up. The Count himself, in disguise, drives the carriage.

En route to the castle, Renfield looks out and sees that there is no one in the driver's seat. A large bat flies before the carriage as if leading the way. This bat, as it gradually dawns on us, is evidently Dracula in metamorphosis.

At the castle, Renfield is greeted by the Count, who is tall, pale, and dark-haired. He carries a candelabrum and is dressed in a tux with a full cape.

Wolves howl outside, and the Count remarks: "Listen to them—the children of the night! What music they make!" Regarding a spider in its web, laying a trap for flies, Dracula observes, "The blood is the life, Mr. Renfield."

Renfield enjoys a supper in which the Count does not join him. They discuss the lease of an old house in London which is called Carfax Abbey.

Dracula says they will set sail for England the following night.

Renfield cuts himself on the finger with a paper clip. The sight of blood excites the Count, but he is repulsed by the crucifix.

Offering Renfield a drink, Dracula explains, "I never drink ... wine."

"… I saw that the cut had bled a little…. When the Count saw [it], his eyes blazed with a sort of demoniac fury…"—Jonathan Harker

Bela Lugosi as Dracula and Dwight Frye as Renfield in *Dracula* (1931) (courtesy Ronald V. Borst of Hollywood Movie Posters)

Dracula shows Renfield to his room. Renfield is soon attacked by three vampire women, two brunettes and a blonde. The Count stops the attack and victimizes Renfield himself.

Along with three boxes of earth, Dracula travels by ship, the *Vesta*, to England. En route, abetted by Renfield, who is now insane, Dracula terrorizes and kills the ship's crew.

The ship weathers a storm and drifts into port at Whitby. The captain is found dead and lashed to the wheel. The rest of the crew are dead as well. The only living person on board is Renfield. A newspaper account tells the story.

Renfield is subsequently linked to the Count because of his having traveled to Transylvania and been driven insane by his experiences there. He is institutionalized in an insane asylum run by Dr. Seward. Renfield catches and eats insects.

After killing a girl selling flowers in the street, the Count goes to the symphony and introduces himself to Dr. Seward, whose asylum is next door to Carfax. Along with his new neighbor, Dracula meets Dr. Seward's daughter Mina, her fiancé John Harker, and her friend Lucy Weston.

In order to get to Lucy in her bedroom that night, Dracula casts a trance over her.

Despite transfusions of blood, Lucy soon dies. During a post-mortem, Dr. Seward notices two tiny wounds on her throat. He observes that "each victim" has the same marks.

Dr. Seward is baffled as to the cause of Lucy's death. Professor Van Helsing knows immediately, based on the symptoms in her death and several other similar ones recently, that a vampire is on the loose. Van Helsing at first suspects Renfield of the vampire attacks. His suspicions are based partly on Renfield's habit of eating live insects in the belief that he can ab-sorb their souls and thereby prolong his own life, and partly on Renfield's frequent escapes from his cell.

Renfield pleads with Dr. Seward to release him. John, meanwhile, is a guest in the residential wing of the asylum. Mina, as Seward's daughter, lives there.

Van Helsing demonstrates Renfield's aversion to wolfbane, which repels vampires.

Dracula turns his attention to Mina. He approaches her room in the form of a bat. Mina has a vivid nightmare about his visit, later saying that he entered her room as a mist. While Dracula is visiting Dr. Seward and the others, Van Helsing notices, in a mirror in a cigarette case, that the Count has no reflection. When asked to explain, Dracula breaks the mirror. He then leaves, whereupon a "large dog," evidently the Count in the form of a wolf, is seen running across the lawn of the asylum.

Van Helsing tells the others of his suspicions concerning Dracula: that he is the vampire, and as such he casts no reflection, can transform himself into a bat or wolf, and rests by day in a box of his native soil. Renfield, having escaped again, enters the room during the conversation.

Shortly afterward, Mina is found outdoors, having been attacked by Dracula.

Lucy, now a vampire, attacks children, who claim to have been with a "beautiful lady." These attacks are described in a newspaper account. Mina reveals that Lucy, though dead and buried, has appeared to her as well. Van Helsing assures Mina that after tonight, Lucy will rest in peace.

Van Helsing places wolfbane in Mina's room and prepares a wreath of it for her to wear in her sleep.

Van Helsing observes that three boxes were delivered to Carfax. He theorizes that these are boxes of Transylvanian soil in which the Count rests during the day.

He further speculates that the Count is unnaturally old.

Renfield escapes yet again. He reveals that the Count has appeared to him and offered him the blood of thousands of rats as a means of prolonging his life indefinitely. It is learned that the Count has bent the bars of Renfield's window, allowing him to escape.

Dracula confronts Van Helsing and tries to hypnotize him. Van Helsing drives him away with a crucifix.

In order to get to Mina, Dracula casts a stupor-like trance over the nurse, enabling Mina to go out onto the terrace. On the terrace, Mina speaks to John with strange seductiveness, but Van Helsing prevents her from attacking him.

Mina reveals that she was forced to drink some of Count Dracula's blood from a cut on his arm. Van Helsing says Mina will become a vampire as a result unless Dracula is killed. Mina's "taint" is shown in her inability to look at the crucifix.

Martin, an asylum attendant, takes a shot at a large bat, obviously the Count incognito. The bat is not harmed.

In order to get to Mina, the Count again casts a trance over the nurse, who removes the wolfbane and opens the door. Dracula abducts Mina and takes her to Carfax.

Renfield escapes a last time and heads for Carfax. Van Helsing and John follow him, assuming he is on his way to meet Dracula.

"... as for things sacred, as this symbol, my crucifix, ... in their presence he take his place far off and silent with respect." —Van Helsing

Edward Van Sloan as Van Helsing and Bela Lugosi as the Count in *Dracula* (1931) (courtesy Ronald V. Borst of Hollywood Movie Posters)

Dracula kills Renfield because Renfield has led his enemies to his hiding place. A frantic search for both Mina and Dracula ensues.

Dracula is killed when Van Helsing stakes him. After Dracula dies, John and Mina are restored to each other.

Commentary

Universal's adaptation of *Dracula*, filmed in the fall of 1930 and released in February 1931, has, of course, a secure place in film history (notwithstanding its unconscionable omission from the American Film Institute's 1998 listing of the 100 greatest American films of the first century of filmmaking). Hugely successful at the box office, it helped Universal survive the Depression, since 1931 was the studio's only profitable year of the decade. It was also the first film to demonstrate that American audiences would buy into a genuinely fantastic or supernatural premise, as opposed to a number of pseudo-fantastic silents of the 1920s in which the supernatural element is explained away at the end. (The most notable of these is the long-lost 1925 mystery *London After Midnight*, directed by Tod Browning, which features Lon Chaney as a *faux* vampire. Browning also directed the 1935 "talkie" remake, *Mark of the Vampire*, with Bela Lugosi, already typecast after *Dracula*, in the role of the bogus Count Mora.)

All that having been acknowledged, the question arises: is Universal's 1931 *Dracula* a particularly good, or particularly faithful, adaptation of Stoker? In many ways, it is neither.

To begin with, the film is not really an adaptation of Stoker's novel *per se*, but an adaptation of the stage play by Hamilton Deane and John L. Balderston, which had been a hit in London, New York City, and the provinces since 1927. At least, the film's opening credits make reference only to the play. But, unlike the film, the play's action starts with Dracula already in England (having arrived, as we ultimately learn, by plane!), Mina Weston already dead and buried, and Lucy Seward already wasting away; Mina and Lucy, notably, have traded names. The play's plot unfolds as a whodunit, with Renfield a suspect in the vampire attacks and the Count initially dismissed because of the impossibility of an every-night commute between Transylvania and England so as to lie in his "native soil." These "mystery" considerations are carried forward into the film. The play's three acts take place in Seward's sanitarium, with the exception of the final scene: Dracula is staked in a crypt under Carfax Abbey, having been able to pass undetected between Carfax and Dr. Seward's asylum by means of a secret passageway.

The film, by contrast, adapts the novel's opening chapters concerning the fateful trip to Transylvania, here taken not by Jonathan Harker, but by Renfield. The story's adapter, Garrett Fort, seems to have felt the need to "explain" Renfield's involvement with the Count. Granted, having Renfield undergo terrifying experiences in Dracula's castle and return from his ordeal insane is as good a way of involving the two characters as any. The downside is that Harker, here called "John," who, after his return from abroad in the novel, is one of several stand-around-and-fret characters, ends up with even less to do, and graduates from fretting into obstructionism. In any event, it is not until Dracula greets Renfield by name, more than eleven minutes into the film, that we learn who our protagonist is.

Dracula, of course, is Bela Lugosi, at the pinnacle of his career, playing the role that both made him and ruined him, the role he had played hundreds of times on stage over the preceding several years, yet virtually had to beg for when the film was made. It is a testimonial to the popularity of this film, and the hypnotic power of this performance, that to this very day, despite the many other versions of *Dracula* that have been filmed in the interim, Bela Lugosi is *still* Dracula to the general public. This also despite Lugosi's having played the role in only two of Universal's endless (and increasingly trivial) series of horror movies of the 1930s and '40s (the other being 1948's *Abbott and Costello Meet Frankenstein*), versus Christopher Lee's portrayal of the Count in two adaptations, six sequels, and a French farce. Let the Count's name be mentioned, and people still lapse into cheesy imitations of Lugosi's vocal mannerisms; let Halloween roll around, and people going to a costume party "as a vampire" still start by renting a cape. (Given the extent to which the Lugosi/Dracula image has become a pop-culture archetype, it is at first surprising to note that an animated character called Count Chocula, created to advertise a cereal by that name, looks more like Stoker's conception: gaunt, and with pointed ears and a cartoon version of Nosferatu's rat-like teeth. Surprising, that is, until one remembers that Universal guards the copyright on their Lugosi image so jealously that they didn't share its ongoing proceeds even with Lugosi's heirs!)

Again having acknowledged all that, the question remains: Is Lugosi the Count Dracula originally envisioned by Bram Stoker? The answer: Of course not. Not even close. Read again Harker's description of him, either as excerpted in the previous chapter of this book, or in its entirety in Chapter 2 of Stoker's novel. Any resemblance between Stoker's Count and Bela Lugosi's is an accident. More to the point, as Christopher Lee remarked in an interview in Leonard Wolf's *A Dream of Dracula*, "Surely it is the height of the ridiculous for a vampire to step out of the shadows wearing white tie, tails, patent leather shoes and a full cloak." The plain truth is that Bela Lugosi, like most of the actors who have played Dracula in film adaptations over the years, is simply miscast ... not to mention overdressed.

Some people defend Lugosi's interpretation on the basis of the actor's authentic Hungarian accent. So? Louis Jourdan has an authentic French accent. But the historic Dracula—that is, Prince Vlad Tepes, a.k.a. Drakulya, on whom Bram Stoker based his fictional character—wasn't Hungarian any more than he was a Frenchman. He was ethnically Romanian, and Romanian is a Romance language whose accent, lent to English, sounds rather like an Italian one. (Lugosi had more than an accent, by the way: he had a language barrier. Even as *Dracula* was being filmed, he could not speak English, having learned his entire role phonetically.)

According to David J. Skal, in his definitive work *Hollywood Gothic*, which traces the evolution of *Dracula* from a novel to a German silent to a stage play and, finally, to the two film versions Universal produced in 1930, the decision to remake Dracula as a suave Mephistophelian gentleman may have arisen from Florence Stoker's vehement objections, not just to the very existence of *Nosferatu*, but to its cadaverous, pestilential Count. Whatever may have motivated the dramatists and screenwriters responsible, the character was turned into a polite, well-dressed man who joined his new neighbors at the symphony. Bela Lugosi brought this reinvention to life in the popular imagination, and there he (actor and role as one) has remained.

To return to Renfield in Dracula's castle: Dracula offers him some wine, explaining his own non-indulgence with the famous and popular phrase, "I never drink ... wine." It comes as yet another surprise to many people that this line is not in

Stoker's novel. Its closest approach is when Dracula excuses himself from joining Jonathan for supper, thus: "You will, I trust, excuse me that I do not join you; but I have dined already, and I do not sup." Stoker or not, the line as spoken by Lugosi has (alongside other non-Stoker elements such as the aforementioned death-by-sunlight syndrome) made its way into what may be referred to as the "Dracula mythos." The line has turned up in a number of the other adaptations over the years, as will be seen. It has also been spoofed, as in *Love at First Bite* (1979, a busy year for Dracula movies), when Dracula (George Hamilton) declines an offer of marijuana with, "I never smoke ... shit."

Shortly afterward, Renfield opens a large floor-to-ceiling window leading to the outdoors. The screenplay has him look out into a courtyard where he sees two coffins loaded into a wagon; this scene was either not shot at all or was cut from the final film. A bat appears at the window, and Renfield swoons. Skal wrote in *Hollywood Gothic* that the wine Dracula has given Renfield is drugged, but the original shooting script gives no such indication; Renfield, in the screenplay, recoils from the bat and bangs his head against the window, knocking himself unconscious. Looking at the scene as it was filmed, there seems to be little other explanation for Renfield's collapse than an unscripted improvisation of drugged wine: he has seen bats already without fainting, and just before he opens the window, his face shows signs of discomfort, as though he's feeling ill ... or drugged.

Renfield is then set upon by the three vampire women. As per the novel—and, interestingly, as in almost every film adaptation in which these women appear—they are depicted as two brunettes and a blonde. The bat has disappeared, and the women advance slowly upon the unconscious Renfield. Dracula, who presumably was the bat, strides in through the open window and, with a gesture of command, motions them back. As they withdraw, the Count victimizes Renfield himself. This scene, played out almost in slow motion, and in the utter silence that still accompanied long stretches of the early talkies, is incomprehensible to someone who has not read the novel, and frustrating to someone who has.

We are then whisked away to the high seas, where we see a sailing ship beset by a storm. Per a caption, this ship is the *Vesta*. Why this apparently arbitrary renaming of the *Demeter* took place, swapping the name of one Greek goddess for another, is anybody's guess. Renfield, an insane stowaway in the ship's hold, assists Dracula in climbing out of his coffin. The Count, his eyes glaring, clearly relishes the hunt ahead. Topside, the sailors battle the wind and waves, oblivious to the even greater danger presented by the vampire in their midst; it's as though the Count isn't on board at all.

And small wonder: he isn't. The scenes of the ship on the stormy sea are stock footage spliced in from an unidentified silent movie. No interaction between Dracula and the sailors is seen, since none is possible; they're in different cinematic universes. As filmed, this sequence is a fraction of what was written in the screenplay, which called for shots of the captain, as per Stoker, lashed to the wheel with a crucifix in his grip, as sailors frantically run to and fro screaming in the gale, the Count stalking and attacking them as Renfield looks on laughing. The scenes on board the doomed ship in *Nosferatu* are much more effective, and much more Stoker. The inevitable effect, in this version, is that of something having been thrown together slapdash.

After the ship's arrival in England, Renfield is found insane in the hold. As we learn from a newspaper clipping that fills

"I was not alone.... In the moonlight opposite me were
three young women."—Jonathan Harker

The vampire women of *Dracula* (1931). Left to right: Dorothy Tree, Jeraldine Dvorak, unknown actress (courtesy Ronald V. Borst of Hollywood Movie Posters)

the screen—an appropriately Stokeresque touch, since the novel, an example of the epistolary format, is ostensibly pieced together from journal entries, letters, and newspaper articles—the ship has drifted into port at Whitby, with a "CREW OF CORPSES". The sole survivor, a "raving maniac" who eats insects, has been committed to Dr. Seward's sanitarium, said to be "near London."

Dracula turns up in London, whose honking, beeping automotive traffic offers the first real clue of this film's period: it is apparently set in the 1920s, which is contrary to Stoker, of course, but consistent with the play. Dracula introduces himself to Dr. Seward and company, cheerfully volunteering the news that he has just moved into Carfax Abbey, next door to Dr. Seward's. In the novel, not only is the Count reclusive to the point of invisibility, but locating his hideout, in Jonathan's long absence, is a matter of considerable vexation for the heroes. As Dr. Seward laments in his diary, "Strange that it never struck me that the very next house might be the Count's hiding-place!... Oh, if we had only [known] earlier we might have saved poor Lucy!"

Furthermore, the Count and Dr. Seward conversationally reveal to us that the asylum is "in Whitby." Whitby, on the Yorkshire coast in northeastern England, is nowhere "near London," contrary to the newspaper clipping. This careless geographic blunder persists: later in the movie, a wolf's howl is heard outside the sanitarium. Dr. Seward, evidently thinking it's a dog, says, "I hardly think there are wolves so near London." Didn't anyone connected with this production own an atlas? British audiences must bellow with laughter.

The film agrees with the novel, and differs from the play, in giving Mina and Lucy their respective names back. But once again, the lengthy drama of Lucy's decline and death is given short shrift: Dracula makes a single visit to Lucy, and the next thing we know, she's on a table in an operating theater undergoing a postmortem. The transfusions that have failed to save her are referred to during this examination; Dr. Seward says she received the last of them "about four hours ago" ("four hours before she died," the screenplay reads). The wounds on her neck are also remarked on, but the film squeamishly does not show them to us. They are said to be the same "on the throat of each victim": evidently the flower-girl Dracula killed has also been examined, and the word "each" (as opposed to "both") implies even more victims.

Considerably later, well after Dracula has already started pestering Mina, Lucy returns as a vampire. Her on-screen vampiric career lasts all of ten seconds, as she meanders in long-shot past a graveyard, to the sound of a crying child. Another newspaper clipping—again per Stoker, except insofar as it is read by Martin, the buffoonish asylum attendant meant to provide "comic relief"—tells us that "the mysterious woman in white" has been victimizing "small girls." Mina then tells Professor Van Helsing that Lucy has appeared to her as well; like so much of the crucial action in this version, Lucy's appearance to Mina takes place offscreen. Van Helsing assures Mina that "after tonight she [Lucy] will remain at rest." And there the matter is dropped, unbelievably, with no further reference made to Lucy or her undead status. Two later scenes in the screenplay tie off this particular plot thread. In the first, Van Helsing and Harker encounter Lucy afoot in the graveyard; in the second, they stake her ... offscreen, of course. These scenes, again, were either never shot, or were cut; either way, their absence results in a glaring loose end.

Van Helsing: how does he get involved in the first place? He turns up, unintroduced, in his laboratory shortly after the post-mortem scene. Dr. Seward is present, along with another doctor who was at Lucy's post-mortem, so viewers are led to assume what the novel makes plain: that Dr. Seward has sought out Professor Van Helsing to ask him to lend his expertise to the baffling case. We are given no clue as to where Van Helsing's lab is; we have been given no indication, by action or dialogue, that Dr. Seward has traveled any farther than a stroll down the block. The screenplay has Van Helsing say that he is "returning to England with Dr. Seward," a cut line that doesn't tell us where they're returning *from*. Mina later says, in a line also cut from the final film, that the first of her enervating "dreams" (i.e., nocturnal visits from Dracula) took place "the night father left for Switzerland." According to Stoker, of course, Van Helsing is Dutch.

Edward Van Sloan's interpretation of the good professor is much as Stoker conceives him, in his age and appearance, his cool competence, his evident faith in both science and religion, and his amusing accent. The warmth and charm of the novel's character are gone, as Van Sloan strikes pose after wooden pose. The one out-and-out gaffe comes in his first scene—his very first line of dialogue, in fact—in which he calls his assistant (mentioned in the screenplay as an "Austrian", although he doesn't wear a label to that effect) a "dumkopf." Stoker's Van Helsing is an endearing gentleman who never insults anyone, not even the Count.

Dwight Frye's pathetic Renfield, too, lingers in memory long enough that Arte Johnson did a spoof of the performance nearly fifty years later in *Love at First Bite*. Pity that, once again, the screenwriter is uncertain what role Renfield is to play in the action once he has helped Dracula attain England. In the novel, Renfield is Dracula's means of entry into Seward's asylum, where Jonathan and Mina are

guests; as Van Helsing explains, Dracula "has been making use of the zoophagous patient to effect his entry into friend John's home; for your Vampire, though in all afterwards he can come when and how he will, must at the first make entry only when asked thereto by an inmate." So, per Stoker, the Count promises Renfield all manner of red-blooded creatures in exchange for ingress, so that he can get to Mina.

None of which is made clear in this version. The need for an invitation is never mentioned, which begs the question as to what Renfield means when he warns Seward, "If you don't send me away, you must answer for what will happen to Miss Mina!" Dracula then appears outside of Renfield's window, staring and silent. Renfield sobs, "Please don't ask me to do that! Don't ... not *her*! Please!" We know Renfield is talking about Mina, but what does Dracula want him to do? And why Renfield? Next thing we know, Dracula is entering the open window to Mina's room as a bat. What has Renfield done to facilitate this intrusion? If he's offered the Count an invitation, we learn of it neither then nor later.

In a later scene, Renfield reveals that the Count has come to him and offered him "'rats ... rats ... thousands, millions of them ... if you will obey me!'" Van Helsing asks what the Count wanted Renfield to do, and Renfield's reply is, "That which has already been done." Martin bursts in and says that the bars on Renfield's window have been bent "as if they was cheese," and Van Helsing declares, "Dracula is in the house!" No kidding. The question remains: what has Renfield done to let him in?

Even the bent bars on Renfield's window offer us no clue. In the novel, after he receives the invitation, the Count comes and goes several times, always through the window of Renfield's cell. Bending the bars is unnecessary: Renfield tells how the Count "slid into the room through the sash, though it was only open an inch wide." This testimony is in keeping with Van Helsing's telling the others, per Stoker, that the vampire can "come out from anything or into anything, no matter how close it be bound." Our only indication that Lugosi's Count has any such power of incorporeality is early in the film, when he breezes through a wall of cobwebs without disturbing them. No further use is made of this capability: we do not see Lugosi dissolving through walls as Max Schreck did in *Nosferatu*. Obviously Lugosi's Count has brute strength, since he bends the bars; but they seem to have been bent to allow Renfield to escape, and not the Count to enter, since we've already seen him enter through *Mina's* window. As filmed, Renfield's part in the Count's designs on Mina is, in the final analysis, unclear and confusing.

Reams of additional dialogue for Renfield are cut from the final film. Some of it has to do with the effort, on Van Helsing's part, to get Renfield to tell what he may know about the location of Dracula's two remaining boxes. One of them has already been found by Van Helsing and Dr. Seward during an infiltration of Carfax, a scene which, incredibly, was cut from the final film, though it corresponds to a major episode from the novel.

Since Lucy has been dispensed with, much of the novel's action surrounding her slow death is transferred to Mina. It is her room that is festooned, not with garlic as in the novel, but with wolfbane, in an effort to protect her that is repeatedly frustrated by the herb's removal. Well-meaning hands are the culprit in the novel, but here Dracula enlists the aid of the help via hypnotism. Stoker's Count goes to no such trouble: in a development that has never been filmed, he simply drugs the domestic staff of Hillingham.

In any case, this part of the film puts the "talk" into talking pictures: Van Helsing expostulates, Dracula threatens, Renfield rants, Dr. Seward frets, John interferes, Mina alternately blubbers and bubbles, and Martin cracks wise in a phony Cockney accent. Nothing much happens until the end, when Dracula snatches Mina and makes a run for Carfax, followed by Renfield and pursued by Van Helsing and John. Nothing much onscreen, that is. As noted earlier, much of this adaptation's action takes place offscreen, to be later described or otherwise commented on by one character or another. The *Vesta's* arrival at Whitby: offscreen; described in a newspaper clipping, as is Renfield's commitment to Dr. Seward's care. Lucy's blood transfusions, her subsequent death, and even the wounds on her throat: offscreen; commented on by the doctors at her postmortem. Most of Lucy's vampiric career, including her victimization of children and her appearance to Mina: offscreen; described later by a newspaper article and by Mina, respectively. The Count's appearance as a wolf running across the lawn of the asylum: offscreen; described by John looking out a window. The bent bars in the window of Renfield's cell: offscreen; described by Martin. The Count's forcing Mina to drink some of his blood from a cut on his arm: offscreen, of course, and described by her later. Martin's potshot at the Count in the form of a bat: offscreen; described by Martin by way of explaining the gunshot…. It goes on and on.

While there is much merit to the argument that horror on film is more effective if suggested rather than graphically depicted, this version takes its non-depiction into the realm of visual stinginess: for example, as John and Mina sit outside on the terrace, even the stars whose beauty they admire are offscreen! The result, coupled with Tod Browning's frequent lapses into nail-your-camera-to-the-floor direction, is often like watching, not a film at all, but what this adaptation started out to be: a play, and an underproduced one at that, with characters staring off into the wings of the stage and describing what they purportedly see there.

John Harker and Professor Van Helsing catch up with Count Dracula in the crypt under Carfax Abbey, which is in keeping with the stage play; the novel's pursuit all the way back to Transylvania proved to be beyond the film's budget. As John frantically searches for Mina, Van Helsing drives an improvised (!) stake through Dracula's heart. This happens, of course, offscreen.

As John and Mina depart in the light of dawn, Van Helsing, for whatever reason, tells them he'll be along "presently." In the screenplay, he says, "I shall remain, and fulfill my promise to Renfield." Even in the context of the original screenplay, it can only be guessed what "promise" he's talking about.

Universal's 1931 *Dracula*, for reasons listed earlier, is a milestone in American cinema. Renting the video and watching it, enjoying what fine (if fleeting) moments of atmosphere it has to offer, reveling in Lugosi's boundlessly influential (if thoroughly non-Stoker) performance, it's a hard movie to dislike. It's a beloved popcorn-muncher, a true American classic of the stature (if not the quality) of *Gone With the Wind* or *The Wizard of Oz*.

That's as may be. As an adaptation of Stoker's original story, it underachieves in any number of ways. The "gist"—centuries-old Transylvanian vampire nobleman travels to contemporary England, afflicts a gaggle of protagonists, and meets his doom at their hands—remains, but it's gasping for breath.

Musical Notes

When sound pictures were in their infancy, soundtrack music, as a distinct and important adjunct of a movie, had not yet been developed, despite the earlier tradition of accompanying silent screenings with either live or recorded music, depending on the means of the theater. As a result, *Dracula* has no musical soundtrack as such, and no music at all composed especially for the film.

The music that accompanies the opening credits is an excerpt from Scene 2 of Tchaikovsky's ballet, *Swan Lake*. The same piece of music serves as the title theme of Universal's 1932 picture, *The Mummy*, with Boris Karloff.

In the scene where Dracula joins Dr. Seward's party at the symphony, we hear brief excerpts from Schubert's *Unfinished Symphony* and Wagner's *Die Meistersinger*. Very little of the dialogue of the scene is spoken over the music; at the time, the debate was still unresolved as to whether music in films would distract from dialogue, should the two overlap.

━━━━◆━━━━

Dracula
(Spanish language version)

Universal Pictures (1931)
Directed by George Melford.
Screenplay by B. Fernandez Cue (a translation of the
English-language screenplay, adapted by Garrett Fort
from the stage play by Hamilton Deane and John L. Balderston).
Running time: 1 hour 43 minutes.
Available on video

Cast

CONDE DRACULA . . . . Carlos Villarias (listed erroneously as "Villar")
EVA . . . . Lupita Tovar
JUAN HARKER . . . . Barry Norton
RENFIELD . . . . Pablo Alvarez Rubio
PROFESSOR VAN HELSING . . . . .Eduardo Arozamena
DR. SEWARD . . . . .José Soriano Viosca
LUCIA . . . . Carmen Guerrero
MARTA . . . . Amelia Senisterra
MARTIN . . . . Manuel Arbo
DRACULA'S WIVES . . . . unbilled

Synopsis

The year is not given, but seems to be in the 1920s. Renfield travels to Transylvania to close a real estate deal with Count Dracula. As we ultimately learn, he has traveled in secret; no one knows of his expedition.

En route, Renfield meets fearful, superstitious people on a coach, who are frightened because it is Walpurgis Night. Later, he encounters people at an inn who are frightened at the mention of Dracula's name. A woman gives him a crucifix, which she says is "for your mother's sake."

The coach continues on its way, taking Renfield as far as the Borgo Pass, where Dracula's own carriage picks him up. The Count himself, in disguise, drives the carriage.

En route to the castle, Renfield looks out and sees that there is no one in the driver's seat. A large bat flies before the carriage, as if leading the way. This bat, as it gradually dawns on us, is evidently Dracula in metamorphosis.

At the castle, Renfield is greeted by the Count, who is tall, pale, and dark-haired. He carries a candelabrum and is dressed in a tux with a full cape.

Wolves howl outside, and the Count remarks: "Listen to them. They are the children of the night! What beautiful music they make!"

Regarding a spider in its web, laying a trap for flies, Dracula observes, "The blood is the life, Mr. Renfield."

Renfield enjoys a supper in which the Count does not join him. Renfield cuts himself on the thumb while slicing some bread. The sight of blood excites the Count, but he is repulsed by the crucifix.

Offering Renfield a drink, Dracula says, "I never drink … wine."

They discuss the lease of an old house in London which is called Carfax Abbey.

"... I moved forward ... holding the Crucifix.... I felt a mighty power fly along my arm; and it was without surprise that I saw the monster cower back...."—John Seward

Carlos Villarias as el Conde Dracula and Eduardo Arozamena as Van Helsing in the 1931 Spanish-language version of Dracula (courtesy Ronald V. Borst of Hollywood Movie Posters)

Dracula says they will set sail for England the following night. He shows Renfield to his room.

Later, Renfield finds a courtyard in which Dracula stands next to a coffin-like box. Two others are loaded on a wagon.

Renfield is attacked by three vampire women, two brunettes and a blonde.

Along with three boxes of earth, Dracula travels by ship, the *Elsie*, to England. En route, Dracula terrorizes and kills the ship's crew as Renfield, now insane, looks on.

The ship weathers a storm and drifts into port at Bristol. The captain is found dead and lashed to the wheel. The rest of the crew are dead as well. A newspaper account tells the story. The only living person on board is Renfield, who is subsequently linked to the Count because of his having traveled to Transylvania and been driven insane by his experiences there.

Dracula's boxes are moved to Carfax by the maritime authorities.

The Count goes to the symphony and introduces himself to Dr. Seward, whose asylum is next door to Carfax. Along with his new neighbor, Dracula meets Dr. Seward's daughter Eva, her fiancé Juan Harker, and her friend Lucia Weston.

In order to get to Lucia in her bedroom that night, the Count casts a trance over her.

Despite transfusions of blood, Lucia soon dies. During a post-mortem, Dr. Seward notices two tiny wounds on her neck. He observes that "each of the victims" has the same marks.

Dr. Seward is baffled as to the cause of Lucia's death. Professor Van Helsing knows immediately, based on the symptoms in her death and several other similar ones recently, that a vampire is on the loose. Van Helsing at first suspects Renfield, who has been institutionalized in Dr. Seward's asylum, of the vampire attacks. His suspicions are based partly on Renfield's habit of eating live insects in the belief that he can absorb their souls and thereby prolong his own life, and partly on Renfield's frequent escapes from his cell.

Renfield pleads with Dr. Seward to release him. Juan, meanwhile, is a guest in the residential wing of the asylum. Eva, Dr. Seward's daughter, lives there.

Van Helsing demonstrates Renfield's aversion to aconite, which repels vampires.

Dracula has already turned his attention to Eva. She has had a vivid nightmare about his visit, later saying that he entered her room in the form of a mist. She has the marks on her neck as well.

While Dracula is visiting Dr. Seward and the others, Van Helsing notices, in a mirror in a cigarette case, that the Count has no reflection. Asked to explain, the Count breaks the mirror.

Van Helsing tells the others of his suspicions concerning Dracula: that he is the vampire, and as such he casts no reflection and must rest by day in a box of his native soil. Renfield, having escaped again, enters the room during the conversation.

Shortly afterward, Eva is found outdoors, having been attacked by Dracula.

Professor Van Helsing and Dr. Seward infiltrate Carfax, but are unable to find the Count.

Lucia, now a vampire, attacks children, who claim to have been with a "beautiful lady." These attacks are described in a newspaper account. Eva reveals that Lucia, though dead and buried, has appeared to her as well. Van Helsing assures Eva that after tonight, Lucia's soul will rest in peace.

Van Helsing places aconite in Eva's room and prepares a sprig of it for her to place on her pillow as she sleeps.

Van Helsing observes that three boxes were delivered to Carfax. He theorizes that these are boxes of Transylvanian soil in which the Count rests during the day. He further speculates that the Count is unnaturally old, but that he can be killed with a stake through the heart.

Renfield escapes yet again. It is learned that the Count has bent the bars on Renfield's window, allowing him to escape.

In order to get to Eva, Dracula casts a trance over the nurse, who removes the aconite from Eva's room.

Renfield reveals that the Count has appeared to him and offered him the blood of thousands of rats as a means of prolonging his life indefinitely.

Soon, at Eva's request, the nurse removes the aconite from the adjoining room as well, enabling Eva to go out onto the terrace with Juan.

Dracula confronts Van Helsing and tries to hypnotize him. Van Helsing drives him away with a cross.

On the terrace, Eva speaks to Juan with strange seductiveness and tries to bite him, but Van Helsing intervenes. Her "taint" is shown in her inability to look at the cross. Eva reveals that she was forced to drink some of the Count's blood from a cut on his arm, which will cause her to become a vampire.

Martin, an asylum attendant, takes a shot at a large bat, obviously the Count incognito. The bat is not harmed.

In order to get to Eva, the Count

again casts a trance over the nurse, who removes the aconite and opens the door.

Van Helsing and Juan go to the cemetery where Lucia is buried and stake her. They then set out for Carfax.

Dracula abducts Eva and takes her to Carfax.

Renfield escapes a last time and also heads for Carfax. Dracula kills Renfield because he believes Renfield has led his enemies to his hiding place.

A frantic search for both Eva and Dracula ensues. The Count tries to attack Eva one last time, but the rays of the rising sun come slanting in through the dungeon window, and he flees.

Dracula is killed when Van Helsing stakes him. After Dracula dies, Juan and Eva are restored to each other.

Commentary

At the dawn of the era of talking pictures, sound technology was so rudimentary that, instead of dubbing a movie into a foreign language for release to overseas markets (or to certain domestic markets, in the case of Spanish), studios found it was just as easy to make an alternate version of the same movie, filming it in a different language. *Dracula* was one property given this treatment by Universal.

When the cast and crew of Tod Browning's opus went home at the end of the day, the personnel involved in the Spanish-language production came in at night. They used the same sets as the daytime production, which enabled the Spanish version to be made for a fraction of what Browning's version cost.

The Spanish version was also shot from a translation of the same screenplay (although, whereas the credits of Browning's film say it was based on the play by Deane and Balderston, the Spanish film's credits describe it as an "*Adaptacion de la obra de BRAM STOKER*"). The director,

George Melford, working through an interpreter, followed the screenplay much more closely than Tod Browning did. One result is that the Spanish version is considerably longer than the English one; another result is that it makes more sense. Since the two films, Browning's and Melford's, are variations on the same story, the differences will be emphasized here.

These differences start with the opening credits. Whereas Browning's film plays its credits over a stylized image of a bat, the Spanish film's credits feature a flickering candle. The candle's flame suddenly goes out, or, more accurately, it disappears: it isn't snuffed or blown out, it just vanishes in a subtle dissolve, with atmospheric results. One is reminded of the candle that blows out in Ruth Harding's window, its curtains billowing gently, near the end of *Nosferatu*, a film which seems to have been an influence on the Spanish *Dracula*. In both instances, we have moved from light into darkness, a signal that we are entering the realm of the vampire. (The same gimmick was used, and still effectively, many years later, in 1978, in the opening credits of John Carpenter's *Halloween*: in a moment illustrative of how effective subtle horror can be, a jack-o'-lantern, already too close for comfort, flickers out, leaving us in the dark.)

Once again it is Renfield who makes the trip to Castle Dracula, despite dire warnings from the locals. It all looks familiar to us, as well it should, what with the use of the same sets and similar costumes. The occasional detail differs, as when the passenger coach passes a roadside bonfire not seen in Browning's film. We are reminded of the blue flames Stoker describes flickering by the roadside, but they were not to be filmed for more than another sixty years yet. And when Renfield is met by Dracula's carriage, its door opens by itself, its hinges screaming, much to Renfield's consternation. This incident, though written into the screenplay, is omitted from the English-language film.

At the castle, which is also well-equipped with loudly self-operating doors, Renfield is greeted by Dracula, played by Carlos Villarias. According to Skal in *Hollywood Gothic*, Villarias was the only one of the Spanish cast allowed to see dailies from the English-language version, and was encouraged to model his performance after Lugosi's. For the most part, he does so successfully. Still, he manages to make the role his own: in closeups of his face, and sometimes just his eyes, when he registers fury or bloodlust, we see an animalistic passion totally unlike Lugosi's squinting deviousness. Of course, one effect lost on an English-only audience member reading the subtitles of the Spanish version is that of Lugosi's outlandish accent; to the non-Spanish-comprehending ear, Villarias' Spanish sounds like anyone else's—as well it may, since the actor was from Spain, not Hungary. (Spanish-speaking audiences were reportedly amused by the wide range of accents of the actors in the film, since the cast came from several different Spanish-speaking countries and the United States.)

Villarias' Count, on the several occasions we see him arising from his coffin, does so with an atmospheric panache lacking in Lugosi's film. Whenever Lugosi is about to arise, Tod Browning pans away; we hear the lid go clunk, then the camera returns its gaze to the coffin, with Lugosi standing beside it, straightening up slowly. Villarias's coffin lid, by contrast, silently and smoothly opens on its own, in such a way as to block our view of the interior of the coffin. A cloud of vapor rises from the coffin and vanishes; like the candle flame in the credits, it simply disappears, by which we know it to be a superimposed special effect. Villarias rises from the coffin, or more accurately, he rises straight

up into view beyond it, since the lid then quietly closes, on its own, without his having to step out of its way. These scenes, utterly unlike Lugosi's analogous ones, are accompanied by music! The brief theme is always the same: a quotation in low strings from Schubert's *Unfinished Symphony*—the same few bars, in fact, heard in Browning's version just after Lugosi, in the concert hall, tells his new neighbors, "There are far worse things awaiting man than death."

As in *Nosferatu*, Renfield cuts his thumb while slicing bread. Villarias' Dracula, noticing the crucifix, doesn't recoil as though warding off a blow, as Lugosi handled the scene; he simply takes a step back with a look of discomfort on his face, much like someone upset at the sight of blood, which is, of course, Renfield's misinterpretation.

After the wine and the paperwork, Dracula leaves Renfield alone in his room. Renfield immediately begins registering a suffocating discomfort which lends more credence to Skal's theory about drugged wine. Renfield crosses to the floor-to-ceiling window and manages to open it.

A reverse-angle shot, looking in from outside, shows us that the three vampire women are standing behind Renfield, watching him. Their sudden appearance is jolting; unlike the women in Browning's film, who make their entrance, as per the screenplay, through a door to an adjoining room, these three vampire brides appear from out of nowhere.

Renfield looks out the window and sees a small courtyard wherein there is a wagon with two coffins loaded on it. This scene, omitted from Browning's film, is in the screenplay, but here it is enhanced: A third coffin, its lid slowly closing on its own, sits alongside the wagon. Dracula stands beside it, staring up at Renfield; he is too far away for us to read his facial expression, but his body language seems to indicate indignation at being spied on. A bat flutters overhead—obviously not the Count, in this version.

Renfield collapses unconscious, and the vampiresses advance upon him. Unlike the interchangeable women of Browning's film, who move as though sleepwalking and regard Renfield as if they're merely curious, these women are presented as three unruly individuals, hungry-looking and dangerous. Contrary to Stoker, but as written in the screenplay, Dracula does not call them off.

The scene shifts to the high seas and Dracula's doomed ship to England. We are shown no introductory title card as in Browning's film, which is but the first difference we notice in the two films' handling of the shipboard sequence. The Spanish film also uses, more sparingly, some footage from the same silent seafaring film, but the sequence on the whole is truer to the shooting script's conception. As the Count rises from his coffin in the ship's hold, a live rat perched atop the coffin is reminiscent of the use of rats in *Nosferatu*. This time, also as in *Nosferatu*, the sailors are aware of the danger in their midst: we see close-ups of two of the crew, and the staring, unblinking eyes of one of them indicates he may have been driven to madness with fright. Dracula emerges from the hold onto the deck and proceeds to stalk the crew, as Renfield, staring out a porthole, laughs maniacally over the howl of the gale. There is not a word of dialogue. The entire sequence lasts a little over a minute, but the effect is nightmarish.

A slight continuity problem arises with the next two scenes. The ship, having made it to England, is boarded by investigators who, as in Browning's film, are heard but not seen. One of them says, "What about the sailors? Where are they?"—which implies that the crew, as per Stoker, are missing, other than the

captain, the shadow of whose body we see gripping the wheel. Perhaps the investigator just needs to keep looking, since the very next shot, after the discovery of Renfield in the hold, is of the newspaper account telling of the ship's arrival with a "crew of corpses" ("*tripulacion de cadaveres*").

While this clipping tells us, as in Browning's version, that "*un loco es el unico sobreviviente*," it mentions neither his fly-eating nor his commitment to Dr. Seward's asylum. But a close look at the clipping (most easily done through the magic of freeze-frame) yields other information not to be found anywhere else. For one thing, it reveals the ship's name to be the *Elsie*, inexplicably enough. Even more baffling is the news that the *Elsie* has ended its voyage "*al puerto Bristol*." Bristol is a seaport in western England, just south of Wales. It must indeed, as one of the investigators observes, have been a "terrible storm" to blow them that far afield; but at least we aren't told here that Bristol is "near London."

The Count again goes to the concert hall in London, if London it is, since, unlike Browning's version, the Spanish film again offers no title card. In any case, Dracula once more tells his new neighbors that he's moved in next door to them. As noted in the previous chapter, this entire premise of a sociable, tell-all Dracula is contrary to Stoker. Here, in the Spanish film, this conception makes even less sense: not only did Renfield, we were told, keep his trip to Transylvania a secret, but—in lines not used in Browning's film—he assured Dracula that he'd burned all their letters. Why all the hush-hush if Dracula's just going to turn around and blow his cover the day he arrives?

Dr. Seward's sanitarium is established conversationally to be in Whitby again. This time around there is no geographic confusion. Whitby is not said at any time to be "near London," and the later line about the wolf howling outside the sanitarium has been altered to an expression of doubt that there are wolves "so close to men." (In fact, in this version, it sounds like a coyote.)

After Lucia's death, the post-mortem scene grants us a look at the wounds on her throat. The two punctures are enclosed inside a football-shaped outline that seems to be meant to mimic the double-crescent imprint of a human bite. Although in this version Dracula does not kill the flower girl in the street en route to the symphony, the wounds are still said to have been found "on the neck of each of the victims."

Van Helsing's involvement is, in this version, less of a mystery. In the lab scene, which here immediately follows the post-mortem, Van Helsing announces that he is "going to England with Dr. Seward to study Renfield's case"—not exactly Stoker, but it does away with the impression we get from Browning's film that Van Helsing just barges into the story uninvited. And the later line about Dr. Seward's having gone to Switzerland is restored, so we know where Van Helsing has come from. Unfortunately, this line alone doesn't make up for the lack of any indication that Dr. Seward has actually traveled anywhere; there's not even a stock shot of Alpine footage inserted to break up the studio-bound staginess into which this version, too, has already settled.

Despite the Spanish version's more extensive usage of Renfield, restoring to him scenes and dialogue either cut or never shot by Tod Browning, the puzzle of his exact importance to Dracula again goes unclarified. We learn that he graduated Oxford School of Law in 1927; we hear him expostulate (in a paraphrase of Stoker) about how the "wings of the fly … represent the aerial power of the psychic faculties"; but at no point does he say the equivalent of, "The Count can't get in here unless he's invited, and I'm just the guy to do it."

Nor does the sequence of events lend itself to this interpretation. During his first meeting with Van Helsing, Renfield pleads with Dr. Seward to release him, or "you will be responsible for what happens to your daughter." Renfield's analogous warning in the novel, as noted, is meant to preclude his inviting Dracula into the asylum, thereby granting him access to Mina, here called Eva. But here, after Renfield is hauled away by Martin, Dr. Seward and Van Helsing go into another room where Eva is telling Juan of her troubling dream about mist and red eyes, a "dream" we recognize as a visit from Dracula. He has already attacked her, the marks are already on her throat, and Renfield's being sent away after the fact would change nothing.

After the incident involving the mirror in the cigarette case, Dracula attacks Eva again, outdoors; judging by her somnambulant look, he has somehow lured her there. Renfield, meanwhile, has escaped again … or has he been released by the Count? And what involvement, if any, does Renfield have in this latest attack?

Caught outside his cell, Renfield reproaches Seward: "I begged you to let me out…. Now it is too late. It has already happened." As noted, it had already happened by the time Renfield issued his *first* warning. How could sending him away have prevented something that had already taken place? How would it have prevented Dracula from attacking again?

Several scenes later, Dracula appears outside Renfield's window, glaring. Renfield pleads with him: "Not her! Never again!" Next thing we know, Renfield is on the loose once more, and Martin discovers the bent bars on the window. (In this version, unlike Browning's, we are shown the bent bars.) The Count, meantime, is indoors, hypnotizing the nurse and making her remove the aconite (as it's known here; it is, in fact, the same thing as wolfbane) from Eva's room.

Renfield reveals to Van Helsing and Dr. Seward the Count's offer of "*ratas*" in exchange for his obedience in doing "what has already been done." Again, we are not told what deed this is; but Van Helsing knows, even before Martin enters with news of the bent bars, what it means: "Dracula is in this house." ("Where else did you expect him to be?" Renfield asks with chilling flippancy, in a line denied Dwight Frye.) It could be that the Count, this time, enters the asylum through Renfield's window—at any rate, we do not see him flitting into Eva's boudoir as a bat—but again, nothing is clarified.

Moments later, Dracula confronts Van Helsing and gloats that "Dracula's blood is already flowing in Miss Seward's veins." As we soon learn, he is referring to his having made Eva drink his blood from a cut on his arm (which again takes place offscreen). Is this what Renfield was referring to as "what has already been done"? If so, what role did his obedience to Dracula play in it? None of these questions is answered in this version, any more than in Browning's—which is a pity, since, of the two, the Spanish version follows the screenplay much more closely. One is forced to conclude that Garrett Fort's screenplay adapts this aspect of Stoker's novel—i.e., the nature of Renfield's involvement in the Count's depredations —poorly.

Other plot threads are woven among these scenes. Lucia returns as a vampire, again offscreen except for a six-second appearance in a graveyard, this time with no crying child heard. She is seen in such a long shot that she could be anybody. And a conversational scene between Juan and Martin reveals that Dr. Seward and "his famous scholar" are in Carfax Abbey, "chasing vampires." Again missing is a scripted scene in which Van Helsing and Dr. Seward, inside Carfax, are frustrated at not having found two of Dracula's three boxes; Van Helsing reproaches himself for having played his hand too soon by showing the Count what the mirror revealed.

As Van Helsing, Eduardo Arozamena is suitably redoubtable; unfortunately, in scenes in which he gets into "staring contests" with the Count, or otherwise expresses surprise or indignation, his eyes become huge and round, the whites completely surrounding the irises. The effect of this frozen gawk, together with his huge potato of a nose, is unintentionally funny. Still, at least he doesn't call anybody a "dumkopf."

On the other hand, Pablo Alvarez Rubio is enjoyable as Renfield, in a performance totally unlike Dwight Frye's. Rubio's Renfield is generally more animated, more relaxed and amiable when lucid, and much more given to histrionic fits. His idea of maniacal laughter isn't croaked, as Frye's is, but screamed.

But the show is stolen by Lupita Tovar as a teenaged Eva. In a development that can be observed to continue in vampire films over the ensuing decades, Eva isn't weakened and enervated by Dracula's attentions, as Helen Chandler's Mina is; instead, after Dracula's blood is infused into her, Eva's libido runs wild. At first, describing her dream, Eva has her misgivings, to be sure: the morning after, she says she felt "as if I had lost my virginity," a line significantly different from the script's "as if all the life had been drained out of me," which is what Chandler says.

But by the time she and Juan go out onto the terrace by night, Eva is wearing a low-cut nightgown totally unlike anything seen in Tod Browning's version, and she laughs so wantonly she makes Juan, and us, nervous. We see what's happening: she's turning into one of the Count's vampiresses, like the three in his castle, right before our eyes. Juan, not having made the trip in this version, doesn't realize the danger he's in until Eva tries bite a chunk out of him. In the analogous scene, Browning maddeningly allows Mina to move out of shot to "attack," if that's the word for it, an already–offscreen John. The contrast here between the two versions, and the two actresses, is startling.

The almost-unseen saga of Lucia ends when Van Helsing and Juan go to the cemetery and stake her; again, the actual staking happens offscreen. An earlier scene in the screenplay, depicting the two men encountering Lucia in the graveyard, still goes unfilmed. Instead, they are seen emerging from the cemetery's front gate, Juan looking a bit ill, Van Helsing reassuring him of the goodness of the deed they've just done. They then set out for Carfax.

So does everybody else: Dracula, who has abducted Eva, and Renfield, who has escaped yet again, head for Carfax, which is briefly seen, as it never is in Browning's version, in an establishing shot which shows the estate's seaside location. When Dracula hurls Renfield over the side of the interior stairwell to his death, we hear the same clunk-and-moan sound effect that accompanies the Count's offscreen staking in both versions. Sophisticated foley artistry, like all other aspects of sound in pictures, was still developing.

As Dracula, who has carried Eva into a locked crypt, prepares to attack her a final, possibly fatal time, the sun's rays angle in through a window grate, and he withdraws. The sunrise upping the ante is in the script, but is only mentioned in Browning's version, as an afterthought: Mina, after her rescue, explains that the sun stopped him. The Spanish version's more graphic depiction again brings to mind the influence of *Nosferatu*, with its lethal dawn.

Once more Juan and Van Helsing

need to improvise both a stake and a hammer to dispatch Dracula. Since they have come, in this version, straight from the staking of Lucia, one would think they would have been better prepared.

As Juan and Eva are reunited, Van Helsing says he plans to stay behind and "do good on my promise to Renfield." This line still makes no sense: in neither the finished film, nor in the screenplay, has he promised Renfield anything.

The Spanish production, in its complete form, was long a near-lost film; an incomplete copy was housed at the Library of Congress. But the entire film, in good condition, turned up in Cuba a few years back, and the film has since been made available on video (typically with a delightful interview with Lupita Tovar, in her 70s, included at the end). Like the Lugosi/Browning film, the Spanish *Dracula* is not what Stoker had in mind, and for most of the same reasons—largely arising from the half-baked, hybrid adaptation of the script from both the novel and the play. But as a curio of filmmaking and a bit of cinematic history, it's a significant find.

It is also, ironically, a better movie than Browning's, in some respects: truer to the screenplay, and with George Melford's direction and George Robinson's cinematography making a fuller realization of the visual potential of the script.

There is still only one Bela Lugosi. But there are two Universal *Dracula*s from 1931, and both are worth a look.

Musical Notes

As is the case with Tod Browning's version, there is no musical soundtrack, as such, to the Spanish version of *Dracula*. The excerpt from Tchaikovsky's *Swan Lake* once more serves as the title music.

In the concert hall scene, a longer excerpt of the same portion of Wagner's

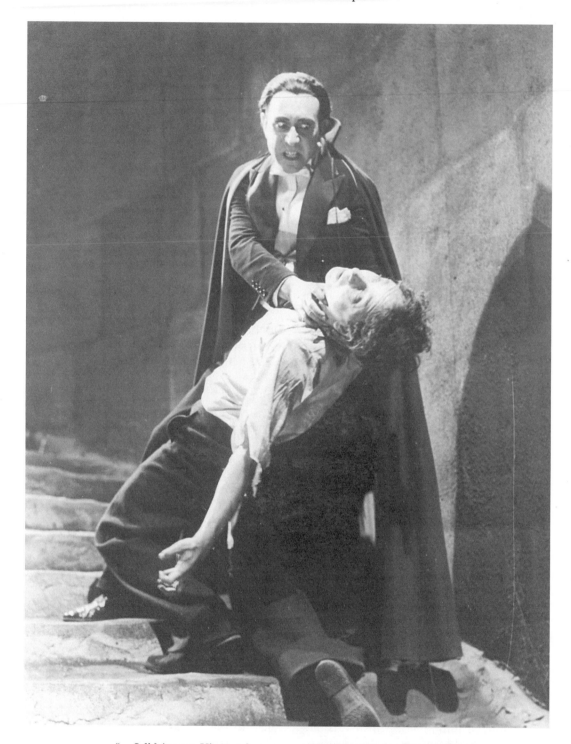

*"… I didn't mean Him to take any more of her life, till I saw His eyes. They
burned into me, and my strength became like water."*—Renfield

**Carlos Villarias as Dracula and Pablo Alvarez Rubio as Renfield in the 1931
Spanish-language *Dracula* (courtesy Ronald V. Borst of Hollywood Movie Posters)**

Die Meistersinger is heard; Melford has his cast talk over the music, evidently unafraid of the possibility that the music and the dialogue would compete for the attention of the film's audience.

The piece of Schubert's *Unfinished Symphony* heard at the end of the concert hall scene in the Browning film is not used in the Spanish version's analogous scene. As noted, it serves several times throughout the film as incidental music accompa- nying Dracula's emergence from his coffin. It works beautifully in that context, by the way. (True aficionados may also have noticed that the same few bars are used by detail-oriented director John Landis in his 1992 *Innocent Blood*, to score the awakening of Don Rickles, of all people, to his new "life" of vampirism. His vampiric career is cut short immediately by a particularly gruesome exposure to sunlight, continuing this trend as discussed earlier.)

Horror of Dracula

(U.K. title: *Dracula*)

Hammer Films (1958)
Directed by Terence Fisher
Screenplay by Jimmy Sangster,
Based on the novel by Bram Stoker
Running time: 1 hour 22 minutes
Available on video

Cast

VAN HELSING	Peter Cushing
COUNT DRACULA	Christopher Lee
ARTHUR HOLMWOOD	Michael Gough
MINA	Melissa Stribling
LUCY	Carol Marsh
JONATHAN HARKER	John Van Eyssen
VAMPIRE WOMAN	Valerie Gaunt
DR. SEWARD	Charles Lloyd Pack
GERDA	Olga Dickie
TANIA	Janine Faye

Synopsis

There is a tomb in the castle inscribed with the single word: DRACULA.

Jonathan Harker keeps a written daily journal. The year is 1885. Jonathan travels to Klausenburg, ostensibly to be Count Dracula's librarian.

The coach will only take him so far, and then he must walk the rest of the way to the castle. Finding a welcoming note, Jonathan enjoys a dinner in which the absent Count does not join him.

A mysterious young woman approaches Jonathan, pleading for his help and warning him that the Count is a terrible person. She leaves abruptly when the Count enters the room.

The Count is tall, thin, and dark-haired. He dresses totally in black and wears a cape. Dracula helps Jonathan with his bags and shows him to his room. He sees and asks Jonathan about a picture of Lucy Holmwood, Jonathan's fiancée.

"His eyes were positively blazing. The red light in them was lurid, as if all the flames of hell-fire blazed in them."—Jonathan Harker

Christopher Lee as Dracula in *Horror of Dracula* (1958) (courtesy Ronald V. Borst of Hollywood Movie Posters)

Jonathan discovers he's been locked into his room. As he writes in his diary, we learn that he has come to kill Dracula.

Someone unlocks the door, and soon Jonathan is attacked in the library by the young woman, who is a vampire. The attack is stopped by the Count.

Jonathan awakens later in his room and learns that he has been bitten.

In desperation, Jonathan climbs out the window of his room. He finds a vault in which the Count reposes in a sarcophagus in a death-like trance, with blood on his mouth. Jonathan also finds the woman in a similar state, whereupon he stakes her. Jonathan tries to kill the Count with a stake, but he fails and is trapped in the vault with him.

Van Helsing, concerned about Jonathan, follows him to the castle. En route, he encounters fearful, superstitious people at an inn. They are frightened at the mention of Dracula's name. As he nears the castle, he is nearly run down by a hearse bearing a coffin.

Jonathan, now a vampire, has to be killed with a stake.

Van Helsing bears the news of Jonathan's death to Lucy's brother, Arthur Holmwood, and his wife Mina, who live in the city of Karlstadt in a neighboring country. Lucy suffers from a mysterious illness which leaves her pale and weak. She also has two tiny wounds on her throat.

Van Helsing keeps a phonograph journal. In it, he reviews some of what he knows about vampires: sunlight is lethal to them, and garlic and crucifixes can ward them off.

Lucy is in the care of Dr. Seward. He is baffled by her illness, so Mina asks Van Helsing for a second opinion.

Van Helsing places garlic in Lucy's room, but it is removed, with disastrous results, by Gerda, the maid. Lucy dies.

Van Helsing gives Jonathan's journal to Arthur and Mina to persuade them of the reality and danger of Dracula.

The maid's little daughter, Tania, claims to have gone for a walk with "Aunt Lucy" after Lucy's burial.

Arthur goes alone to the graveyard. Inside the tomb, Lucy's coffin is empty. Later that night, Lucy returns to the tomb with Tania, only to be confronted by Van Helsing and Arthur. After trying to sweet-talk Arthur, she retreats from a cross, which burns her forehead, and re-enters her tomb. She is then staked by Van Helsing, whereupon the peace of true death is seen on her face. The mark of the cross has disappeared.

Van Helsing tells the others of his suspicions concerning Dracula: The Count is centuries old, but he has no supernatural powers such as transformation into a bat or a wolf. He must rest by day in a box of his native soil.

Dracula turns his attention to Mina. While Arthur and Van Helsing are off trying to learn where the hearse bearing Dracula's coffin went, the Count sends Mina a message supposedly from Arthur and lures her to an undertaker's where he has been hiding out. Afterwards, he disappears.

Mina's "taint" of having been attacked by Dracula is shown by a scar in the palm of her hand, made by a cross.

Dracula is somehow able to get to Mina again. Afterwards, she receives a blood transfusion from Arthur.

Dracula's hiding place is discovered, in the cellar of Arthur and Mina's home. It is an inside job, Mina having obviously acted in collusion to place him there.

Dracula flees, abducting Mina as he goes.

Van Helsing and Arthur pursue Dracula back across the border to his castle. They rescue Mina, who is being buried alive by Dracula. While Arthur comforts her, Van Helsing pursues Dracula into the castle.

A violent confrontation ensues. Dracula is killed in the library when Van Helsing pulls down a curtain to admit the morning sunlight. As Dracula dies, his body crumbles to dust, which blows away.

After Dracula's death, the scar fades from Mina's hand.

Commentary

From the minute the music starts, you know you're in trouble. The first thing you see, perched atop a stone pillar, is a sculptured imperial eagle. Symbol of Dracula's ancient martial heritage, the eagle can trace its pedigree all the way back to the empire that gave Romania its name. As the music throbs and booms, and the credits come up in blood-red Gothic letters, the camera stares at the eagle as though afraid of what it may do. The feeling you get is that you've been caught doing something you shouldn't, or that you're trapped somewhere you don't want to be.

Welcome to Castle Dracula. There is no way out.

Soon the camera starts tiptoeing, as it were, past the eagle, warily keeping it in sight, only reluctantly panning away in search of an exit. It sees a side doorway and enters it—insanely going *downstairs*, into the bowels of the castle. And it takes you with it.

The image of the passageway dissolves into a view of a gloomy interior—a crypt. You are drawn closer and closer to a frightful object described by Stoker as follows: "There was one great tomb ... lordly [and] huge it was, and nobly proportioned. On it was but one word DRACULA."

Just at that moment, the music abruptly stops. Blood—nobody's blood, blood from nowhere, unless we're watching a symbolic premonition of the ultimate fate of Jonathan Harker—suddenly spatters onto the nameplate. The first few drops appear suddenly, via jump-cut, like an orgasmic rush; the rest drip audibly in the deafening silence following the end of the music. The blood is exaggeratedly red in this, the first of all color adaptations of *Dracula*. The screams of the audiences of the 1950s must have been delicious.

Horror of Dracula is a textbook case of how a thumbnail sketch of a literary adaptation can yield a ripping good movie. The original U.K. title was simply *Dracula*, but Americans already had a movie by that title, a movie which, in those pre-VCR days, had seen occasional theatrical re-release and was therefore still in the public's mind. Besides, Universal Studios, ever since the release of Hammer Films' *The Curse of Frankenstein* in 1957, had been watching Hammer like an imperial stone eagle, prepared to swoop down and sue at the first sign of anything vaguely resembling copyright infringement. It was Universal-International, in fact, that ended up releasing *Horror of Dracula* in the States. As it happens, since the movie, as evidenced by the above synopsis, takes such extensive liberties with Stoker's novel, it makes sense to give it the variant title, which it bore not just in the States but elsewhere outside Great Britain (*Le Cauchemar de Dracula* in France, for example).

Unlike the Universal versions of 1931, *Horror of Dracula* places the story back in Stoker's Victorian era. Like the novel, it begins with Jonathan Harker's journal entry of May 3; unlike the novel, it pinpoints a year: 1885. While Stoker never tells us the exact year the action of his novel takes place, he does, as Leonard Wolf points out in *The Annotated Dracula*, give us a clue. We are told that September 22, the day the Count is seen by Jonathan and Mina in the daylit streets of London, falls on a Thursday. Wolf posits 1887 as the year in question, since its September 22 was a Thursday, but he cautions: "Any five-year period before or after 1887 will do."

Jonathan hoofs the last leg of his journey from "the village of Klausenburg." Strange to say, the name of Transylvania is never mentioned in this version; but "Klausenburgh," one of Harker's stopovers in the novel, is the earlier Saxon name of the modern city of Cluj-Napoca, in central Transylvania, giving us a clue as to Jonathan's whereabouts.

Dracula's castle is not the "vast ruined castle" of the novel, with its "broken battlements show[ing] a jagged line against the moonlit sky." In the late afternoon sunlight of Jonathan's arrival, the castle is more than picture-"esque": it is, in fact, a painting, and an unconvincing one, of a mittel-European fantasy castle, backdropped by snowy peaks and approached by a wooden bridge over a rushing stream. A cannon reminds us at a glance of the violent history of this strategic crossroads of eastern Europe, and of the part this fortress no doubt played in it. Yet at this late date in history, when, as Stoker has the Count remind us, "The warlike days are over" (Dracula, remember, meets his final end before the onset of the bloody 20th century), Jonathan is able to enter the castle ungreeted and unchallenged. In a world where the coach will not bring Jonathan within several kilometers of the castle, Dracula hardly needs to worry about intruders or thieves. One is reminded of the ancient tale of Prince Vlad Tepes of Wallachia, a.k.a. Dracula, that during his reign he left a jewel-encrusted solid gold goblet next to a roadside spring for travelers to use. Nobody stole it. Nobody dared.

Jonathan is soon approached by a mysterious young woman who pleads for his help. As he will learn soon enough, she is, of course, a vampire; this moderately-budgeted version evidently couldn't afford the full harem of three women. (The other two turn up in *The Brides of Dracula* in 1960.)

For the time being, Jonathan is met, finally, by Dracula, played by an energetic young Christopher Lee, who bounds up the stairs two at a time as he shows Jonathan to his room. Mr. Lee's international fame was secured by this role, which, as noted earlier, he went on to reprise in most of the rest of the Hammer series (the sole exception being *The Legend of the Seven Golden Vampires*). Fortunately, unlike Bela Lugosi, Mr. Lee found that there was life after Dracula; in addition to non-Dracula horror movies from Hammer and Amicus, he also worked in more "mainstream" films, such as *The Three/Four Musketeers* (1974/75) and the James Bond entry, *The Man with the Golden Gun* (1975).

How is he as Dracula? Is he what Bram Stoker envisioned? Yes and no: In appearance he differs insofar as he is not an old man with white hair and a full mustache. His all-black attire coincides with Stoker, and although his use of the full cloak effectively accentuates his height and slim build, it is debatably too much of a gimmick that might, in at least a scene or two, have been dispensed with. Otherwise, he is very much what Stoker's novel describes: he is tall and lean, physically powerful, aristocratic and arrogant, and utterly malevolent. It could be argued that Christopher Lee, in this and other appearances as Dracula, is so far the last actor to play the Count as a totally unsympathetic villain, a monster so long dead that hardly a trace of humanity remains.

Except one: he has a library. Unlike Stoker's Dracula, who travels to London evidently bent on some sort of plan of conquest (as Harker speculates, "perhaps, for centuries to come he might, amongst [London's] teeming millions, ... create a new and ever-widening circle of semi-demons to batten on the helpless"), this Dracula, when he's not preying on the locals, is a reclusive country squire who just wants to be left alone with his books. World conquest? At his age? Not likely. Besides, as a tyrannical member of the ruling class, this Dracula is less in the mold of an expansionist Hitler than that of his countryman Nicolae Ceausescu: he is content to exploit and abuse the populace of that backwoods portion of the world that is rightfully his. Meantime, his big plan is just to get his library in order. Dracula hires Jonathan Harker as a librarian. Only after Jonathan betrays his trust and stakes the Count's best girl does this Dracula stir from his home and embark on a quest for revenge. It could be argued that he has a case. (Bibliophiles will also note that Jonathan misses quite an opportunity. The Count, Van Helsing later tells us, may be "five or six hundred years old." Imagine the collection one could amass in that time! "There are a large number of volumes to be indexed," the Count dryly observes. No doubt.)

Jonathan, as it turns out, is too dense for the part of undercover vampire hunter: when the dishy vampiress again begs him for help, it doesn't once seem to occur to him that this woman, whom he has twice encountered afoot in a known vampire's home, and both times at night, just may be part of the problem. It doesn't seem to enter his mind that maybe Dracula locks him into his room for his own protection. He lets her get too close, she puts the bite on him, and the Count immediately intervenes.

The Count is just in from a successful blood-hunt: his mouth is smeared with it; his eyes are reddened with it. His sudden, furious appearance, and his two-fisted disruption of the vampiress's attack, while completely unlike the way Bela Lugosi handled the same scene, are true to Stoker's vision: "Never did I imagine such wrath and fury, even to the demons of the pit. His eyes were positively blazing. The red light in them was lurid.... His face was deathly pale, and the lines of it were hard like drawn wires.... With a fierce sweep of his arm, he hurled the woman from him...." But, contrary to Stoker, this violent scene is played out without any dialogue. We do not hear the Count's reprimand, "How dare you cast eyes on him when I had forbidden it?... This man belongs to me! Beware how you meddle with him, or you'll have to deal with me." Nor do we hear him say, "I promise you that when I am through with him you shall kiss him at your will." As a result, this scene, pitting a vampire against a vampire for no evident reason, makes very little sense as filmed ... which arguably makes it the more frightening. Are they two dogs scrapping over a bone, i.e. Jonathan, or what?

As it turns out, the Count has no more dialogue at all. His last line—the ironic "Sleep well, Mr. Harker"—comes barely ten minutes into the film. In the first sequel in which the Count appears, *Dracula, Prince of Darkness*, he has not a word of dialogue. Nor does he speak in 1968's *Dracula Has Risen from the Grave* until more than twenty minutes into the story, so we've heard the last from him for a while. For the rest of this version, he casts off the pretense of being a conversational human being and becomes the boogeyman, seldom seen and never heard.

As if he's not in enough trouble, Jonathan mixes in when the Count pulls the vampire woman off him. He tries to protect the woman whose bite has possibly just doomed him—and who is still trying to lunge at him! The Count, of course, has no time for this interference with his domestic affairs; he coldcocks Harker and carries the woman from the room. Jonathan awakes in his own room: even after his impertinence, the Count has, like a gentleman, returned the unconscious Jonathan to his bed, again locking him in for his own protection. The Count has also discreetly refrained from reading Jonathan's diary, as evidenced by Harker's still being alive.

Not knowing when to quit, Jonathan pushes his luck too far at last: he escapes from his room, finds the crypt, and stakes the woman. Her screams wake the Count—it is right at sunset—and the Count decides he's had enough of his troublesome houseguest. Jonathan doesn't make it out the castle alive.

This is, of course, quite a major departure from Stoker, and one that many readers of the novel find upsetting. But when I mentioned that *Horror of Dracula* is a textbook example of a good movie which is at best a tentative adaptation of its source, the textbook I had in mind was *Writing Screenplays That Sell*, by Michael Hauge. Of adaptations from novel to film, Hauge writes (emphasis his): "*You must be truer to your screenplay than to your original source.* If, in order to fulfill the requirements of film structure and character, you have to alter or eliminate parts of the original material, then do it." Jimmy Sangster does it. Jonathan Harker, who survives Castle Dracula in the book only to become just another fretful, ineffectual character unable to protect Mina from the Count, has served his purpose in this version. Whereas, in the novel, he helps the Count fill out the paperwork for a move already planned, in *Horror of Dracula*, it is his bungled attempt as a vampire hunter that draws the Count out in the first place. Having staked the Count's mate, Jonathan motivates him to look for another. Dracula chooses Jonathan's fiancée, Lucy Holmwood. Sangster, having bumped off the superfluous Jonathan, has also neatly set the stage for the doom of Lucy, as per the novel. By pairing off Jonathan and Lucy, Sangster lets the dead bury their dead.

When Van Helsing arrives at the castle, in addition to having to stake Jonathan,

he discovers the diptych frame in which Jonathan had carried two pictures of Lucy, pictures which, in a popular non-Stoker touch, Dracula had seen and asked about. Only a shred of one of the two pictures now remains: Dracula has yanked them out, leaving only the frames. A sentimental treasure has been chillingly reduced to an ID photo.

Due to the budget constraints of this version, Dracula doesn't take a sea voyage to London, not even via footage pirated from another film. Instead, he takes a hearse to the town of Karlstadt, wherever that may be. There is a Karlstadt in Germany, but in order to get there from Klausenburg in central Transylvania, Dracula would have to travel across modern-day Hungary and Austria. The impression the movie gives is that it's an overnight trip, so Karlstadt is evidently a fictional town somewhere in Transylvania. There is a border crossing guard in the story, so Karlstadt must be in a neighboring "state," province, or district. (The border crossing, we're told, is at "Ingstadt," itself apparently a fictional town and therefore not much help here.) As for its name, "Karlstadt" here compares with the "Carlsbruck" seen the same year (1958) in Hammer's *The Revenge of Frankenstein*, and with the "Karlstaad" seen in 1964's *The Evil of Frankenstein*. The creation of a generic Germanic archetypal town is what goes on here, comparable to Universal's having set part of its Frankenstein series in the never-land town of Visaria.

It is ironic that in this, the first British adaptation of *Dracula*, the Count doesn't go to London. In Hammer's series, he doesn't finally turn up in England until *Taste the Blood of Dracula* in 1970. Still, *Horror of Dracula* is so very British that articles have been written about it by reviewers who didn't notice that it *isn't* London that Dracula invades. Seems like the undertaker's address in the movie—

on "Friederickstrasse"—would have provided a clue.

This Dracula, like Stoker's, doesn't announce his arrival in town by turning up in polite society at the concert hall; beyond being merely reclusive, he is actively hiding out. Our first clue of the Count's presence in Karlstadt is Lucy's sudden illness. The baffled Dr. Seward is here no more than a general practitioner who makes house calls; unlike Stoker's Seward, he is neither one of Lucy's suitors nor does he run an asylum.

Which means, of course, that this version features no Renfield. Though written years before Michael Hauge's book, Sangster's take-no-prisoners approach to streamlining Bram Stoker's overlong, overpopulated story still serves as a prime illustration of what Hauge seems to have had in mind. While some of the novel's readers harbor a grudge against *Horror of Dracula* for this exclusion, I'd rather see Renfield omitted outright than reduced to an irrelevant grotesque, or worse, to comic relief, both of which have happened. (The Renfield character turns up, under another name, in 1965's *Dracula, Prince of Darkness*.)For all it omits from Stoker's story, *Horror of Dracula* is the first adaptation to give full narrative scope and weight to the ordeal of Lucy, her "illness," death, and resurrection as a vampire. Much of the action surrounding Mina or Eva in the 1931 versions is restored to Lucy: the nightly visits from Dracula; the placement of garlic (as opposed to wolfbane) in her room; its fatal removal by a well-meaning household member. For the first time onscreen we see Lucy as a vampire from something other than a great distance. We see in action—not in newsprint—her preference for young children: Lucy lures away not just any little girl, but a girl she knows and loves, Tania, the maid's daughter. "In Roumania," Summers writes in *The Vampire in Europe*, "and other lands the vampire first attacks his own household." Lucy, who dies single and childless, seeks to prey on the child closest to her. We see her initially empty coffin; the later confrontation at her tomb, accompanied by the child; her attempt to schmooze Arthur Holmwood (her fiancé in Stoker; her brother here); her retreat from a cross (which sears her forehead as the communion wafer does Mina's in the novel); and her staking (graphically done, for the standards of the time), after which the peaceful look of true death is seen on her face. In these segments of *Horror of Dracula*, Stoker's story is being filmed more faithfully than ever before.

A possible continuity problem arises in Lucy's tomb. Van Helsing tells Arthur, "I've watched her tomb each night since she was interred three days ago. Tonight she ventured out for the first time." This is puzzling, since Tania has already told Arthur and Mina of a "little walk" she and "Aunt Lucy" took together earlier. That encounter, in order to be in agreement with Van Helsing's observation, must have taken place earlier the same night. This is entirely possible, since we learn that the confrontation at the tomb happens just before dawn. But it begs the question why Tania isn't guarded more closely after having already seen Lucy once.

In any case, there is a definite anachronism in the same scene. Bundling Tania up in his own coat, Van Helsing says, "You look like a teddy bear now." Teddy bears, of course, derive their name from Theodore Roosevelt, U.S. President from 1901 to 1909, and a well-known hunter and outdoorsman, hence his association with wildlife such as bears. In 1885, Roosevelt was an up-and-coming young player in the Republican Party politics of New York State, still a long way from the international fame and popularity that awaited him.

In another substantial departure from

"As he had placed [it] on [her] forehead, it had seared it—had burned into the flesh as though it had been a piece of white-hot metal."—Jonathan Harker

**Lucy (Carol Marsh) is seared by the cross in *Horror of Dracula* (1958)
(courtesy Ronald V. Borst of Hollywood Movie Posters)**

Stoker, and indeed from folklore, Van Helsing tells Arthur that the Count is incapable of transformation into a wolf or bat. To be sure, in European folklore, metamorphosis into a bat was a later development, mainly because the various species of vampire bats (of the genera *Desmodus*, *Diphylla*, and *Diaemus*) are found only in the Americas, ranging from Mexico through Central and South America, plus certain Caribbean islands. In the novel, Quincey Morris tells of his experience "on the Pampas" (i.e., in central Argentina) with "one of those big bats they call vampires": a favorite horse of his was killed, he says, by a single bat in a single night. This is a wildly improbable story, since vampire bats aren't "big" at all, and the amount of blood they take in any one attack is minuscule; the main threat they pose, to livestock or to people, is the spread of rabies. In any event, after the discovery of vampire bats by European explorers, the bat joined the ranks of things into which a vampire could transform himself, which included, according to Heinrich von Wlislocki, "a black cat, a black dog, a beetle, a butterfly, or even a simple straw." Jimmy Sangster's script dismisses all of this folkloric heritage. Certainly this decision disappoints, since it limits Dracula so much; but on the other hand, it provides a way for a moderately-budgeted film to spare itself, and us, the embarrassing sight of phony rubber bats on strings.

Hammer's Dracula series, discussed more fully in a later section of this book, followed through with this tendency to demythologize the Count: although he can hypnotize, Dracula never attains the power to transform, to summon rats or fogs or tempests, or to walk through walls. In other, non–Dracula Hammer vampire efforts, e.g. *Vampire Circus* (1971), transformation into bats can be found; yet in *Kiss of the Vampire* (1964; extensively tampered with and retitled *Kiss of Evil* for American TV), the vampire cult are *destroyed* by ensorceled bats.

Mina's secret tryst with Dracula is revealed when a cross brands her palm, again analogous to the communion wafer's searing her forehead in the novel. Despite their vigil, Van Helsing and Arthur are unable to prevent Dracula from attaining Mina's room again. How does he get into the house? It is learned that he is already concealed within: in the mocking words of Renfield in the Spanish version of 1931, "Where else did you expect him to be?" The "inside job" pulled by Renfield in the novel is here perpetrated by Mina herself.

After Dracula abducts Mina, a breakneck chase back to his castle ensues. Let's freeze-frame the action and have a look at the pursuers and other interested parties.

The late Peter Cushing was already an established actor, both on stage and in film, by the time he landed the role of Van Helsing. Hammer was obviously delighted to have him on board, especially in the wake of the previous year's success with *The Curse of Frankenstein*: in the opening credits for *Horror of Dracula*, his name appears *before* the film's title. (In the title role, Christopher Lee, who had been Mr. Cushing's *Curse of Frankenstein* co-star, only rates a "with" listing, after the "also starring" Michael Gough and Melissa Stribling, as Arthur and Mina.) Mr. Cushing makes the role of Van Helsing totally his own, and much as Stoker wrote him: a man of unwavering belief in both science and faith, a man of intellect and charm, a man of courage and action. Losing only the awkward and inconsistent accent Stoker gave the character, Mr. Cushing went on to reprise the role in several of Hammer's sequels.

Michael Gough, another Hammer regular and an accomplished character actor (well-known in recent years as the butler, Alfred, in the *Batman* films), plays

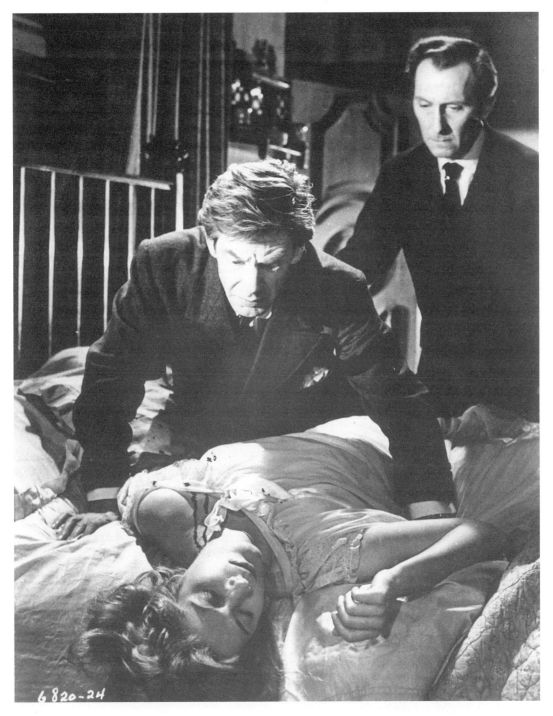

"There on the bed, seemingly in swoon, [she] lay ... more horribly white and wan-looking than ever."—John Seward

Peter Cushing (right) as Van Helsing, Michael Gough as Arthur Holmwood, and Melissa Stribling as Mina in *Horror of Dracula* (1958) (courtesy Ronald V. Borst of Hollywood Movie Posters)

Arthur Holmwood with just the right mix of resolution and befuddled dimness. When Mina turns up early one morning, smiling, looking like the cat that ate the canary, with her wrap clutched snugly around her throat, he observes that she looks "pale"; later, when the cross burns her hand, he has the nerve to act surprised.

As Mina, Melissa Stribling is attractive and intelligent in a married-woman-in-trouble sort of way. Carol Marsh, as Lucy, effectively makes the transformation from braided not-so-innocent to (in Stoker's words) "the Thing in the coffin" that "writhe[s]" when staked. John Van Eyssen's Jonathan Harker is, if anything, even more of a nebbish than usual; good riddance. The misnamed Valerie Gaunt is the Count's curvaceous and wonderfully green-eyed cryptmate. Mercifully brief comic relief is provided by George Benson as the venal border guard, and by Miles Malleson as an impish undertaker. (Malleson returns in *The Brides of Dracula*, as an equally impish, and highly unethical, doctor; seeing the two movies back-to-back, one wonders if the two characters aren't evil twins working in cahoots.)

Back to the chase, which is made the more urgent by its once again being a race against the sunrise. After Arthur rescues Mina from being buried alive, which presumably would have hastened her vampiric resurrection, Van Helsing follows Dracula into the castle. It all ends where it began, in the Count's library, where Van Helsing yanks down the curtains and lets the morning sun stream in. Anybody who wants to comment on the symbolic nature of the scene—the scholar and scientist letting in the light which dispels the darkness of medieval superstition—go ahead, but the ghost of the late Terence Fisher, who reportedly prided himself on his films' lack of subtlety, will laugh in your face.

Van Helsing forces Dracula into the shaft of light with a "cross" formed with two candlesticks. This bit of winging-it was Peter Cushing's suggestion. As he tells it in his autobiography: "... the script demand[ed] Van Helsing carry so many crucifixes, it read as if he was a traveling salesman in these relics, and could have been risible.... Rather than take yet another one from my pocket, I asked Terry if there could be some candlesticks on the long ... table, which I could grab and clash together in the form of a cross." It works, and Dracula is incinerated, crumbling, while *still alive*, to an ashy dust that blows away afterward. As Stoker has Mina describe the scene: "It was like a miracle; but before our eyes, and almost in the drawing of a breath, the whole body crumbled into dust and passed from our sight." The film ends with an image paraphrased from Stoker: the cross-shaped mark in Mina's palm disappears, as the mark on her forehead vanishes in the novel.

Cutting Stoker's plot back to its bare bones, eliminating the deadwood of the book, *Horror of Dracula* not only captures the essence of the novel; it distills it. There has never been any pretense surrounding this film. It is, as its overseas title announces, a horror movie, and a good one. As a version of Stoker's story, it is one of the most freely adapted and, ironically, therefore one of the best.

Musical Notes

James Bernard's main title, whose three-note theme reflects the three syllables of Dracula's name, is a modally-based piece that varies between 4/4 and 3/4 time. Structurally, it is in the form ABA'. The A section introduces the melody in brass and woodwinds, with no strings; percussion is provided by timpani, suspended cymbals, and gongs. The B section is totally chromatic, featuring strings in unison octaves at first, which then spread into harmonized parts. The brass then joins in to usher in the A' section, similar to the A section except that the full orchestra is now present. The melody is now played by the brass as well, and ornamented by strings. The overall effect of this loud, brash piece, just over two minutes long, is heart-pounding and intimidating.

This theme, along with the other selections from the soundtrack of *Horror of Dracula*, is now available on a CD titled "Dracula: Classic Scores from Hammer Horror," released by Silva Screen Records America, Inc. (SSD 1026). The CD also includes selections of Bernard's music from *Dracula, Prince of Darkness, Dracula Has Risen from the Grave,* and *Taste the Blood of Dracula,* as well as music from *Vampire Circus* by David Whitaker, and from *Hands of the Ripper* by Christopher Gunning. The music was digitally recorded for the CD in September 1989 by the Philharmonia Orchestra, directed by Neil Richardson.

El Conde Dracula

(U.S. title: *Count Dracula*)
(U.K. title: *Bram Stoker's Count Dracula*)

A Towers of London Production (1970)
Directed by Jess (Jesus) Franco
Screenplay by Peter Welbeck
Running time: 1 hour 38 minutes
Available on video (The title *Bram Stoker's Count Dracula*
appears on the tape.)

Cast

JONATHAN HARKER	Frederick Williams
COUNT DRACULA	Christopher Lee
DR. SEWARD	Paul Muller
VAN HELSING	Herbert Lom
RENFIELD	Klaus Kinski
MINA	Maria Rohm
LUCY	Soledad Miranda
QUINCEY	Jack Taylor
DRACULA'S WIVES	unbilled

Synopsis

The year is 1897. Jonathan Harker travels to Transylvania to close a real estate deal with Count Dracula.

En route, Jonathan meets fearful, superstitious people on a train who are frightened at the mention of Dracula's name. He also encounters people at an inn who are frightened since it is the eve of St. George's Day, and the forces of evil will take command at midnight.

The next day, he encounters passengers on a coach who are also frightened to be in the company of someone who goes to meet Count Dracula.

The coach only takes him as far as the Borgos [*sic*] Pass, where Dracula's own carriage picks him up. The Count's carriage is driven by Dracula himself, in disguise. He offers Jonathan a flask.

En route to the castle, the carriage is pursued by wolves. Dracula dismounts and sends them away.

At the castle, Jonathan is greeted by the Count, who is tall, thin, and white-haired. The Count carries a candelabrum and dresses totally in black. He has a white mustache and noticeably sharp teeth.

The Count makes excuses as to the absence of his servants and shows Jonathan to his room. A large mirror on the wall shows that the Count has no reflection.

Jonathan enjoys a supper in which the Count does not join him. They discuss the sale of the old house the Count wishes to purchase.

Dracula sees and asks about a picture of Jonathan's fiancée, Mina, and her best friend Lucy Westenra.

Dracula tells Jonathan about Transylvanian history.

Wolves howl outside, and the Count remarks: "Listen to them—the children of the night. What music they make!"

Jonathan later discovers that he has been locked into his room.

"I didn't quite dream; but it all seemed to be real.... I had a vague memory of something long and dark with red eyes..."—Lucy Westenra

Christopher Lee as the Count and Soledad Miranda as Lucy in *El Conde Dracula* (1970) (courtesy Ronald V. Borst of Hollywood Movie Posters)

A woman comes to the castle pleading for the return of her child.

Jonathan is attacked by three vampire women, two brunettes and a blonde. The attack is stopped by the Count, who gives them a child to feed on.

Jonathan later awakes in his room. Looking out a window, he watches as Dracula turns into a bat and flies away.

Jonathan learns he has been bitten. In desperation, he climbs out his window and down an outer wall.

Jonathan finds a vault in which the Count reposes in a sarcophagus. He's in a death-like trance, and appears to be younger, his white hair having turned dark gray.

Jonathan flees in terror. He makes a desperate leap to escape, not to be heard from again for many weeks.

Along with an unspecified number of boxes of earth, Dracula somehow travels to England.

Jonathan is nursed back to health by Dr. Seward in Van Helsing's private clinic near London. Renfield is also a patient in Van Helsing's care. Renfield catches and eats insects.

Dracula's house is near the clinic. His boxes are taken to the house by a moving company.

Mina and Lucy come to fetch Jonathan. Lucy suffers from a mysterious illness which leaves her pale and weak. She stays on at Van Helsing's clinic to be cared for.

Lucy walks in her sleep. Mina follows her and sees her, at a distance, being preyed upon by Dracula, who disappears.

Lucy has two tiny wounds on her throat. Mina believes them to be pinpricks inflicted when she pinned a shawl around Lucy's throat before walking her back to her room. Lucy's illness baffles Dr. Seward.

Lucy is engaged to Quincey Morris, a young nobleman. She receives blood transfusions from Quincey, but because of nightly visits from Dracula, she continues to waste away.

Renfield is linked to the Count because he traveled to Transylvania and returned insane, his young daughter having been killed by Dracula. Renfield escapes when Dracula moves into his nearby home.

Lucy soon dies.

Van Helsing tells the others of his suspicions regarding Dracula: the Count can transform himself into a bat or a wolf; he "throws strange shadows … upon the earth"; he rests by day in a box of his native soil.

Lucy is buried.

Lucy, now a vampire, victimizes children. Van Helsing leads Quincey and Jonathan to the graveyard. Inside the tomb, Lucy's coffin is empty. Later that night, they discover that Lucy has returned to her grave. Van Helsing stakes Lucy. Quincey then decapitates her.

After everyone compares notes, it is discovered that the Count's residence is right next door to Van Helsing's clinic. Van Helsing gives Jonathan and Quincey crucifixes, which he says will repel the Count.

After Van Helsing suffers a mild stroke, Jonathan, Dr. Seward, and Quincey infiltrate the Count's house. They learn that some of the boxes of earth are missing. While in the house, they are attacked by taxidermized animals.

Meanwhile, Mina pays Renfield a visit. He tries to kill her.

A crucifix halts the attack of the animals, and the party sanctify the Count's house.

Jonathan is shocked to see Dracula in the streets of London, looking younger still, his hair having turned black.

Dracula turns his attention to Mina. Sending her a message supposedly from Jonathan, he lures her to the opera, where he attacks her. Afterwards, he disappears.

Dracula books passage aboard the *Czarina Catherine*, a ship bound for the Black Sea port of Varna. Renfield's psychic link to Dracula enables the others to learn his destination.

Dracula confronts Van Helsing and tries to abduct Mina. When Van Helsing produces a cross, Dracula flees.

Jonathan and Quincey pursue Dracula to Transylvania. They precede him into the castle and stake the three women. As Quincey stakes the last of them, blood squirts into his face.

There is a tomb in the castle inscribed with the single word: DRACULA.

Just before sunset, Dracula approaches the castle. He is in a box loaded onto a wagon driven and guarded by peasants. A violent confrontation ensues.

Dracula is killed when Jonathan and Quincey burn him in his coffin and dump him off a cliff.

Commentary

By the end of the 1960s, Christopher Lee had starred in his first three Hammer Dracula efforts, with the fourth and fifth due to come out in 1970. By this time it was clear that the studio was not interested in the dramatic potential of Dracula as a character and was content to use him as a one-dimensional boogeyman. Mr. Lee lamented the limited range of Hammer's Dracula, but, as a working-stiff actor, he continued to play the role. Fortunately, unlike Mr. Lugosi before him, Mr. Lee found other work available, and so was beginning to look to the day when he would never again don the cape and fangs … unless he could play the role as Bram Stoker had written it.

Around that time the rumors started to be heard on this side of the Atlantic: that a major new adaptation of *Dracula*, faithful to the novel, big-budgeted, was about to be/was being/had just been filmed, in anticipation of the novel's 75th anniversary in 1972. The rumors were irresistible: not only was Christopher Lee fulfilling his long-desired wish, but he was opposite Vincent Price as Van Helsing, under the direction of long-time collaborator Terence Fisher! Fans and followers in the States sat back and waited.

And waited: 1970 came and went with no sign of the film's release stateside; just a few atmospheric-looking stills in the occasional monster-movie magazine. Then, silence.

What happened? Apparently either some international financing sources fell through or else never materialized. The film that was ultimately made, an Italian-Spanish-German co-production titled *El Conde Dracula*, did in fact star Mr. Lee in the title role. But Vincent Price was not on board, the role of Van Helsing being played instead by veteran character actor Herbert Lom. And instead of Terence Fisher, the film was helmed by Jess Franco.

Jess Franco, a.k.a. Jesus Franco, a.k.a. Jeff Frank, is the director of more than 150 films under almost as many pseudonyms (not one of which, surprisingly, is the legendary nom-de-anonymous-director Allen Smithee). Mr. Franco is undeniably prolific, having made as many as a dozen films

in a single year. Many of his films, such as *A Virgin Among the Living Dead*, *Sadisterotica*, and *Kiss Me, Monster*, deal with horror, gore, erotica, fantasy, or a mix of these elements, so he brought some experience, and experience in the genre, to *El Conde Dracula*. But although he has a fan following on an international scale, including a website called "The FrancoFile," the sad fact is that he doesn't have enough talent to direct traffic. *El Conde Dracula* is a dull, cheap-looking failure.

The trouble starts even before the story does. A ludicrous title card informs us that Bram Stoker wrote his novel "over fifty years ago"; it was nearly 75 years by then. The title goes on to boast of the film's intent to "retell [the story] exactly as he wrote" it—always a red flag, especially when adapting a longish novel (editions of *Dracula* tend to run over 400 pages) into a movie less than two hours long.

A very non-Stoker Jonathan heads into Transylvania. The actor, Frederick Williams (possibly a pseudonym, since his English is as badly dubbed as anyone else's), is quite Mediterranean-looking, and bears a scar on his upper lip. Hardly Stoker's non-streetwise young man, this fellow could be a barroom brawler. When he reveals his destination to his fellow travelers, they snub him with dirty looks aplenty, unlike the well-meaning yokels of the novel, who do everything they can to convince Jonathan not to continue his journey.

When Dracula greets Jonathan at the castle, we see that he is, indeed, presented much as Stoker describes him in Chapter 2 of the novel: once again tall, lean, pale and black-clad, as Christopher Lee has played him several times before, he now has, for the first time, white hair and a full white mustache. Jonathan is visibly shaken by the sight of the Count's sharp canines as he speaks of "the children of the night" and, for the first time on screen, recites some of his family's (and, indeed, his own) contributions to the history of Transylvania. Lee's portrayal is restrained, low-key and literate, not the one-note, red-eyed, hissing caricature of most of the Hammer series. If (*if*) this film has any saving grace at all, Lee's performance is it; one finds oneself frequently wishing it had been featured in a better movie. But, alas, Jess Franco (a.k.a. Clifford Brown, a.k.a. Dave Tough) is behind the camera, and his too-frequent, headache-inducing zoom shots aren't going to let you forget it.

This "exactly as he wrote [it]" adaptation continues to wander from Stoker: once again the non-Stoker episode of the picture of Mina and Lucy is included; fair enough, since so many versions feature a variation on this theme, no doubt because this technique is a convenient way for a screenwriter to introduce absent characters into the story. Plus, Mina and Lucy's names, and their relationships to Jonathan and to each other, are correct here.

But for some reason, the name of Carfax is never given. And when the Count shows Jonathan to his room, they come face-to-face with a mirror that fills an entire wall. This is in dire contrast to Jonathan's observation in the novel: "There are certainly odd deficiencies in the house ... in none of the rooms is there a mirror. There is not even a toilet glass on my table...." Jonathan stands before this wall of glass, baffled at the Count's absence of reflection, while the Count seems blithely indifferent to having his cover thus blown. A similar scene in a bedroom is funny in *The Fearless Vampire Killers*; it's supposed to be. Here it's just ridiculous.

Looking out the window of his room, Jonathan observes the Count, not climbing down a wall as per Stoker, but turning into a bat and flying away. At least, that's one's best guess as to what is supposed to be seen. This moment is one of

many that are defeated by the film's stifling cheapness.

Another budgetary short-circuit: we are given no clue as to how Jonathan, after his leap from Castle Dracula, turns up in Van Helsing's (!) clinic, near London. We are similarly afforded no hint as to how Dracula has turned up in England as well. The makers of earlier versions overcame the budgetary challenge of the trip to England, either by the use of stock seafaring footage (both 1931 versions), or by shortening the Count's journey to a day trip (1958). Franco just ignores the logistical problems and insultingly hopes we won't notice.

After Lucy falls ill, no effort is made to protect her from Dracula's nightly visits; i.e., no garlic is placed in her room, nor wolfbane, nor crosses. She receives a blood transfusion from her fiancé Quincey Morris, who is here a hybrid character: he has the name of the Texan in the novel, but he is an Englishman with a title, like Arthur Holmwood, Lucy's fiancé per Stoker, who is absent here. Lucy's third suitor from the novel, Dr. Seward, here has no such interest; and he is merely Van Helsing's employee, instead of the head of the asylum, as Stoker has it.

Lucy is played by a young actress named Soledad Miranda, who, before her untimely death in late 1971 at the age of 27, appeared in several other films by Franco, including the provocatively-titled *Vampyros Lesbos* (1970). As Lucy, she is as pretty as a porcelain doll, and almost as lively. Christopher Lee reportedly experienced an on-camera chemistry with Ms. Miranda unlike that of any other actress with whom he'd worked. Pity that this quality, like a vampire, doesn't show up on film. After Lucy's resurrection, Ms. Miranda's appearance in the coffin—eyes staring, mouth bloodied—effectively evokes Dr. Seward's description from the novel: "She seemed like a nightmare of

Lucy as she lay there; the pointed teeth, the bloodstained, voluptuous mouth—which it made one shudder to see—the whole carnal and unspiritual appearance, seeming like a devilish mockery of Lucy's sweet purity." The trouble here is, she looks and acts the same before death as after. Ms. Miranda, blessed with exactly one facial expression, evidently couldn't act her way out of a paper bag.

Lucy is staked by Van Helsing and decapitated by her fiancé—the reverse of who-does-what in the novel. It is interesting that Quincey's beheading tool of choice is a shovel. In the novel, Jonathan unsuccessfully tries to kill Dracula with a shovel: "There was no lethal weapon at hand, but I seized a shovel which the workmen had been using to fill the cases, and lifting it high, struck, with the edge downward, at the hateful face. But as I did so the head turned...."

Montague Summers, in *The Vampire: His Kith and Kin*, concludes: "When the stake has been thrust with one drive through the Vampire's heart his head should be cut off, and this is to be done with the sharp edge of a sexton's spade, rather than with a sword.... The only certain methods of destroying a Vampire appear to be either to consume him by fire [make a mental note of this method], or to chop off his head with a grave-digger's shovel." Thus the style of Lucy's beheading, while non-Stoker, has folkloric precedent.

Renfield, played as a near-catatonic by the late Klaus Kinski, once again has his mysterious link to Count Dracula "explained" in terms of his once having traveled to Transylvania and had terrible experiences in the vicinity of Castle Dracula. This time these experiences involve the death of a young daughter whose existence would be news to Stoker. When Mina pays Renfield a visit, he tries to kill her; in the novel, he tries to warn her

about Dracula, and ends up giving his own life trying to save her from him.

Whereas, in *Horror of Dracula*, Mina usurps the absent Renfield's role as inside operative, here Renfield returns the favor: it is he, and not Mina, whose psychic link to Dracula enables the vampire-hunting party to learn that the Count has fled to Varna. He also, unlike the Renfield of the novel, survives the story, despite a fall from an upstairs window during an escape attempt.

Van Helsing, in detailing the characteristics of the vampire to the others, says that he "throws strange shadows ... upon the earth." Little is made of this strange, non-Stoker observation (in the novel, of course, the Count throws no shadow at all). The comment seems to trace its pedigree to *Nosferatu*, and may, in concept, have helped pave the way for the mischievous shadowplay of *Bram Stoker's Dracula*.

Van Helsing, for impenetrable reasons, suffers a stroke in this version. (The closest this incident comes to being in the novel is that "stroke" is an anagram for "Stoker".) His debilitation means that Jonathan, Quincey, and Dr. Seward must go without him to the Count's unnamed house. There they are attacked by a group of taxidermized animals. This incident is not only non-Stoker, it is so badly and unconvincingly filmed as to be laughable. There is no sense of menace from these stuffed carcasses at all. Nor does Jess Franco's hyperactive zoom lens, repeatedly bringing the animals into extreme close-up, make them seem dangerous or frightening. Up to this point, the adaptation has been rocky at best, with most of its problems arising from its threadbare budget. At this point, with that paltry budget applied to an attempted effects scene which is both beyond its capabilities and untrue to both the letter and the spirit of the novel, we can no longer pretend we're

"It made me shudder to think of so mutilating the body of the woman whom I had loved. And yet the feeling was not so strong as I had expected."—John Seward

Left to right: Jack Taylor as Quincey, Herbert Lom as Van Helsing, Soledad Miranda as Lucy, Frederick Williams as Jonathan Harker in *El Conde Dracula* **(1970) (courtesy Ronald V. Borst of Hollywood Movie Posters)**

watching anything with a credible claim to be a definitive, or even an adequate, adaptation of Stoker.

Dracula's luring of Mina to the opera is a non-Stoker incident which borrows from Dracula's trip to the concert hall in the 1931 adaptations, as well as from his luring Mina to the undertaker's parlor, also in the name of her husband (albeit a different husband), in *Horror of Dracula*.

Jonathan and Quincey proceed to Dracula's castle in Transylvania, again without the incapacitated Van Helsing. This is the only film version of *Dracula*, other than the first *Nosferatu*, in which Van Helsing is not in on the final effort to run

Dracula to earth. His absence from the crucial later scenes of the story leads one to suspect budget problems were again the culprit: that it was beyond this film's meager budget to have Herbert Lom—an established professional, but no megabucks superstar—go the distance, and that the stroke was written in as a cost-cutting measure to bail him out early. This is admittedly speculation, but Van Helsing's disappearance certainly adds to the film's air of poverty.

As Quincey stakes one of the vampire women, blood squirts into his face. This insult, borrowed by *Fright Night* and burlesqued in *Dracula: Dead and Loving It*, has its basis in folklore, if not in Stoker's novel. Paul Barber, in *Vampires, Burial, and Death*, writes: "Sometimes the corpse is covered with a hide or cloth [before staking], ... to prevent the vampire-killers from being spattered by the vampire's blood.... It is presumably this phenomenon that is described in Romanian folklore, where the blood of the staked vampire is said to spurt high into the air.... In reality, of course, the pressure derives from the forcing of the stake into the bloated body, which compresses the body cavities. When killing revenants, people must have learned early on to cover them with something so as to avoid violently disgorging fluids."

As the Gypsies approach the castle, Quincey and Jonathan roll a couple of boulders down onto them. One of the boulders strikes a horse squarely on the head ... and the animal doesn't even seem to notice! Franco's Transylvania, it seems, is paved with foam rubber.

Jonathan and Quincey burn Dracula in his coffin, treating him to a non-Stoker demise. As noted earlier, cremating the body of a vampire is a sure way of getting rid of him. But, as Barber points out, "Because of the high water content of the average adult human body, the energy requirements of cremation are high.... Without ... a special furnace it becomes quite difficult to burn a body at all.... The problem ... lies not in creating a hot enough fire—that is easy—but in conveying enough of that heat to the body and for a long enough time to bring about its destruction...." Which is to say, touching a torch to the body, as is done here, won't get the job done. Barber continues, "Cremation, which seems to us so tidy a form of body disposal, is actually not tidy at all, and certainly not quick...." Except, of course, in bad films. And in *El Conde Dracula*, we're looking at one: Dracula goes up like a scarecrow from Oz. His face

melts into a cheap, bug-eyed mask, and Jonathan and Quincey, two interlopers far from home—*sans* Van Helsing, *sans* Mina, *sans* Dr. Seward—dump him off a cliff. There is no sense of triumph or victory, and the whole movie leaves a bitter aftertaste.

To give credit where it's due: though it falls far short of its boast to retell Stoker's tale "exactly as he wrote [it]," *El Conde Dracula*, plotwise, was the closest adaptation of *Dracula* filmed up to that point. For all its other distortions, it depicts a few details from the novel never seen before or since: Dracula's dismounting from the driver's seat to chase away the wolves that pursue his carriage to the castle; the Count's white mustache, and the intermediate, gray-haired stage of his returning youth; the woman who comes to the castle and pleads for the return of her child (though the denouement of that scene—in which wolves, summoned by Dracula, kill her—goes unfilmed). The "gist" of the novel survives: Jess Franco, working from a script by producer Harry Alan Towers (under his pseudonym Peter Welbeck), treats his source material with respect and refrains from making it into one of his exercises in soft-core graveyard porn. If he'd only been able to treat it with a budget, and with talent, the results could have been special.

After its completion, release of *El Conde Dracula* was held up by litigation. Its arrival in Great Britain, where it had only a limited release, was delayed by a couple of years. The film evidently was never released theatrically in the U.S. at all, but did finally surface on TV and on video. It's worth a look for the curious, but don't expect much.

Musical Notes

Bruno Nicolai's main theme is in the key of B-minor, 4/4 time, at a moderate tempo. Performed by a full orchestra, its short intro features tremolo strings, and the subsequent melody, performed by the brass instruments, is accompanied by a broad, pseudo-Bachian organ in addition to the orchestra. Overall, the theme is obnoxiously repetitive and overused, if mercifully short. It is apparently not available on a recording. However, with Franco's growing international cult, that may change: a soundtrack album for *Vampyros Lesbos*, for example, is now available.

Dracula

Dan Curtis Productions (1973)
Directed by Dan Curtis
Screenplay by Richard Matheson
Running time: 1 hour 40 minutes
Available on video

Cast

COUNT DRACULA . . . . Jack Palance
ARTHUR HOLMWOOD . . . . Simon Ward
VAN HELSING . . . . Nigel Davenport
MRS. WESTENRA . . . . Pamela Brown
LUCY . . . . Fiona Lewis
MINA . . . . Penelope Horner
JONATHAN HARKER . . . . .Murray Brown
DRACULA'S WIVES . . . . Virginia Wetherall
Barbara Lindley
Sarah Douglas

Synopsis

The year is 1897. On behalf of his employer, Mr. Hawkins, Jonathan Harker travels to Transylvania to close a real estate deal with Count Dracula.

A letter from Dracula reaches him on the way.

The coach to Bukovina only takes Jonathan so far as the Borgo Pass, where Dracula's own carriage picks him up. The Count's carriage is driven by Dracula himself, in disguise.

En route to the castle, the carriage is pursued by wolves.

At the castle, Jonathan is greeted by Dracula, who is tall, dark-haired, and dressed totally in black. Although he is not wearing a cape at this particular moment, he frequently does so later on. The Count has noticeably sharp teeth. Jonathan enjoys a supper in which the Count does not join him.

Jonathan and Dracula discuss the sale of an old house in England, which is called Carfax.

Dracula sees and asks about a picture of Jonathan's fiancée, Mina, and her best friend Lucy Westenra. Lucy's picture looks exactly like Dracula's long-lost 15th-century love, so he evidently believes she has been reincarnated. Lucy is engaged to Arthur Holmwood. Carfax is near Lucy's home, Hillingham, not far from Whitby.

Dracula tells Jonathan about Transylvanian history.

Dracula tells Jonathan he must stay at the castle for a month, and he tells him to write false letters home.

Jonathan discovers he has been locked into his room.

Jonathan cuts himself shaving. The sight of the blood disturbs the Count.

Jonathan discovers the library. There he finds a painting which identifies the Count as Vlad the Impaler.

Jonathan is attacked in the library by three vampire women, two brunettes and a blonde. The attack is stopped by the Count.

Jonathan watches helplessly as Dracula's final travel preparations are made.

*"Then the Count turned ... and said in a soft whisper:—
'Yes, I too can love...'"*—Jonathan Harker

**Jack Palance as the Count and Fiona Lewis as Lucy Westenra in *Dracula* (1973)
(courtesy Ronald V. Borst of Hollywood Movie Posters)**

In desperation, Jonathan climbs out his window and up an outer wall. He finds a vault in which the Count reposes in a coffin-like box. The Count is in a death-like trance. Jonathan tries to kill the Count with a shovel, but fails.

Dracula departs, leaving Jonathan at the mercy of the three women.

Along with ten boxes of earth, Dracula travels by ship, the *Demeter*, to England. The ship is wrecked at Whitby. A dead seaman is lashed to the wheel, a crucifix in his hand. The rest of the crew are missing.

Mina is visiting Lucy at Hillingham. Lucy suffers from a mysterious illness which leaves her pale and weak. Her illness baffles the doctor.

Lucy walks in her sleep. Lucy's mother sends for Van Helsing, a friend of Arthur's family, to come take a look at her. Van Helsing places garlic and crosses in Lucy's room, and makes a wreath of garlic for Lucy to wear in her sleep, since garlic and crosses repel vampires.

In order to get to Lucy, Dracula casts a trance over Arthur. The next morning, Lucy is found outdoors, having been attacked by Dracula.

Lucy receives a blood transfusion from the maid but continues to waste away because of nightly visits from Dracula.

The window to Lucy's room is broken by a wolf which has escaped from a nearby zoo, under the Count's control. Lucy's mother, who is in the room, faints.

Afterwards, Lucy is found outdoors, dead.

Lucy is buried. Soon afterward, now a vampire, she comes to Arthur at Hillingham. After trying to sweet-talk Arthur, she retreats from a crucifix and flees the house.

Van Helsing leads Arthur to the graveyard. They discover that Lucy has returned to her grave. Van Helsing stakes her.

Dracula, meanwhile, rests by day in a box of his native soil. When he emerges and discovers what has become of Lucy, Dracula is heartbroken.

Dracula turns his attention to Mina.

Van Helsing, Arthur, and Mina travel to nearby Whitby. Dracula infiltrates the hotel where they are staying, but he is chased away by the staff. Gunshots do not harm him.

While at Whitby, Van Helsing and Arthur determine that all of the Count's boxes were transferred to Carfax.

Van Helsing and Arthur infiltrate Carfax and count the boxes, determining some to be missing. They burn the boxes they find.

Dracula enters Mina's bedroom and attacks her. Van Helsing and Arthur soon arrive and confront him. He reveals to them that he is centuries old.

Mina is forced to drink some of Dracula's blood from a cut on his chest. Drinking Dracula's blood will create a psychic link between him and Mina so that he can compel her to obey him. It will also cause her to become a vampire.

Van Helsing must rely on Mina's psychic link to the Count to determine where he is. Dracula is on board the *Czarina Catherina* [sic], a ship bound for the Black Sea port of Varna.

Van Helsing and the others travel by rail to Transylvania. Realizing that the Count can also use Mina to learn their whereabouts, Van Helsing and Arthur falsely tell Mina they are returning to England.

Van Helsing and Arthur proceed to the castle on horseback. They go into the castle and stake the three women. Jonathan, now a vampire, also has to be killed with a stake.

Mina's "taint" is shown by a scar in the palm of her hand, made by a cross.

At the castle, a violent confrontation with Dracula ensues. Dracula is killed in the library when Van Helsing pulls down a curtain to admit the morning sunlight, and then stabs him in the heart with a spear.

Commentary

After the success in the late 1960s of his Gothic TV soap opera *Dark Shadows*, producer/director Dan Curtis moved on to theatrical films based on his creations. The first was *House of Dark Shadows* (1970), an old-fashioned if blood-soaked vampire saga in which almost the entire Collins family is slaughtered; a follow-up, *Night of Dark Shadows* (1971), deals with witchcraft and reincarnation.

Curtis then ventured into making television productions of the well-known Gothics, with mixed results. His adaptation of *Frankenstein*, while one of the most faithful to the novel, is hampered by such a low budget that the novel's final chase into the Arctic wastelands is reduced to a frantic foot race through back alleys. There seems to be virtually no budget for makeup: Bo Svenson, as the monster, sports a few latex scars and is obliged to grimace and talk out of one side of his mouth. Curtis also adapted *The Picture of Dorian Gray*, followed by a version of *The Strange Case of Dr. Jekyll and Mr. Hyde*, with Jack Palance in the dual role, and also called upon Palance to play the title role in his version of *Dracula*.

The screenplay for this adaptation was written by Richard Matheson, accomplished novelist and screenwriter. As the author of the apocalyptic 1954 novel, *I Am Legend*, about the last living man on earth holding his own against a world of vampires, Matheson was no stranger to vampire fiction. His script is generally faithful to Stoker's novel, importantly refusing to trivialize it. At the same time, his adaptation bears several similarities to *Horror of Dracula*, as will be seen; Curtis puts his own stamp on the production, introducing parallels to *House of Dark Shadows*.

What puzzles is the number of times the script sets up familiar situations and then fails to follow through on them. Early on, for example, as Jonathan travels by coach, one of the other passengers asks his destination. When he tells them he's bound for Castle Dracula, the others look at him like he's just said he's on his way to the post office. The aghast reactions of the novel are gone. Later, after his arrival at the castle, Jonathan cuts himself shaving. The Count enters the room, notices the blood on Jonathan's face, and ... nothing happens. The mirror doesn't reveal Dracula's lack of reflection; nor does the Count recoil from a crucifix around Jonathan's neck. He just stands there looking, if anything, slightly nauseated. Jonathan is baffled, and so are we.

As Dracula, Palance is, of course, nothing like Stoker's vision of gaunt pallor, but he's no more miscast than many another actor has been. And he acquits himself well, conveying an air of quiet, soft-spoken menace combined with the physical power of a very old soldier who was there when it was all happening. As Harker innocently observes early on in the novel, "In his speaking of things and peo-

ple, and especially of battles, he spoke as if he had been present at them all."

This adaptation is, in fact, the first to state explicitly that the Count is none other than Vlad the Impaler. Prince Vlad Tepes (1431-1476), occasional ruler of Wallachia, is evidently the person referred to in the novel when Van Helsing identifies the Count as "that Voivode [warrior-prince] Dracula who won his name against the Turk, over the great river on the very frontier of Turkey-land." Or, as the Count himself puts it, apparently blowing his own horn: "Who was it but one of my own race who crossed the Danube and beat the Turk on his own ground? This was a Dracula indeed!" (In *El Conde Dracula*, Chrisopher Lee speaks these very words, but we aren't given to understand that they apply to an actual historical personage who turns out to be Dracula himself.) In the play by Deane and Balderston, Van Helsing identifies the Count as "the terrible Voivode Dracula himself"; but the 1931 shooting script goes no further in that direction than to point out, when Dracula first greets Renfield at the castle, that he "wears a decoration," i.e., a medal. That medallion annually is reproduced, more or less, in plastic for use with Halloween costumes by people who typically have no idea that it designates Count Dracula as a war hero.

That status is restored to Dracula by this version, filmed as it was shortly after the 1972 publication of Florescu and McNally's *In Search of Dracula*, which placed the identity of the historical Dracula before the attention of the general public. Here the identification comes about when Jonathan, poking around in the castle, discovers the library. In the library, oddly enough, is an open coffin; on the wall above it there hangs a heroic equestrian portrait identified by a plaque (in English, improbably) as "VLAD TEPES, Prince of Wallachia, 1475." The resemblance between the Count and this portrait—executed in a 19th-century Romantic style, well beyond the Prince's living years—is, of course, disturbingly remarkable, even if it bears no resemblance at all to surviving portraits of the real Vlad.

The gimmick of the centuries-old portrait and its resemblance to the vampire is not found in Stoker's novel; Matheson borrows it from *Carmilla*, by J. Sheridan Le Fanu. It is Carmilla, ostensibly eighteen, whose face turns up on an ancient canvas. It is appropriate, therefore, that the detail that disturbs Jonathan most about Dracula's portrait is a woman's face: the prince's consort, included as a background detail, is a dead ringer for Lucy Westenra.

By this time, Dracula has already seen the familiar photo of Mina and Lucy ... and recognized Lucy's face. As the similarity between the photo and the portrait indicates, and as a series of treacly flashbacks makes clear, Lucy is evidently the 19th-century reincarnation of the Count's long-lost 15th-century love. Here Matheson and Curtis introduce into the popular conception of Dracula one of the most significant and lingering of the non-Stoker elements: that of the "reincarnation romance," the notion that Lucy, or Mina, is Dracula's lost love or dead wife reborn.

Dan Curtis himself had dealt with this theme before. In *House of Dark Shadows*, Barnabas Collins concludes that his 18th-century fiancée, Josette Dupree, has been reborn as Maggie Evans, tutor of the Collins' young son David. Again, the tip-off is Maggie's resemblance to Josette's portrait. In both movies, a music-box theme accompanies the scenes of the "reincarnation romance"; in *House of Dark Shadows*, the music box is actually seen, while in *Dracula*, it is only heard on the soundtrack.

Folklorically, the premise of the "reincarnation romance" is problematic. While vampires survive death, we have no record of folkloric vampires surviving for centuries: the longevity of vampires such as Count Dracula, Carmilla, Lord Ruthven, and Varney the Vampire is the stuff of fiction. The assumption they have in common is that of a noble or otherwise well-connected vampire whose grave is hard to find or is protected by servants, by force of law, or both. But in folklore, most vampires, like most people, were peasants; they were buried in shallow graves, and were easily found and easily disposed of. Their survival of death did not lead to eternal earthly "life."

Still, if we posit the existence of an untouchable noble vampire—ensconced in his castle, hidden in his crypt, surrounded by armed servants, and distant cousin of the Emperor in Vienna—we can accept, as a fictional premise, the idea of one of them surviving for centuries. If, having accepted that premise, we then wed it to the idea of reincarnation—*and* make the final stretch that a transmigrated soul would always wear the same face—then the "reincarnation romance" becomes a workable innovation in vampire fiction. But it is not found in Bram Stoker's novel. Indeed, Dan Curtis' inspiration may have been the 1932 Universal film, *The Mummy*, with Boris Karloff, and its series of non-sequels, the Kharis movies of the 1940s, in which the reanimated mummy is convinced that he's found the reincarnation of the Egyptian princess who'd turned his head several millennia before. Then again, a 1960 Italian film, *L'Ultima Preda del Vampiro* (unpromisingly titled *The Playgirls and the Vampire* for its U.S. release), also includes a "reincarnation romance."

Whatever its source, the theme is here introduced into the Dracula saga for the first time. (True, both Dracula and the "reincarnation romance" concept had been featured *together* in a movie before, in 1972's *Blacula*, whose basic premise—a vampire locked in a coffin for 200 years emerges and finds his long-lost love reborn—is cribbed from *House of Dark Shadows*. But the afflicted romantic of that story is not Dracula himself, but the African prince who has the misfortune of being the title character.) It is Lucy's photo, and the news that her estate of Hillingham is "quite near Carfax," which makes up the Count's mind as to which of Jonathan's offered houses he plans to buy. (As we later learn, both estates are near Whitby; none of this version's action takes place in London.) As in *Horror of Dracula*, Jonathan has again unwittingly doomed Lucy, whose face he later discovers circled in a copy of the same photo, unaccountably presented as a newspaper clipping.

Jonathan is no less doomed himself: when Dracula departs for England, he leaves Jonathan at the mercy of the three women. And they get him. Again as in *Horror of Dracula*, Jonathan doesn't make it out of Castle Dracula alive.

Dracula's journey by ship to the shores of England is omitted for the sake of a TV movie's budget, but we see the end of it. "Whitby, England, five weeks later," a caption tells us: Dracula stands on the beach near the shipwreck, on board which the body of the lone remaining crew member (later identified as a "seaman," not specifically the captain) is lashed to the wheel, a crucifix in his hand, his mouth in a frozen gape of terror. The wind blows off the North Sea, billowing the Count's cape and the fallen remains of the sails. While not the letter of Stoker, the scene is effectively eerie. Like all the best horror scenes in film, it hints at more than it shows.

Shortly after Dracula's arrival, Lucy falls ill. (Alert viewers will recognize the actress who plays Lucy, Fiona Lewis, as the maid in 1967's *The Fearless Vampire Killers* who tries to ward off a Jewish vampire with a crucifix.) Lucy's illness puzzles

"the doctor," we are told; we never see him onscreen. Dr. Seward does not survive in this version even as an ear-nose-and-throat specialist. As in *Horror of Dracula*, there is no asylum; there is no Renfield; nor is there a Quincey Morris, the protagonistic party again being reduced to Mina, Lucy, Arthur (their relationships restored to the way Stoker wrote them), and, soon enough, Van Helsing. The Professor is not Dutch, but again a nononsense Englishman, like Peter Cushing without the charisma. (Palance, the only non-British member of the cast, gives Dracula an unusual type of foreignness: he's an "ugly American.")

For the first time, we see Lucy's window broken by a "wolf," obviously a German shepherd with a badly-teased coat. As per Stoker, the wolf is an escapee from a nearby zoo (in this case, Scarborough, which is near Whitby), and not the Count himself in metamorphosis, as some versions have it. In fact, even though it is not stated here as explicitly as in *Horror of Dracula*, the Count seems incapable of any such transformations. His only powers, again, are a form of souped-up hypnotism that crosses over into mind control, and unusual physical strength. When Dracula, attempting to get to Mina, infiltrates the Whitby hotel where she and the others are staying, his violently physical encounter with the hotel's staffers recalls the highhanded, arrogant power with which Christopher Lee's (Hammer) Dracula fends off attackers.

The only blood transfusion we see Lucy receive is from the maid ... about the only person in the novel who *isn't* a donor. Blood types weren't classified until 1901, or several years after *Dracula* was published. As has often been pointed out, Lucy would, in real life, have been killed by the riot of random transfusions she receives in the novel, from Arthur, Quincey, Dr. Seward, and even Van Helsing. For this reason, most film versions wisely soft-pedal the transfusions.

Nothing avails. Lucy is ultimately found outdoors, dead, propped upright and staring vacantly. Here begins so close a parallel to *House of Dark Shadows* that, for a few moments, this version amounts to a remake of the earlier film, as Dan Curtis revisits similar scenes in identical visual language. In *House of Dark Shadows*, Carolyn is also discovered dead, propped up, and staring vacantly. In both films, the camera moves in for a close-up of the dead woman's face; in both, the close-up dissolves, with the sound of a church bell tolling, to the burial; in both, the burial is carried out under sheets of rain, the mourners huddled under black umbrellas, the pallbearers hatless in the downpour, a cleric reading from a service for the dead; in both, a wizened sexton opens the iron gate to the family vault (Collinses and Westenras can afford to be buried in style); and both sequences end with the blackness of the tomb's interior and the sound of the iron gate booming shut. But for the horse-drawn hearse of the later film, these two sequences are interchangeable. Since this version of *Dracula* is, after all, a TV movie, Curtis picks up the pace a tad: the sequence is about thirty seconds shorter than in *House of Dark Shadows*.

The borrowing continues in the next scene, although its source changes. Lucy turns up at Hillingham and, looking in through a window, pleads with Arthur to let her in because she's cold. This scene resembles the one in *Dracula, Prince of Darkness* wherein the late Helen turns up outside our dense heroine's window at Father Sandor's monastery, pleading to be let in because she's cold. Arthur, it turns out, is here no less dense: he opens the window, too.

Dracula's response to Lucy's subsequent staking is one of histrionic heartbreak. Please. Stoker's Dracula is many

things, but sentimental isn't one of them. A man over four hundred years old has surely figured out by now that it doesn't pay to get too attached to anyone. People die every day.

Dracula later infects Mina (here annoyingly rhymed with "henna") with his blood as Arthur and Van Helsing watch; she is in his hands and therefore in danger for her life. But having done the deed, he calmly walks past them out the door. This is the one point in the film where Dan Curtis's direction falls appallingly flat.

The story concludes with the pursuit back to Dracula's castle in Transylvania. Dracula's castle and Carfax are, in this version, both well-kept, well-furnished, welcoming, clean, and comfortable, each looking like a tourist resort. Such cheery accommodations are not, of course, what Stoker describes. "The walls of my castle are broken," the Count tells Jonathan in the novel; "the shadows are many, and the wind breathes cold through the broken battlements and casements." Much later in the novel, Jonathan describes Carfax in terms of manifest neglect: "The walls were fluffy and heavy with dust, and in the corners were masses of spider's webs, whereon the dust had gathered till they looked like old tattered rags as the weight had torn them partly down." Evidently the owners of the locations involved, which are not identified in the film's credits but are possibly ancient English manor houses, didn't agree to having their properties enhanced with all that atmosphere. While the locations are handsome and deflect a reliance on stagebound interiors, and on paintings or models for exteriors, the film's atmosphere suffers as a result.

After the two men stake the vampire women, Harker attacks them like a wild animal. He is knocked into a pit full of stakes and impaled on one of them, in a manner reminiscent of the often-reprinted

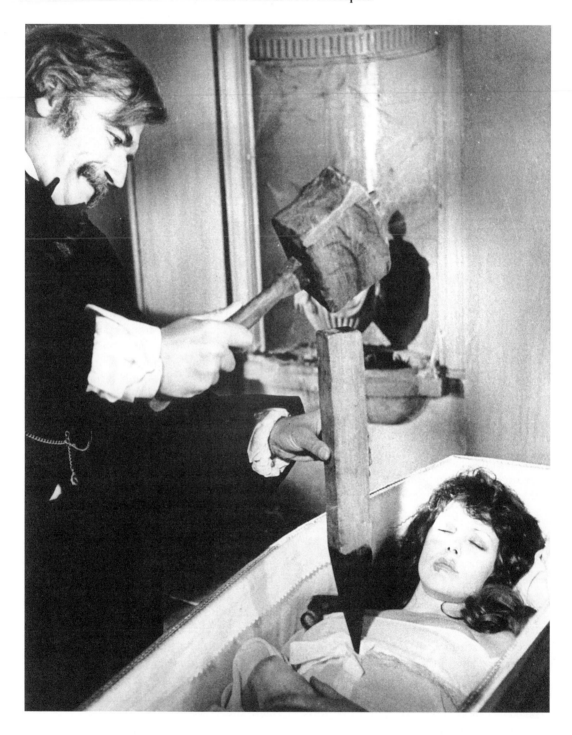

"A moment's courage, and it is done."—Van Helsing

Nigel Davenport as Van Helsing and Fiona Lewis as Lucy in *Dracula* (1973)
(courtesy Ronald V. Borst of Hollywood Movie Posters)

woodcut images of Vlad the Impaler amid a forest of his victims. Fairly strong stuff for TV.

In a final nod to *Horror of Dracula*, Van Helsing and Arthur corner Dracula in his library, resulting again in a scuffle that sends stacks of books tumbling. Van Helsing again pulls down the curtain that admits the sun. Dracula, this time, doesn't crumble, die, or even blister; he staggers around as though painfully dazzled. Tired of waiting for him to keel over, Van Helsing grabs a spear and pins the Count to an upended table, like a bug in a collection. Even then the Count doesn't crumble or fade as the novel describes it; this version may have lacked the budget for such an effect. In any event, the result is anticlimactic, and it leaves much the same downbeat aftertaste as is experienced at the end of *El Conde Dracula*.

Part of the reason for this letdown is yet another failure on the part of the script to follow through on the setup of a familiar scene. Shortly before the end of the movie, Mina, looking for spiritual solace, grabs a cross which burns her hand; this scene is analogous, of course, to the branding of Mina's forehead in the novel with a communion wafer, and is even more similar to the comparable scene in *Horror of Dracula*. Yet, in this version, when Dracula dies ... nothing. We do not see the scar fade from her hand. Again we sense no feeling of triumph, and the lack of this graphic assurance of Mina's salvation from Dracula's curse—which is much of the reason Dracula is pursued to Transylvania in the first place—has a lot to do with the hollowness of the victory. A final dose of irrelevant information about Vlad the Impaler, scrolled over his equestrian portrait to the sound of a military march, doesn't help.

In this telling of the tale, the spirit of Stoker's novel survives, and handsomely so, despite some misfires and disappointing decisions, and despite the inclusion, for the first time, of the "reincarnation romance." There are better versions, in terms of style, imagination, and fidelity to the novel, so this one can't be said to be in any way definitive. But it is worth a look, since there are certainly also worse versions to be had.

Beware: if you rent the videotape, there is a version of the video release hosted by Elvira, Mistress of the Dark. This *Dracula* may or may not be anybody's favorite, but it's certainly better than to deserve her attentions. Fortunately, there are also now copies available which dump Elvira in favor of a brief end-of-movie interview with Jack Palance.

Musical Notes

The soundtrack music was composed by Robert Cobert. The main title is in 4/4 time, with a fast underlying rhythm, suggestive of Jonathan's speedy travel, in contrast with a slower melody. This melody is initially played in C minor by an oboe solo which is soon joined by woodwinds; the key briefly changes to C# minor, at which point the strings take the melody. With a return to C minor, an English horn solo of the melody begins, with the strings and low winds joining in shortly. The title theme ends chromatically, with the main melody played by bass strings and bass clarinets.

This theme, along with the music-box love song, the military march at the movie's end, and several other selections from the soundtrack, is available on a CD titled "Vampire Circus," from Silva Screen (SSD 1020). The CD features music from thirteen vampire movies in all, including *Vampire Circus* itself, plus the title theme from the *Forever Knight* TV series.

Count Dracula

BBC-TV (1977)
Directed by Philip Saville
Screenplay by Gerald Savory, based on *Dracula* by Bram Stoker
Running time: 2 hour 30 minutes
Not available on video. (Even stills are hard to
come by, as evidenced by their paucity here.)

Cast

COUNT DRACULA . . . . Louis Jourdan
PROFESSOR VAN HELSING . . . . Frank Finlay
LUCY WESTENRA . . . . Susan Penhaligon
WILHELMINA WESTENRA . . . . Judi Bowker
RENFIELD . . . . Jack Shepherd
DR. JOHN SEWARD . . . . Mark Burns
JONATHAN HARKER . . . . Bosco Hogan
QUINCEY P. HOLMWOOD . . . . Richard Barnes
MRS. WESTENRA . . . . Ann Queensberry
BOWLES . . . . George Raistrick
SWALES . . . . George Malpas
MR. HAWKINS . . . . Michael MacOwan
BRIDES OF DRACULA . . . . Susie Hickford
Belinda Meuldijk
Sue Vanner
PASSENGERS ON COACH . . . . Bruce Wightman
Izabella Telezynska
O.T.

Synopsis

Via a gruesome stained-glass window, Dracula is identified as Vlad the Impaler.

The year is 1892. On behalf of his employer, Mr. Hawkins, Jonathan Harker travels to Transylvania to close a real estate deal with Count Dracula.

Another passenger on a coach explains to Jonathan that a gesture he saw directed toward him by peasants at the inn is a charm to ward off the evil eye. The passengers are frightened because it is the eve of St. George's Day, when all the forces of evil take command at midnight. They are further frightened at the mention of Dracula's name. A woman gives Jonathan a crucifix, which she says is "for your mother's sake."

The coach only takes Jonathan so far as the Borgo Pass, where Dracula's own carriage picks him up. The Count's carriage is driven by Dracula himself, in disguise. He offers Jonathan a cloak and a flask.

At the castle, Jonathan is greeted by Dracula, who is dark-haired and dressed totally in black. Although he is not wearing a cape at this particular moment, he frequently does so later on. The Count has noticeably sharp teeth, pointed fingernails, and hair in the center of his palms.

Dracula helps Jonathan with his bags and, making excuses as to the absence of his servants, shows Jonathan to his room.

Jonathan enjoys a supper in which the Count does not join him. The table settings are of solid gold.

Wolves howl outside, and Dracula remarks: "Listen to them—the children of the night. What music they make!"

*"We Transylvanian nobles love not to think that our bones
may lie amongst the common dead."*—Count Dracula

Louis Jourdan as Dracula in the 1977 BBC-TV production *Count Dracula* (Photofest)

Jonathan and Dracula discuss the lease of an old house in London, which is called Carfax. Carfax is near an asylum run by Dr. Seward.

Jonathan cuts himself shaving. In his shaving mirror, he sees that Dracula has no reflection. Dracula breaks the mirror by dropping it out the window. The sight of the blood excites the Count, but he is repulsed by the crucifix.

Dracula sees and asks about a picture of Jonathan's fiancée, Mina Westenra, and her sister Lucy.

Jonathan discovers the library.

Dracula tells Jonathan he must stay at the castle for a month in order to help him perfect his English. He tells Jonathan to write letters home and falsely say that all is well.

Looking out his window, Jonathan sees the Count climb head-first down an outer wall.

Back in England, Mina and Lucy go to Whitby for the summer.

Lucy becomes engaged to Quincey P. Holmwood, a Texan, having also been courted by Dr. Seward.

Jonathan again sees the Count climb head-first down an outer wall.

Jonathan is attacked in the library by three vampire women, two brunettes and a blonde. The attack is stopped by the Count, who gives them a child to feed on. Jonathan later awakes in his room.

Jonathan realizes he is a prisoner in the castle. He tries to mail a shorthand letter to Mina by tossing it to some workers outside the castle with a gold piece. But they give the letter to the Count, who returns it to Jonathan. The Count again instructs Jonathan to write false letters home, this time to say he has already left Transylvania.

Jonathan confronts Dracula about his being detained. The Count tells him he is free to leave whenever he pleases, but when he tries, wolves bar his way.

Renfield is a patient in Dr. Seward's asylum. He catches and eats insects. He is linked to the Count because his particular pathology makes him vulnerable to the Count's influence.

In desperation, Jonathan climbs out his window and down an outer wall. He finds a vault in which the three women repose in coffin-like boxes. Each is in a death-like trance, with blood on her mouth.

Jonathan also discovers the Count in a similar state. He tries to kill the Count with a shovel, but fails. Jonathan flees in terror, not to be heard from again for many weeks.

Along with fifty boxes of earth, Dracula travels by ship to England. En route, as is ultimately learned from the ship's log, Dracula terrorizes and kills the members of the ship's crew. As the ship weathers a storm, its dead captain lashed to the wheel with a crucifix in his hand, a wolf, evidently Dracula in metamorphosis, lurks among the cargo.

The ship is wrecked at Whitby. Other than the captain, the rest of the crew are missing. A newspaper account tells the story.

The paper also reports that Mr. Swales, a colorful old local salt who used to visit Mina and Lucy during their walks in a seaside cemetery, is found dead shortly after the ship's arrival.

Dracula flits around Lucy's window in the form of a bat.

Lucy walks in her sleep. Mina follows her to the cemetery and sees her, at a distance, being preyed upon by Dracula, who disappears. She pins a shawl around Lucy's shoulders and walks her back to their room.

Lucy has two tiny wounds on her throat, which Mina blames herself for making with the shawl pin. Lucy suffers from a mysterious illness which leaves her pale and weak. Her teeth seem to be longer and sharper.

Dracula's boxes are moved to Carfax by a moving company.

Next door, Renfield becomes excited at Dracula's arrival. He begins catching birds as well, and he asks Dr. Seward for a kitten.

Jonathan is nursed back to health in a convent hospital in Europe. Mina goes abroad to fetch him, and they are married shortly after their reunion.

Returning with her mother to their London estate, Lucy is placed in the care of Dr. Seward. Her illness baffles him, so he sends for Professor Abraham Van Helsing, his former professor, to come from Amsterdam to take a look at her.

Lucy receives a blood transfusion from Quincey, but because of nightly visits from Dracula, continues to waste away.

Dracula comes to Renfield's window and promises him more insects, blood, and years of life.

Renfield attacks Bowles, an asylum attendant, cutting his wrist and lapping up the blood from the floor. "The blood is the life!" he cries.

Van Helsing places garlic in Lucy's room and makes a wreath of garlic for her to wear in her sleep, since garlic repels vampires. But it is removed, with disastrous results, by her mother.

The window to Lucy's room is broken by a wolf, evidently the Count himself. Lucy's mother, who is in the room at the time, dies of a heart attack.

The wounds disappear from Lucy's throat overnight. On her deathbed, Lucy speaks with strange seductiveness to Quincey. Van Helsing prevents him from kissing her. Shortly afterwards, Lucy dies.

Jonathan and Mina return from Europe. Jonathan is shocked to see Dracula on the streets of London, driving their coach.

Mina is crushed to learn that her mother and her sister have both died and have been buried for two days.

Van Helsing leads Dr. Seward to the graveyard. Inside the tomb, Lucy's coffin is empty. Afterwards, they find a child nearby who claims to have been with a "bloofer lady." The child's neck has been bitten.

Van Helsing later reveals that the wounds in the child's neck were not made in the same way as Lucy's wounds, but were made *by* Lucy.

The next night, Van Helsing returns to the graveyard with Dr. Seward and Quincey. Again, Lucy's grave is empty.

Lucy returns to the graveyard only to be confronted by Van Helsing and the others. After trying to sweet-talk Quincey, she retreats from a crucifix and re-enters her tomb.

Quincey stakes Lucy, whereupon the peace of true death is seen on her face. Van Helsing then stuffs her mouth with garlic and decapitates her.

Mina and Van Helsing read Jonathan's diary to learn what they can of Dracula.

Jonathan travels to Whitby, where he determines that all of the Count's boxes were transferred to Carfax.

Van Helsing, Jonathan, Mina, Dr. Seward, and Quincey agree to join forces against Dracula. They realize that the boxes of his native soil are where he must repose during the day.

Mina pays Renfield a visit. He reveals to her that his habit of consuming live things is based on his belief that he could thereby absorb their souls and prolong his own life.

Van Helsing decides it would be best to exclude Mina, a mere woman, from the group effort to hunt down Dracula.

Van Helsing, Dr. Seward, and Quincey infiltrate Carfax, where they encounter a horrid smell, and count the boxes, determining some to be missing. They sterilize the boxes they find with crumbled communion wafers.

Dracula turns his attention to Mina. He enters her bedroom as a mist. Mina has a vivid nightmare about his visit.

Mina visits Renfield a second time and describes her dream to him. He can tell Dracula has been able to get to her.

Renfield pleads with Dr. Seward to release him.

Later that night, Dracula enters Renfield's cell via the window. He kills Renfield because of Renfield's refusal to kill Mina, and because Renfield tries to attack him.

Dr. Seward keeps a phonograph journal.

In order to get to Mina, Dracula casts a trance over Jonathan. He again enters her room as a mist. In a trancelike state, Mina drinks some of Dracula's blood from a cut on his chest. Van Helsing and Dr. Seward burst in on this scene and confront Dracula with a crucifix and a communion wafer. He vanishes.

Mina's "taint" is shown by a scar on her forehead, made by a communion wafer.

Van Helsing and the others seek out the rest of Dracula's boxes and sterilize them with crumbled communion wafers. As they work, Van Helsing tells the others that, according to his research, the Count is apparently centuries old. Dracula confronts them as they sterilize the last of the boxes. He flees, leaping out a window. Gunshots do not harm him.

Drinking Dracula's blood creates a psychic link between him and Mina so that he can compel her to obey him. She also shows signs of becoming a vampire.

Van Helsing must rely on Mina's psychic link to the Count to determine where he is.

Van Helsing and the others pursue Dracula to Transylvania.

The pursuers split up: Mina and Van Helsing travel by carriage, while Quincey, Dr. Seward, and Jonathan proceed on horseback.

Near the castle, Van Helsing and Mina are approached by the three vampire women. Van Helsing encloses Mina in a circle of crumbled communion wafers, which neither she nor the women can cross. He then holds the women at bay until they leave.

The next day, Van Helsing goes alone into the castle and stakes the women.

Just before sunset, Dracula approaches the castle. He is in a box which is loaded onto a wagon driven and guarded by armed peasants. A violent confrontation ensues, in which Quincey is badly wounded.

Dracula is killed when Van Helsing stakes him. After Dracula's death, his body turns to dust, and the scar fades from Mina's forehead.

Commentary

The BBC's production of *Count Dracula*, originally shown in the U.S. as a three-part miniseries, is, simply put, the most faithful adaptation of the novel yet filmed, Francis Ford Coppola's boasts to the contrary. It's true that the production bears the marks of a TV budget: it was shot on a mix of film and video, which gives it an occasionally uneven look and feel; there are special effects which border on cheesiness, and gimmicky visual effects which are, more often than not, just intrusive. Fortunately, the film doesn't depend heavily on special effects, or on visual gimmicks, for its effectiveness, and so survives these debits.

That having been said, we start immediately with a non-Stoker scene: Jonathan's departure for Transylvania, as he bids farewell to Mina. Contrary to Stoker, we learn that Mina and Lucy are sisters. Even in this most faithful of versions, some streamlining is necessary:

making Mina and Lucy sisters instead of best friends neatly explains why they are always together. (The two actresses bear no evident family resemblance, but that can be explained in terms of which parent each sister takes after.)

Just after the opening scene, the credits imply an identification of Count Dracula with Vlad the Impaler by means of an image in an all-blue stained-glass window, backlit by lightning. The window depicts one of the now-familiar scenes of impalement: Prince Vlad at table, facing a forest of his victims. The camera zooms in on the inverted face of one of these unfortunates; the image of his silent scream fades to black, leaving an afterglow of two red eyes in the darkness. This brief moment captures more unspoken horror than many films contain in their entire running times.

Harker, depicted as the eager, youthful pup Stoker envisions, heads off for Transylvania. We learn much later that the year is 1892—in fact, by the date on the plaque on Lucy's coffin. The scene aboard the coach is filmed as Stoker wrote it, even including such well-researched attention to detail as having the locals cross themselves in the Eastern Orthodox manner (concluding right, then left), as opposed to the Roman Catholic manner (left, then right) more familiar in Western countries and seen, for example, in Universal's 1931 versions.

The locals also express concern, as they do in the novel, that it is the eve of St. George's feast day. St. George, the legendary dragon-slayer, is an internationally popular saint; he is the patron saint of England and is much revered in East Orthodox countries, such as Romania, as well. His feast day is April 23, so the eve, of course, would be the 22nd. But Stoker has Jonathan receive this warning, according to the date of his journal entry, on May 4. Stoker, with his eye for detail, remembers the 11-day discrepancy between the

Gregorian calendar, adopted by Great Britain in 1752, and the Julian calendar still in use in certain Eastern European venues in his day. Nor is it necessarily an error that the helpful passenger of this film gives the date as "the fourth of May," since some Eastern Orthodox nations adopted the Gregorian calendar for civic purposes while retaining the Julian calendar for church observations. To this man, May 4 and April 22 mean the same thing: the eve of St. George's Day.

Of this momentous day, Montague Summers writes: "Throughout the whole of Eastern Europe, indeed, the feast of S[t]. George, 23 April, is one of the most important celebrations of the whole year … upon the eve of the saint the power of vampires, witches and every evil thing is at its height … throughout Transylvania, Walachia and Bavaria precautions of various kinds are … taken." Whereas this film (and *El Conde Dracula*) depict the peasantry as nervous about St. George's eve, both of Universal's 1931 versions have them frightened because it is Walpurgis Night. Walpurgis Night is the night before the feast day of St. Walburga, which is May 1. Since May Day was also the pagan spring celebration of Beltane, and owing to the Christian-era equation of paganism with witchcraft and Satanism, the night of April 30 came to have an evil reputation, especially in parts of Germany, as a night when witches consorted with Satan in the deep woods. Walpurgis Night is the night Jonathan nearly meets his doom in "Dracula's Guest," originally the first chapter of the novel, published after Stoker's death as a short story.

We never see a long, establishing shot of the castle: suddenly we're there, entering the gate and clattering into the courtyard. Dracula's first appearance at the castle is too close for comfort as well. Whereas some other versions first show the Count at a slight distance, in silhouette, or both, here he is first seen in TV close-up, as a talking head: opening the door, he startles Jonathan with his sudden appearance.

As the Count, Louis Jourdan does not look the way Stoker describes the character. He is a good-looking man of about fifty, with a neat, jarringly contemporary haircut. Since much of the rest of this adaptation is faithful to the novel down to the last detail, this attempt to sanitize the Count's appearance is initially both puzzling and disappointing. Yet it works, almost in spite of itself; for even though Dracula is attractive here at first glance, further scrutiny reveals that he does, in fact, match Stoker's description in a number of its details. Most obvious is his habit of dressing, in Stoker's words, "in black from head to foot, without a single speck of colour about him anywhere." He also has the sharp teeth, the pointed nails, and the hairy palms Harker sees and describes in the novel. He has the imperiousness of ancient nobility. And he does not seem to blink, which is not a characteristic Stoker mentions, but which is unnerving nonetheless. All told, whereas our first inclination upon seeing the Count greet Jonathan at the door is to think, "Aw, *he's* not scary," as the story progresses, this handsome, charming man starts to give us the creeps, described by Jonathan in the novel as "that vague feeling of uneasiness that I always [have] when the Count is near." By the time Dracula, lying in his box in the crypt, opens his eyes and stares blankly at Jonathan (to the sound of a thunderclap, no less), he is as horrifying a sight as any Count in any other adaptation, and we realize that, if anything, this Count's good looks are a snare and a trap.

The Count's overall manner, too, while possessed of the arrogance of nobility that Stoker gives him, is here also suave and unctuous, as reflected by alterations in his dialogue. The scene in which Jona-

than's shaving mirror reveals Dracula's lack of reflection (via a special effect that misfires slightly: Jonathan and his own reflection are out of synch by about a half-second) is filmed much as Stoker wrote it, except for what the Count has to say about the mirror. In the novel, he refers to it as "a foul bauble of man's vanity. Away with it!"—and tosses it out the window. In this version, just before dropping it out the window (this is the only adaptation in which he does so), Dracula observes: "The trouble with mirrors is that they don't reflect quite enough. Don't you think?" He chuckles once, and then the smile vanishes from his face as quickly as turning off a light switch as he lets the mirror drop. He seems to be trying to maintain his composure in the face of this infraction of his unspoken house rules. (Jonathan's subsequent beardedness confirms that there are, in fact, no other mirrors in the castle.)

Much of the Count's other dialogue is similarly rewritten. In the crucial scene wherein Mina drinks his blood, he refers to her in the novel as "my bountiful wine-press" (see Isaiah 63: 2-3 for the apparent inspiration of this gruesome metaphor), informing her that, due to her ingestion of his blood, "you shall cross land or sea to do my bidding." In this adaptation, the word "bountiful" becomes "beautiful" (which does nothing, of course, to alleviate the sanguinary nature of the metaphor), and he promises her, "We shall cross land and sea together." He sounds as insincere as an adulterer promising his young mistress he'll leave his wife for her. The Count clearly does not love Mina, just as he does not in the novel; he is a reptilian seducer, and a successful one, which is why he does not, in this version, have to *force* her to drink his blood.

Some of the Count's revisionist dialogue borders on the ludicrous. Confronting Van Helsing and Jonathan as they sterilize his boxes, Dracula demands, "The blood of a human for me, a cooked bird for you: where is the difference?" This lame rationalization is not only anachronistic in tone—a late-20th-century attempt to paint vampirism as just another "alternative lifestyle"—it also is unworthy of the man whom Stoker depicts as saying, "I have been so long master that I would be master still—or at least that none other should be master of me." This is hardly a man who feels the need to go around explaining himself to others, especially in terms of weak analogies.

On the whole, though, the Count's non-Stoker dialogue works, not to lessen his villainy, but to make it, in effect, the more dangerous because the more attractive. And it makes him difficult to pin down, even with a simple yes-or-no question. Earlier in the story, when Jonathan, puzzled by the absence of servants, asks him point-blank whether they are alone in the castle, Dracula answers (if it can be called an answer), "How could one be alone in this castle? In its most remote corners, the past—the living past—is present, surrounding us." Jonathan is understandably dissatisfied with this bit of obfuscation. This Count, schooled in four centuries of statecraft, is more than just a vampire; he is also, God help us, a politician!

Immediately after the incident with the shaving mirror, Dracula asks about the picture of Mina and Lucy, the non-Stoker incident insinuating itself even into this most faithful of versions. We have already been introduced to the two women, but the picture allows them to catch Dracula's eye as well. No reincarnation-romance nonsense here, but when Jonathan tells the Count that the sisters habitually go to Whitby for the summer, we see the Count make a mental note of it. And when Jonathan later notices Whitby circled on a map—which the Count has, with arrogant carelessness, left lying around—

Jonathan realizes he has said too much, and we know that he's put his foot in it again.

Jonathan sees Dracula climb head-first down an outer wall of the castle, not once, but twice, as in the novel. The special effect used is obviously the old TV-*Batman* ploy of having the actor "climb" a horizontal surface filmed by a camera at an angle. Nonetheless, it is the first time in the history of adaptations of *Dracula* that this scene has been filmed at all (although a variation on it is seen in Hammer's 1970 production, *Scars of Dracula*).

The attack of the three vampire women (one of whom, unaccountably, is French!) is a highlight of this version. Most of the details of the scene as written are depicted, including the women's chilling laughter, which Stoker describes as being "like the intolerable, tingling sweetness of waterglasses when played on by a cunning hand." The scene lapses into a surreal, dreamlike style, incorporating overlapping images, distortion of sound and color, slow motion, and dreamy flashbacks of Mina's face and voice, to create a sense of seduction and disorientation. The scene's conclusion, in which the women feast with red-eyed glee on the baby Dracula gives them, is one of the most horrifying moments in this or any vampire film. It was, in fact, too strong for PBS, which foolishly censored the scene, deleting the baby after the film's first few American airings.

Back in England, Lucy becomes engaged to a hybrid character, Quincey P. Holmwood, a Texan, who is, of course, an amalgam of Quincey P. Morris and Arthur Holmwood. Again, even this most faithful of versions must streamline Stoker's too-numerous characters. One of Quincey's first utterances in this version starts with the words, "Whoa thar, little lady," which runs the risk of making him seem an insulting caricature. But even in the context of the scene, it's clear that he's affecting this manner of speech for the amusement of the ladies. This intention is in agreement with the novel; Lucy says of Quincey that "he found out that it amused me to hear him talk American slang, and whenever I was present, and there was no one to be shocked, he said such funny things." Certainly the actor manages a better Texan/American accent than the phony British accents attempted at a staging of *Dracula* in October 1975, by the Little Theater of Pasadena, Texas.

Dracula's ship, the name of which is not given in this version, founders off the shore of Whitby, courtesy of some interesting but unconvincing special effects, which are adequate if you're willing to meet them halfway—rather like the effects used in live theater, which may serve to illustrate rather than realistically depict. It is preferable to see a limited budget ingeniously lent even to semi-convincing effects such as these, than to see scenes pirated from another movie, as was done in the 1931 versions. (Granted, this adaptation does, early on, borrow a few snippets of footage to suggest aspects of Jonathan's trip to Transylvania: a few seconds of grainy black-and-white footage of a train, plus a shot of snow-covered mountains ostensibly glimpsed from the window of the coach. But these are brief impressions only, and not the wholesale lifting of a momentous plot point such as a shipwreck.)

As stated earlier, several of this adaptation's effects misfire slightly: prime among these Jonathan's uncoordinated reflection. To the list can be added a communion wafer which starts to smoke just *before* it touches Mina's forehead. Plus, this version's Dracula-as-bat, mercifully seldom and briefly seen, is as wooden as anybody's. (There are shots of live bats—they appear to be fruit bats or flying foxes—which turn up in the sisters' bedroom, or even in their beds. Context seems to indicate that these are surreal images, not to be taken literally.) The wolf briefly seen appears to be a wolf, and not a dog. Since no mention is made of Berserker, the wolf that escapes from the zoo, we are left with the assumption that the wolf that breaks Lucy's window is the Count himself. This is not in accord with the novel, but since we've already seen Dracula in lupine form on the deck of the doomed ship, there seems little point in dragging another wolf into the story.

Dracula's first victim on English soil is Mr. Swales, an eccentric old sea dog. This is the only version of the story ever filmed that includes this character, and it features him as Stoker wrote him: garrulous, colorful, and curmudgeonly. (There is a Swales in the Frank Langella version, but he is an altogether different character gratuitously given a name from the novel.) The sight of Mr. Swales' body—his hand a claw, his eyes staring, his throat torn out, the gulls crying as though it's any other morning—is chilling.

As Professor Van Helsing, Frank Finlay brings Stoker's character to life. Finlay is a slight man—the Van Helsing of the novel is physically more imposing—but he nonetheless embodies Van Helsing's scientific and medical expertise, his unwavering religious faith, and the authority with which he wields both. Finlay's use of Van Helsing's accent is nonintrusive, and he fully realizes Van Helsing's charm: if Lucy weren't already bedridden, his bedside manner would sweep her off her feet.

After Lucy's return as a vampire, the childish term "bloofer lady" is heard in a film adaptation for the first time ever. The sight of livid teeth marks on the child's neck—shown, not described in a newspaper account—is another of this version's most horrifying moments, a glimpse of the unspeakable. It fortunately proved not to be too much for PBS.

This version appropriately makes full use of the religious content of both the novel and of folklore. Some latter-day vampire films (*Fright Night* comes to mind) introduce such nonsensical notions as that a crucifix won't serve to repel a vampire unless the person wielding it "has faith." None of that here. Nor do we find any of the modern tendency to shy away from referring to vampires as spiritually evil and in league with the Devil. "We must recruit disciples," Dracula says, in a non-Stoker line which is nonetheless appropriate, "just as your Leader has done." This utterance establishes Dracula as an anti-Christ figure. In the same scene, Van Helsing holds him at bay with a crucifix; Dracula stares it down, a cruciform light pattern reflected across his face. While he doesn't recoil with one of the standard cringes that Christopher Lee found so limiting, nor does he come a step closer to Van Helsing. Prayer frequently accompanies the activities of the vampire hunters; the film closes with a prayer of gratitude, in fact. After her "dream" of Dracula, Mina genuinely frets that her soul is bound for Purgatory. And Renfield's dying words here, after he explains that he "would not send her soul to Purgatory," are a prayer.

Jack Shepherd's Renfield is the best interpretation of the character ever seen on film. He is younger than the 59 years Stoker gives him, but he is prematurely grey, bearing the look of a man who has been to hell and has not quite found his way back. The script gives him a sympathetic treatment, never hinting that his bizarre diet and behavior should be viewed as funny. Our first view of Renfield, through an overhead fish-eye peep-hole, emphasizes his isolation, both within his cell and within his world, as he stands on a chair and gropes for a fly. His later recital of "The Fly", from William Blake's *Songs of Experience*, is not only thematically appropriate, but serves to emphasize Renfield's intelligence and education. It becomes clear to us, in fact, that Renfield is not insane, but disturbed; in his own words, as written by Stoker and paraphrased here, he is "a sane man fighting for his soul." He is also, of course, the only character in the story who knows what's really going on, since he knows the Count's whereabouts, and his designs on Mina; yet he is powerless to do anything about it, since he is in the Count's thrall.

Refreshingly, this version doesn't try to "explain" Renfield's involvement with the Count in terms of past traumas in Transylvania or any other such non-Stoker contrivances. Their communion is as much of a mystery as it seems to be. Perhaps no better explanation is needed, or is possible, than the one posited by Dr. Richard Noll in his book, *Vampires, Werewolves, and Demons.* "Renfield," Noll writes, "was already well on his way to becoming a clinical vampire, and in the figure of Renfield, Stoker provides a human counterpart to the supernatural vampire. As they are of like natures, it was only to be expected that they should be drawn to one another, at least telepathically ... the motivation of their abnormal behaviors is the same—the ingestion of the lifeforce (blood) of living beings to sustain their own lives. With these two vampiristic characters—one human, the other supernatural—Stoker successfully weds psychiatry and folklore, clinical and legendary phenomena, and yet is true to the unique image of vampires drawn by each of these traditions."

Indeed, Dracula's chief interest in Renfield in this version seems to be to recruit a new vampire. There seems to be no other reason for the Count's visits to Renfield than to entice him further into vampirism with offers of blood and "years of life." Dracula needs nothing from him in return, which is where this version drops the ball concerning Renfield: he is not the Count's "key" to admittance to the asylum, nor are Jonathan and Mina guests in the residential wing. By the time Renfield pleads with Dr. Seward to release him, Dracula has already attacked Mina, at her home in Hampstead. He pleads for his release in an effort to save his own life, which is certainly understandable, but which robs him of the heroic poignancy of his death in the novel, coming about, as it does, as a result of his trying to save Mina. Here Renfield "saves" Mina's life insofar as he refuses to attack her himself. Dracula then kills Renfield for his ingratitude and disobedience. "I have sent you," he says, "a human being—a living person. She's initiated. Take from her, and give to her. The two of you will live forever." The idea of Dracula sharing Mina with Renfield, creating a sort of hellish threesome, isn't Stoker—it may be far beyond anything Stoker was willing to hint at, even using vampirism as a sexual metaphor—but it's certainly interesting.

When Jonathan sees Dracula in the streets of London, it is in circumstances other than those described in the novel. Jonathan and Mina, just back from Europe, are dropped off at Mina's home by a cab. The driver is none other than Dracula himself. It's not Stoker, but it's a nice touch: not only because it's the second time in the story the Count has been Jonathan's driver incognito, but because it constitutes the Count's notification to Jonathan that he is in town—and he knows where Mina lives. As noted earlier, it is at her home where Dracula ultimately gets her.

(There is an odd bit of discontinuity in the scene wherein Mina ingests Dracula's blood. Van Helsing and Dr. Seward burst into the room—twice. Given this version's propensity for the surreal, it's tempting to think that this double entrance is the result of Dracula's playing tricks with time and space. The other possibil-ity is simply a mistake in editing. As care-fully put-together as this film is within its budget restraints, the latter possibility is a bit hard to believe. But it looks like a mis-take, even if it isn't.)

Judi Bowker brings to the role of Mina the sort of timeless beauty that lends itself well to period pieces, rather like that of Helena Bonham-Carter. (Ms. Bowker was also Andromeda in *Clash of the Titans* in 1981, and Clare, St. Francis of Assisi's main squeeze, in 1973's *Brother Sun, Sister Moon*). Ms. Bowker's Mina has not only the fragile beauty and vulnerability the Victorian gentlemen of the story would be willing to die for, but also the strength and intelligence needed to win their respect. When Jonathan expresses doubt that the Count could force Mina, who has ingested the vampire's blood, to work against his pursuers, Mina, her beauty marred by the scar on her forehead and her sharpening teeth, asks with chilling matter-of-fact-ness, "Do you think that I don't look at myself in the mirror?" "Madam Mina," Van Helsing observes correctly, "you are the wisest of us all."

After Mina's contamination by Drac-ula, and her resulting ability to know his movements, the film cuts, literally, to the chase. "There's only one place he'd feel really safe," she says; and the next thing we know, we're in Transylvania, protracted trips on antique trains and sailing ships being beyond the range of this version's budget.

Except for the absence of the snow described in the novel, the scene depict-ing Van Helsing and Mina approached by the three vampire women is filmed as Stoker wrote it, and is nightmarishly effective. Mina's simultaneous laughter and tears are the soul of this scene's hor-ror.

The chase concludes with an exciting gun battle near the castle, a scene more like something out of a western than what we've come to expect from vampire films. At its end, the Count, who has made it into the courtyard of the castle, is staked by Van Helsing right at sunset. This is not quite the ending Stoker describes, but it again calls to mind a classic western: *The Man Who Shot Liberty Valance* (1962), wherein a newsman is told, when the facts are in conflict with the legend, "Print the legend."

The final scene has the party gathered under a tree, with Van Helsing offering up a sincere prayer of thanksgiving for the success of their enterprise. With this conclusion, free of pseudo-hip revisionism; with the disappearance of the scar from Mina's forehead, and with the non-Stoker survival of Quincey (propped up against the base of the treetrunk in the background), victory, relief, and release are experienced.

And the essence of Stoker's novel not only survives, but is revered and celebrated. It is not surprising to learn that this version was produced by the BBC as part of the "Great Performances" series. It has yet to be excelled.

Musical Notes

Kenyon Emrys-Roberts composed a score with a variety of effective and appropriate themes which enhance the quiet menace and dreaminess of the film. Quotations from "Dies Irae" sneak into the music a time or two. The main theme, in A minor and 3/4 time with a moderate tempo, is in a very modern style, performed on hammered dulcimer, harp, vibraphone, chimes, and other instruments.

No recordings of this soundtrack appear to have been made available.

Dracula

Universal Pictures (1979)
Directed by John Badham
Screenplay by W. D. Richter
Based on the play by Hamilton Deane and John L. Balderston,
and on *Dracula* by Bram Stoker
Running time: 1 hour 49 minutes
Available on video

Cast

COUNT DRACULA . . . . Frank Langella
VAN HELSING . . . . Laurence Olivier
DR. SEWARD. . . . . Donald Pleasence
LUCY. . . . . Kate Nelligan
MINA. . . . . Jan Francis
JONATHAN HARKER. . . . . Trevor Eve
RENFIELD. . . . . Tony Haygarth
SWALES. . . . . Teddy Turner

Synopsis

The year is not given, but seems to be sometime in the very early 20th century.

Along with an undetermined number of boxes of earth, Count Dracula travels by ship, the *Demeter*, to England. En route, as the ship weathers a storm, Dracula terrorizes and kills the members of the crew. A wolf, evidently the Count in metamorphosis, lurks among the cargo.

Dr. Seward runs an insane asylum at Whitby. Mina is visiting Dr. Seward's daughter, Lucy, in the residential wing of the asylum.

The ship is wrecked at Whitby. The wolf, later described as a "dog" and "probably the ship's mascot," leaps to shore and runs away.

Jonathan Harker has carried out a real estate transaction with Count Dracula through the mail. The house in question is called Carfax.

The ship's captain is found dead and lashed to the wheel, a crucifix in his hand. The rest of the crew are dead as well.

Dracula's boxes are moved to Carfax by Renfield, who had previously lived at Carfax himself. As Renfield completes the task, Dracula attacks him in the form of a bat. Renfield is subsequently linked to the Count as a result. Carfax is near Dr. Seward's asylum. Accepting a dinner invitation, Dracula enters into the society of his new neighbor, his daughter Lucy, her best friend Mina Van Helsing, and Lucy's fiancé, Jonathan. The Count is tall, thin, and dark-haired. He is dressed in formal evening attire, including a cape.

During dinner, which the Count does not eat, he says, "I never drink ... wine."

A clue as to the fate of the ship's crew has been found in the ship's log, in which the final word of the final entry is "nosferatu."

Swales, an employee of Dr. Seward's, cuts himself on the finger while carving some meat. The sight of blood distracts the Count.

Mina suffers from a mysterious illness which leaves her pale and weak. It also makes her vulnerable to the Count's influence.

Later that night, in order to get to

"And you, their best beloved one, are now to me, flesh of my flesh;
blood of my blood; kin of my kin…"—Count Dracula

Frank Langella as the pompadoured Count and Kate Nelligan as
Lucy in *Dracula* (1979) (courtesy Ronald V. Borst of Hollywood Movie Posters)

Mina's bedroom window, the Count climbs head-first down an outer wall. He enters the room in a mist.

Renfield, lingering at Carfax as a servant, catches and eats insects.

The next morning, Mina is unable to catch her breath. Her illness baffles Dr. Seward, and she dies suddenly. Two tiny wounds are observed on her throat.

Dr. Seward notifies Mina's father, Professor Abraham Van Helsing, who lives in Amsterdam. Dr. Seward also speculates that Mina may have injured her throat fastening her shawl.

Jonathan goes to Carfax. Dracula, who already knows of Mina's death, explains, "News of death travels fast." They finalize the paperwork on the sale of Carfax.

Renfield is committed to the asylum.

Mina is buried.

Van Helsing arrives from Amsterdam.

Dracula turns his attention to Lucy. She accepts a dinner invitation to Carfax. Dracula tells Lucy of Transylvanian history.

Mina, now a vampire, kills the infant son of a woman who is an inmate at the asylum.

Wolves howl outside Carfax, and Dracula remarks, "Listen to them—the children of the night. What sad music they make!" He and Lucy start an awkward friendship that soon blossoms into an awkward romance.

The next night, Van Helsing leads Dr. Seward to the graveyard.

Meanwhile, Dracula enters Lucy's room in a mist. After he takes some of her blood, Lucy in turn willingly drinks some of Dracula's blood from a cut on his chest.

Van Helsing and Dr. Seward learn that Mina's grave is empty. Van Helsing follows a tunnel from the grave to an old mine shaft, where he encounters Mina. After trying to sweet-talk him, she retreats

from a crucifix, which burns her forehead. Van Helsing, with Dr. Seward's help, stakes her.

Lucy receives a blood transfusion from Jonathan. Van Helsing places garlic in her room.

Dracula pays a visit. There is a large mirror on the wall in which Dracula casts no reflection. When Van Helsing points this out, Dracula breaks the mirror.

Van Helsing further incriminates Dracula by showing him some garlic, which repulses him. Dracula reveals that he is at least five hundred years old. He tries to hypnotize Van Helsing, who drives him away with a communion wafer. Dracula flees in the form of a wolf, leaping out a window.

Van Helsing tells the others what he knows about Dracula. They are skeptical.

The next day, Van Helsing cuts Mina's heart out.

When the nurse leaves Lucy alone for a moment, she makes a run for Carfax to warn Dracula. The others chase her down and stop her.

Van Helsing and Jonathan infiltrate Carfax, where they encounter a horrid smell. They find the box of earth in which Dracula reposes by day, since sunlight would kill him.

Dracula confronts them. Jonathan tries to kill him with a shovel, but fails.

They are able to sterilize, with crumbled communion wafers, the one box of earth they find. The rest of the Count's boxes are missing.

In a padded cell at the asylum, Lucy speaks to Jonathan with strange seductiveness. Her teeth seem to be longer and sharper. Van Helsing prevents her from biting Jonathan.

Renfield tells a spider in his cell that he'd like to have a kitten.

Dracula climbs up the outer wall of the asylum and enters through Renfield's window, breaking the bars. He kills Ren-

"At that moment, the remnant of my love passed into hate and loathing; had she then to be killed, I could have done it with savage delight."—John Seward

Jan Francis as Mina in *Dracula* (1979)
(courtesy Ronald V. Borst of Hollywood Movie Posters)

field because he thinks Renfield tried to warn the others about him.

Dracula abducts Lucy, climbing head-first down the outer wall of the asylum as he does so, and takes her to Carfax.

From there, Van Helsing and the others pursue him to Scarborough. Dracula is on the *Czarina Catherine*, a ship which is just leaving port on its way to Romania.

The pursuers split up: Van Helsing and Jonathan catch a boat out to the ship, while Dr. Seward stays on shore in case Dracula has thrown them off the trail.

Dracula and Lucy are found in a box in the cargo hold. Lucy is showing increasing signs of becoming a vampire.

A violent confrontation ensues, in which Van Helsing is mortally wounded. Gunshots do not harm Dracula. He is killed when he is hauled out of the cargo hold into the sunlight.

After Dracula's death, Jonathan and Lucy are restored to each other, and Van Helsing dies.

Commentary

The numerous troubles with this production of *Dracula* start in the opening credits, where we are advised that the screenplay is based on the Deane/Balderston play, *and* on the novel by Bram

Stoker, at the same time and in that order. Basing the screenplay on both sources is problematic because they are incompatible. Basing it more on the play than the novel virtually guarantees that the point of the novel will get lost in the confusion. And it does.

Ironically, the 1931 Bela Lugosi version, which claims only the play as its basis, restores the trip to Transylvania omitted by the play (though changing the traveler from Jonathan to Renfield). This version starts *in medias res*, with Dracula's ship, tossed on stormy seas, already nearing the English shore. (We know the ship's name to be the *Demeter* only from the film's closing credits, which list the name of the actor who plays the "Captain of Demeter.") Starting the story thus is a bad omen: like many of the ship's crew, this film will spend much of its running time lost at sea.

The *Demeter* is shortly beached at Whitby; none of this version's action takes place in London. The environs of Whitby are where we find both Carfax, an impossibly Gothic rockpile on the Yorkshire coast (sort of like Mont St. Michel North), and Dr. Seward's asylum, a teeming, seething human zoo. We are taken from the deck of the doomed ship into the pandemonium of the asylum, where Dr. Seward has lost control of his inmates, panicked by the storm. We are several minutes into the story by this time, and nothing has made sense yet.

In a hoary bit of pop Freudianism, the asylum's residential quarters are upstairs, with the inmates' cells below. Mina and Lucy are in an upstairs bedroom. We quickly learn that their identities are reversed, as per the play, and that Lucy is a law student and an outspoken, *fin-de-siecle* feminist. (Though the play is set in the 1920s, the exact year of this version is never given; perhaps the car Jonathan drives could afford a clue as to the earliest possible date.) The film takes the scrambling of relationships a step further than the play: Lucy here is again Dr. Seward's daughter, but Mina is not Mina Weston, but Mina Van Helsing. Whereas Mina is already dead and buried by the time the play's action begins, here she is already sickly and pale before Dracula sets his four paws on English soil.

Since none of this film's story is set in Transylvania, much of the novel's Transylvania action has been transferred to England. Jonathan meets Dracula at Carfax to finalize the paperwork of the sale. When Lucy meets Dracula at Carfax for their heavy dinner date, he says his line about the "children of the night" in response, as always, to the howling of the wolves outside—a neat trick, since wolves have been extinct in the wild in Great Britain since the 18th century. (Even within the context of this story, the presence of wolves makes no sense. When the Count tells Renfield that he habitually locks the doors of Carfax because "There are wolves in Transylvania," Renfield retorts, "Not 'ere, there ain't!" Scriptwriter W. D. Richter forgot that, if you're going pull your audience's leg, you should at least be consistent about it.) And Dracula ultimately goes crawling up and down the outer walls of the asylum, instead of his Transylvanian homestead.

But the Count first appears by making a big entrance at Dr. Seward's place, where he has been invited for dinner. Frank Langella is, of course, woefully miscast as Dracula. Not only is he utterly unlike anything Stoker envisioned, but his youthful, even boyish good looks completely undermine any attempt on our part to believe that he is centuries old, or that he is evil, or that he is frightening. Langella followed in the footsteps of Bela Lugosi by reprising on film the role he had played on stage, in this case a 50th anniversary Broadway revival of the

Balderston/Deane play. The 1977 production was famous for its set design by Gothic cartoonist Edward Gorey, and for its campy, tongue-in-cheek approach to the play. Langella's pseudo-Byronic lothario may have worked in such an ambiance, but in this film, which takes itself oh-so-seriously, the interpretation falls flat.

In a 1979 print interview with Langella (source unknown), he said that this version introduced a "new" concept: Dracula as a sex symbol. Has this man ever heard of Christopher Lee? A woman friend of mine about my age, who also grew up catching the Hammer films in their first theatrical runs, assures me that the first time she saw Mr. Lee play Dracula, she found it remarkably stimulating when he *kissed* the heroine before biting her. New concept, indeed. Langella also noted he eschewed the use of fangs because he felt that the strength of his performance shouldn't have to rely on such props. This view is not only inconsistent with his female victims' sprouting of fangs, it also begs the question why he didn't adopt the same attitude towards the cape with the "Dr. Strange" collar.

By and large, the rest of the cast fare no better in this devastating rewrite. Laurence Olivier is miscast and squandered as a doddering, whimpery Van Helsing. Donald Pleasence is miscast and grotesque as a crass, boorish Dr. Seward; the image lingers in mind of the doctor sloppily eating breakfast the morning of Mina's death. Trevor Eve's Jonathan Harker is as useless and ineffectual as ever; he even answers, "I suppose so," when asked if he and Lucy will marry. Kate Nelligan's Lucy is the film's sole standout performance: she is beautiful, smart, and strongwilled, and it's truly disturbing to see this smart woman let the Count snowjob her as he does.

Richter's script is particularly brutal to Renfield, reducing him to an ignorant Cockney lout, a surly vagrant squatting in the abandoned Carfax before its purchase by the Count. This "connection" between the two characters is the laziest, most simplistic "explanation" yet attempted. Renfield is not only irrelevant to the story's proceedings, he is inexcusably made into comic relief, his gratuitous munching of cockroaches included for its "ick factor" value. Just before his pointless death, as he calls to the misnamed Mr. Swales for help, he makes a reference to "hundreds and thousands and millions" of rats, paraphrasing Stoker out of context in a way that makes no sense at all.

Richter's script, in addition to its basis on both the novel and the play, reveals a familiarity with vampire lore and fiction, and with the macabre in general, that borders on the pedantic. The scene in which Dracula enters Mina's bedroom window by first clawing free one of its small panes of glass could (except for Dracula's inverted posture) have been lifted from Augustus Hare's famous account of the Croglin Grange vampire: "... she became aware that the creature was unpicking the lead [that held the windowpane in place]! The noise continued, and a diamond pane of glass fell into the room. Then a long bony finger of the creature came in and turned the handle of the window, and the window opened, and the creature came in...."

Van Helsing's use of a white horse to confirm the presence of a vampire in Mina's grave, while not from Stoker, has its precedence in folklore, as reported by Barber: "One may also detect vampires and revenants by leading a horse through the graveyard, over the graves, because it will balk at stepping over the grave of a vampire. Among the Albanians, such a horse should be white...." Mina is, by the way, buried in a grave, not in a tomb as every Lucy ever filmed has been; and Van Helsing's unlikely pursuit of Mina down *through* her grave into an underlying mine shaft has less to do with Stoker than with Henry Kuttner's brilliant, claustrophobic horror story "The Graveyard Rats."

Finally, when Lucy visits Dracula at Carfax for dinner (at an unseemly time: Van Helsing, the father of her deceased best friend, is arriving at the train station, and Lucy can't be bothered to ask the Count for a rain check), he says to her: "If at any time my company does not please you, you will have only yourself to blame for an acquaintance who seldom forces himself, but is difficult to be rid of." This non-Stoker line is a close paraphrase of a bit of dialogue from "The Mysterious Stranger," an anonymously-written German vampire story from 1860. What on earth is it doing *here?*

So Richter establishes that he knows his way around the literature. Is that any excuse to subject us to so much bad writing? Why does Mina, who has suffered blood loss as a result of Dracula's visit, die of an apparent asthma attack? Why is she buried in England instead of at home in Holland? And why so quickly that her grieving father doesn't make it across the Channel in time for her funeral? Are we really to believe that Annie, an insane woman, would be allowed to keep her infant with her in the asylum? Why doesn't Mina's body reflect in a mirror even though, as a vampire, she was shown reflecting in a pool of water just a few scenes earlier? Why does Van Helsing feel the need to cut her heart out *after* she's been staked? It goes on and on. And so does the film: Why is it so overlong, even though the opening and closing sequences of the novel are omitted?

What *does* work in this version? Director John Badham is a strong visual stylist, so the film, a big-budget, handsomely-mounted production, often works as eye candy. Its almost monochromatic ambiance of darkness, mist and fog is appropriate both to the subject matter and

to the seaport setting. The throbbing musical score by John Williams (see below) is suitably passionate for this interpretation—more so, indeed, than the film itself succeeds at being. The special effects, for the most part, are quite good and often startling, even when fairly simple in execution—for example, the scene in which Dracula, fleeing from Van Helsing's communion wafer, leaps out a window and is a wolf before he hits the ground.

Incidentally, audiences are often baffled by the Count's utterance of "Sacrilege!" when confronted with the Host here. This odd line is from the play, not the novel, and may be in recognition of the status of the historic Prince Vlad Tepes as a defender of the faith. First as a practitioner of Eastern Orthodoxy, later in life as a Roman Catholic, Vlad the Impaler fought the Turks and built a number of churches and monasteries. Van Helsing's rejoinder in the play—"I have a dispensation"—is a paraphrase of Stoker's "I have an Indulgence," which is met with skepticism by Leonard Wolf: "All that the Indulgence can grant to Van Helsing is a remission of temporal punishment for a sin he had committed and that was already forgiven. The Indulgence, which is a sort of 'payment' from the Treasury of Grace, cannot be given for sins about to be committed." And the uses to which Van Helsing puts the Host in the novel and in various film versions are, Wolf adds, "absolutely impermissible since, in Catholic belief, the sanctified wafer *is* the Body of Christ Himself. The Host, therefore, may not be used in any profane way, no matter how exalted the end in view." In brief, the novel's scenes of Van Helsing using bits of crumbled communion wafers—to "sterilize" Dracula's boxes, to enclose Mina in a protective circle, and so forth—constitute as large a misstep as Lucy's multitudinous blood donors. It is, indeed, sacrilege, and it's ironic that it is the Count, of all people, who points it out.

The Count's return trip to Transylvania aboard the *Czarina Catherine* is immediately aborted here. In a clumsily-staged contrivance, Dracula is hauled out of the ship's hold with a hook and pulley and run up a mast into the killing sunlight. This incident is ripped off from the death of Dr. Polidori (James Mason) in the 1973 TV movie *Frankenstein: The True Story*; Polidori, who has a phobia of electrical storms, is run up a mast by the monster at the height of a storm at sea and is immediately killed—blasted to a skeleton, no less—by lightning, an unlikely event but a nightmarish image. By contrast, Dracula's thrashing around on the hook, like somebody with an ice cube down the back of his shirt, is, like much of this movie, unintentionally funny. The use of color-distorted NASA footage of the sun is inconsistent with the visual style of the rest of the film, and Dracula's latex sunburn makeup is cheesy and underachieved, unworthy of this film's other, more effective visuals.

After Dracula dies, his cloak, like a bat-shaped kite, glides away on the ocean breeze. Lucy smiles mysteriously. Sequel? Thankfully, no; Dracula will be back, but not *this* Dracula, fortunately.

In the elusive interview referred to earlier, Langella summed up this version's revisionist take on Dracula as "a nobleman with a problem." Stoker envisions the Count as a nobleman who *is* the problem, who travels to England as his first stop on a grand tour of world conquest. This film posits a Count who makes the trip apparently just to wear a big shirt and chase girls. In the swirl of altered characters and distorted plotting, the "gist" of Stoker's novel is here, like Lucy herself (or Mina, as this version would have it!), raped, murdered, and buried.

"Van Helsing answered:—'The Host ... I have an Indulgence.' It was an answer that appalled the most sceptical of us."
—John Seward

Laurence Olivier as Van Helsing in *Dracula* (1979) (courtesy Ronald V. Borst of Hollywood Movie Posters)

Musical Notes

John Williams was one of the busiest composers of big-budget Hollywood film soundtracks of the 1970s and 1980s. His style lent itself well to movies dealing with fantastic subject matter, such as *Star Wars* (1977), *Jaws* (1975), *The Fury* (1978), and *Close Encounters of the Third Kind* (1977).

His main title theme for *Dracula* starts in C minor, later modulating into F minor, and is in 4/4 time at a moderate tempo. It is performed by a full orchestra, with the melody played by the strings.

The soundtrack album for this *Dracula* is available on CD from Varese Sarabande (5250).

Nosferatu, Phantom der Nacht

(U.S. title: *Nosferatu the Vampyre*)

Werner Herzog Filmproduktion (1979)
Released in the U.S. by 20th Century-Fox
Written and directed by Werner Herzog
Running time: 1 hour 47 minutes
(Some English-language TV prints run 1 hour 36 minutes.)
Recently released to video after long unavailability.
Both German and English versions are uncut and are in widescreen format.

Cast

COUNT DRACULA . . . . Klaus Kinski
JONATHAN HARKER . . . . Bruno Ganz
LUCY . . . . Isabelle Adjani
RENFIELD . . . . Roland Topor
VAN HELSING . . . . Walter Ladengast

Synopsis

The year is not given, but seems to be in the early to mid-19th century. On behalf of his employer, Renfield, Jonathan Harker travels to Transylvania to close a real estate deal with Count Dracula. The house he plans to sell the Count is in Wismar, right across the street from the house where Jonathan lives with his wife, Lucy. Jonathan leaves Lucy in the care of his friend Schrader and his wife Mina.

En route, Jonathan meets fearful, superstitious people at an inn. They are frightened at the mention of Dracula's name, and because they believe the forces of evil will take command at midnight.

A woman gives him a crucifix and a book about vampires, which he reads that night.

Next day, the coach refuses to take him to Borgo Pass, and so he must walk. Later, Dracula's own carriage picks him up.

At the castle, Jonathan is greeted by Count Dracula. The Count is thin and very pale, and dresses totally in black. He is completely bald and has noticeably

sharp teeth, pointed fingernails, and pointed ears. As they step inside, Dracula picks up a candelabrum.

Jonathan and Dracula discuss the sale of the old house.

Jonathan enjoys a supper in which the Count does not join him. The Count makes excuses as to the absence of his servants.

Wolves howl outside, and the Count remarks: "The children of the night make their music."

Jonathan cuts himself on the thumb while slicing bread. The sight of blood excites the Count.

Jonathan awakes the next morning and learns that he's been bitten.

Unable to get a letter to Lucy, Jonathan keeps a written daily journal.

As they further discuss the sale of the old house, Dracula implies that he is centuries old. He sees and asks about a picture of Lucy. The picture clearly excites the Count, and he quickly closes the deal, prepared to pay any price.

Jonathan reads more from the book about vampires.

Jonathan is attacked by the Count.

Meanwhile, back in Wismar, Lucy walks in her sleep. Van Helsing, a local doctor, checks her out. The Count's attack is stopped by a psychic cry from Lucy.

Jonathan again awakes in the morning to learn he's been bitten.

Jonathan finds a vault in which the Count reposes in a sarcophagus in a death-like trance. Jonathan flees in terror.

Jonathan realizes he is a prisoner in the castle. He watches helplessly as Dracula makes his final travel preparations. Dracula departs, leaving Jonathan at the castle alone. Jonathan makes a desperate leap to escape, not to be heard from again for several weeks.

Along with twelve boxes of earth, Dracula travels first by cart, then by river boat, and finally by ship, to Germany.

Back in Wismar, Renfield, who seems to have become involved with the Count by unknown means before Jonathan's trip to Transylvania, is now a mental patient in Dr. Van Helsing's care, having been institutionalized after Jonathan's departure. He is said to catch and eat insects. "The blood is the life!" he cries, attacking one of the asylum attendants.

Jonathan, meanwhile, is nursed back to imperfect health in a convent hospital. He then heads for home, though he is not yet fully recovered from his ordeal.

En route to Germany, Dracula terrorizes and kills the crew of the ship. The ship drifts into port in Wismar.

The ship's captain is found dead and lashed to the wheel. The rest of the crew are missing. The crew's fate is ultimately learned from the ship's log.

Renfield becomes excited when Dracula arrives in port.

Panic breaks out when it is learned that the ship, swarming with rats, has brought the plague to town.

Dracula moves his boxes to his new home himself. As he does so, he sees and is repulsed by a cross.

The day after Dracula's arrival, Jonathan is brought home by others. He is in a dazed state and does not recognize Lucy. Sunlight hurts him.

Dracula turns his attention to Lucy. He visits her, uninvited, in her bedroom, where a large mirror on the wall shows that he has no reflection. He tells Lucy that he envies the happiness she and Jonathan share. Having read Jonathan's diary, Lucy knows who Dracula is. She is unafraid of him and tells him to go away.

Renfield escapes from the asylum and seeks out the Count, who sends him far away.

Lucy reads the same book about vampires that Jonathan has read. Among other things, the book says vampires can change into bats and wolves, and that sunlight can kill them.

Lucy tells Van Helsing of her suspicions regarding Count Dracula. He does not believe her.

Mina is found dead of a vampire's bite. Van Helsing is still unconvinced, although he, too, has read Jonathan's diary and the book about vampires.

Lucy goes to the Count's house and sterilizes the boxes with crumbled communion wafers.

Based on what she reads, Lucy concludes the only way to kill the Count and rid her town of the plague is to sacrifice herself: she must entice the Count to come to her by night, then keep him at her side until daybreak.

Lucy encloses Jonathan in a circle of crumbled communion wafers, which form a barrier that he cannot cross.

Dracula is killed when he stays too long at Lucy's side. The sun rises, blinding and immobilizing him. Afterwards, Van Helsing, finally convinced, stakes him.

After Dracula's death, Lucy dies. Van Helsing is arrested for murder, although no legal authority survives in the badly depopulated town.

*"There was no letter for me. I hope there cannot be anything
the matter with Jonathan."*—Mina Murray

**Klaus Kinski as Dracula and Bruno Ganz as Jonathan in *Nosferatu the
Vampyre* (1979) (courtesy Ronald V. Borst of Hollywood Movie Posters)**

The circle of communion wafers is removed by the maid, and Jonathan, now a vampire, escapes on horseback.

Commentary

Like the title sequence of *Horror of Dracula*, the opening shots of *Nosferatu the Vampyre* let you know immediately that you're on the vampire's turf. You find yourself face-to-face with a row of mummies, the first few of whom died as infants. Their shriveled limbs look as brittle as twisted twigs, and their slack-jawed countenances look for all the world like soundless screams of agony. The hand-held camera strolls along, staring at them closely, lingering on one or another. At one point, the camera's gaze drops to take in a poignant detail: the fine boots of one of the mummies, the only articles of its clothing that haven't rotted with time.

You may recognize these mummies as denizens of Guanajuato, a vast cemetery in Mexico; you may realize that they are of 20th-century origin, and therefore outside the time period of *Dracula*; you may know that they are now a tourist attraction. No matter. For a moment they represent the vampire's view of humanity: doomed. In the Count's centuries of earthbound afterlife, he has seen everyone he ever knew, everyone he ever loved, end up like this: dead and too dumb to fall over. Small wonder that he later says to Jonathan, "Can you imagine enduring centuries, and each day experiencing the same futilities?" It is a non-Stoker question, but it flows smoothly from a paraphrase of Stoker that immediately precedes it: "I don't attach importance to sunshine now, or the glittering fountains of youth. I love darkness and shadows, where I can be alone with my thoughts." Welcome to the darkness and shadows, home of this Dracula, of this frail living shadow, who would, like any shadow, vanish in the light.

David Pirie, in his 1977 book *The Vampire Cinema*, concludes that the flood of vampire films that had been released worldwide from the 1950s through the 1970s—in England, the U.S, France, Italy, Spain, Mexico, the Philippines, and even Japan—had at last run its course. "It seems," he writes, "that much of the vampire cinema has come to an end ... if the vampire has begun to leave the cinema, it is because he no longer plays inside our own heads, and has ceased to be a part of western civilization's dreams and nightmares." It can be charitably observed that Mr. Pirie spoke too soon, and that he did well to start the book's final paragraph with the word "However,..." Not only was 1977 also the year of the BBC's unsurpassed adaptation, but by the summer of 1979 there were no fewer than three films in theaters that were not just about vampires, but about Dracula. One was the spoof *Love at First Bite*; the other two were adaptations, more or less, of the original story: the Frank Langella fiasco discussed in the previous chapter, and Werner Herzog's perverse, darkly funny remake of *Nosferatu*.

Nosferatu the Vampyre is a love-it-or-hate-it movie. Many American audience members find its stately European pacing to be like watching paint dry; many others seem to think its absurd humor is unintentional. The opening sequence detailed above is a make-or-break moment for some: to find themselves looking at dozens of actual dead bodies, *and* in the first few minutes of the movie, strikes them as about as entertaining as a graphic Holocaust documentary, so they bolt. But in fact, the opening sequence comes off as an elaborate bluff on Herzog's part: it turns out to be a nightmare Lucy is having, and nothing else in the film that follows can match the blunt shock-trauma of those withered, leathery faces. (Even the plague rats are fluffy and cute—white lab rats, far too sanitary for the task of infecting a city.)

The opening credits make no reference to Bram Stoker's novel, leaving us with the impression that this *Nosferatu* is based only on the earlier film of which it is a remake. Yet Herzog's screenplay retrieves a number of scenes, details, and bits of dialogue from the novel. There is, for example, a character named Mina, analogous to the character referred to as Lucy Westenra (or Ruth Harding) in the 1922 original; here again, the names of Lucy and Mina are reversed, with Lucy being Jonathan's wife. The peasant woman at the inn, who gives Jonathan a book about vampires as per the 1922 film, also gives him a crucifix *a la* the novel. The "children of the night" line is restored, if paraphrased, and Jonathan again keeps a written journal.

The three women are still absent, which is in keeping with this depiction of Dracula as absolutely isolated and alone. The ever-popular non-Stoker incident involving the picture of Lucy is included, and enjoys a special significance beyond the odd compliment ("What a lovely throat!") of the 1922 version. While the "reincarnation romance" spin is not put on it, the picture prompts Dracula to close the deal on the unnamed house quickly: he is understandably eager to live across the street from such a beauty as Isabelle Adjani. Since Lucy's pallor is the equal of his own, promising little in the way of a blood feast, one may wonder what he sees in her. In the answer lies the difference between the 1922 vampire and this one.

While the pallid, skeletal baldness of Max Schreck's 1922 Count is recreated here—complete with the pointed teeth, nails, and ears—the overall effect is quite different. Max Schreck's vampire is a rigid cadaver, someone who has been so long dead that very little resemblance to a living human being remains. His Count is sketched in the stark relief of an antique German woodcut playing card, angular and flat. Klaus Kinski, by contrast, still has a haunted human face that peers out at us from behind the distorted features. Kinski, the only actor ever to play both Dracula and Renfield in separate adaptations, creates a Count weighed down by the immense sadness of his centuries of existence, a man of infinite regrets who wants to taste more of life than just blood. In Lucy's face, he sees an impossible, hopeless hope to be loved, and so he strands Jonathan at the castle and sets off to pursue her.

The arrival of Dracula's ship, drifting into port at Wismar as though guided by an invisible hand, is beautifully done, a scene of quiet menace and portent. The subsequent visitation of plague on the city is more fully realized here than in the 1922 film, complete with an apocalyptic frenzy of the doomed and dying populace dancing and feasting in the streets and squares as society breaks down.

While Stoker's narrative again is largely abandoned the moment the ship arrives, Herzog continues to restore details from the novel omitted by the earlier film. We learn, from Lucy's reading of the same book of vampires Jonathan read earlier, of the vampire's power to transform into a bat; it never happens in this version, although the opening dream of the mummies concludes with a stunning slow-motion view of a bat in flight. Mina, the

Lucy character here, is found dead, not of plague, but of a vampire's bite. Her death is abrupt, not the gradual lapsing into vampirism undergone by Lucy in the novel; that fate is here reserved for Jonathan, who never recovers from his ordeal in Dracula's castle.

Dracula makes his intentions clear by intruding upon Lucy as she prepares for bed one evening. Lucy's dressing mirror, like Jonathan's shaving mirror in the novel, reveals the Count's lack of reflection, although he does cast a fearsome shadow. He is so wrapped up in his attention to Lucy that the mirror is here of no concern to him and so escapes unbroken. The Count is not after her blood this time out; he is making instead an uninvited and unwelcome social call in which he expresses a wish to be more than a new neighbor to Lucy and Jonathan. In effect, he wants to be her back-door man. It is, of course, an incredibly inappropriate request, especially coming from the man who has ruined Jonathan; and it is pathetic, reducing Dracula to a beggar of love. While it is unusual for the lonely downside of Dracula's earthly afterlife to be depicted in films, it is Mina who says in the novel, "That poor soul who has wrought so much misery is the saddest case of all." What Mina advocates, though, is that the vampire hunters exterminate Dracula in a spirit of mercy, not of hatred; she doesn't recommend they welcome him into their wives' beds. Lucy, naturally, will have no part of it here, and sends him packing.

But when Lucy tells Van Helsing what she knows about the Count, he doesn't believe a bit of it. He is here a town doctor who dismisses vampirism as mere superstition. Lucy, having read the book and Jonathan's diary, knows the source of the plague, knows who it is who has harmed Jonathan, and knows what must be done. Van Helsing reads the book and the diary, too, but is unconvinced by them, and even by the death of Mina.

Lucy then must take several Stoker-inspired matters into her own hands. It is Lucy who goes—alone—to the Count's house to sterilize his coffin-like boxes with crumbled communion wafers (appropriately asking God's forgiveness before sprinkling the shredded wafers into the rat-infested boxes). It is Lucy who traps Jonathan in a corner of the room by enclosing him in a semicircle made up of fragments of the crumbled Host. And it is Lucy who tries to convince Van Helsing by saying to him, "Faith is the amazing faculty of man which enables us to believe things which we know to be untrue." This line is paraphrased from the novel, wherein it belongs to Van Helsing. (Lucy also pirates a line from Dr. Seward, a non-player in this film, when she asks Van Helsing, "Is it possible we've all gone mad and will wake up one day in straitjackets?")

Renfield, meanwhile, has fled from the story. Depicted as a giggling pinhead, Renfield is here, as in the 1922 film, Jonathan's employer, in mysterious league with the Count; he sends Jonathan to Transylvania and his ultimate doom. He is again institutionalized after Jonathan leaves town, this time in Van Helsing's care. His diet of insects is mentioned, but not depicted, as the theme of his own incipient vampirism is not developed. While he ultimately escapes his confinement, he is never mistaken by the townspeople as the source of the plague, and is therefore spared the rooftop chase of the earlier film. He seeks out Dracula, who regards him with contempt, but who nonetheless gives him his marching orders: "Go to the north, to Riga," he says, "and the army of rats and the Black Death go with you." Riga, the capital of Latvia, is another seaport; as such, it may prove useful as a springboard for further travel and conquest by the Count. Dracula's command therefore has a hint of "Prepare ye the way of the Lord" in it. And Renfield doesn't miss the cue: "Thy will be done. Amen!" he cries.

Dracula's assault on Lucy is overtly sexual—he hikes up her nightdress and keeps his hand firmly on her breast the whole time—but it can hardly be called erotic in any enjoyable sense. The initial bite is executed by a slight forward jerk of his head, whereby his two foremost teeth, like a bat's as in the 1922 original, puncture the flesh of her neck. It's as sexy as pricking your finger. Dracula's subsequent gulping and slurping the unseen rush of blood that emerges is comically repulsive.

Dracula is again done in by sunlight when he stays too long at Lucy's bedside. Van Helsing, convinced too late, drives a stake into Dracula's heart, even though the Count, immobilized by sunlight, may already be dead. Van Helsing is immediately arrested for his troubles, although society has fallen apart so badly that his arrest depends largely on his own cooperation. (His arrest is not without precedent: Van Helsing, again played by Edward Van Sloan, is also arrested at the beginning of 1936's *Dracula's Daughter* for having staked the Count at the end of the Bela Lugosi version.)

Meanwhile, something is happening downstairs. Jonathan, long haggard and amnesiac, suddenly perks up, clutching his chest as he hears the sound of Van Helsing's hammer blows. With a new and strange light in his eyes, he urges the arrest of Van Helsing and has the maid sweep up the "dust" that encircles him. Deftly stepping out of the circle as soon as it is broken, he tears the cross from around his neck, and we see that his nails have become talons like the Count's. With an enigmatic hint of a smile—his teeth, too, are now sharp and protruding—he calls for his horse, saying, "I have much to do ... now."

*"Strangely enough, I did not wish to hinder him. I suppose it is a part of the
horrible curse that such is, when his touch is on his victim."*—Mina Harker

**Klaus Kinski as Dracula and Isabelle Adjani as Lucy in *Nosferatu the Vampyre* (1979)
(courtesy Ronald V. Borst of Hollywood Movie Posters)**

The impression given is not simply that Jonathan has become a vampire, but that he has become *the* vampire, the Count's soul having fled from his ancient body into Jonathan's much newer one, a carefully-prepared vessel conveniently waiting downstairs. Is such a metempsychosis what the Count had in mind all along? Has he manipulated Lucy into making such a thing possible? Was it Jonathan's "body" he was after the whole time, and not Lucy's? We aren't told for certain, but it seems likely from the film's context.

The final image has "Jonathan," wrapped in a fluttering black cloak, escaping on his horse. He rides away, across a windswept stretch of sandy beach, until he becomes just a dark dot on the horizon.

What rough beast, we may wonder, slouches toward Riga to be born?

And what becomes of the "gist" of Stoker's novel? Does it survive? First, we must remember that this *Nosferatu* is a remake of the earlier one, and not an adaptation of the novel *per se*. Still, as in the 1922 film, Stoker's story is mostly intact until Dracula's ship arrives in port. Afterward, the novel's plot is mostly abandoned, as the film follows instead in the footsteps of Henrik Galeen's 1922 script: the plague devastates Wismar, and Lucy takes it upon herself to put a stop to the Count. As noted, Herzog's version includes details from the novel that are omitted from the 1922 film; in the Wismar sequences, these details mostly have to do with Lucy's taking over Van Helsing's activities. So far, Stoker survives in spirit, if not in letter.

It is in its ending that the newer *Nosferatu* not only varies from the original, but from the spirit of the novel. We are given no indication that the plague ends, and Dracula seems to have survived his own death. If it is not literally the Count himself now indwelling Jonathan, at least his evil has survived him and is primed to spread abroad. This is an ending that owes more to films like Polanski's *The Fearless Vampire Killers* (1967) or *Count Yorga, Vampire* (1970), with their snatching-defeat-from-the-jaws-of-victory endings, than to Stoker's novel. "Jonathan" snatches the crucifix from around his neck and tosses it away: God is absent, or indifferent, or impotent, or fictitious, or asleep, or dead. Here is, perhaps, the deepest rift between Stoker's novel and Herzog's film.

Still, this *Nosferatu*, by its perverse reimagining of the original story, demonstrates how wildly differing variations on a theme can spring from the same source. Considering this film alongside the other 1979 version of *Dracula*, and remembering that they are both ostensibly second-generation adaptations of the same novel, is a bit dizzying. One can only wonder what Bram Stoker would have thought of either film.

Musical Notes

The music accompanying the film's opening scene featuring the mummies is a slow, funereal piece in 4/4 time and a tonality of D. It includes synthesized voices chanting wordlessly in a pseudo-Gregorian-New-Age style, to which winds and strings are later added. Underlying all, ominously, is a heartbeat: we are, remember, dealing with the *living* dead. This theme, repeated several times throughout the film, is performed by the German art-rock band Popol Vuh (who took their name

from a Mayan codex), fronted by keyboardist/synthesizer artist Florian Fricke. The soundtrack album (the band's eleventh) was originally released on vinyl by the French label Spalax (SPA-14112). More recently, the soundtrack has been released as a CD (Sarga M17285), also a French import, most readily available from sources on the Internet. The film's music also features an excerpt from Wagner's *Das Rheingold*, which the film's credits indicate is available on Decca LC1071, likely to be a vinyl release. The Vokal-Ensemle Gordela's rendering of "Zinzkaro" is featured, as is Charles Gounod's "Sanctus," from the Cacilienmesse. The "Sanctus" is used ironically to score the film's final shot: the disappearance of "Jonathan" into the distance.

Nosferatu in Venice—Commentary

Nosferatu the Vampyre spawned a belated and bizarre not-quite-a-sequel, 1988's *Nosferatu in Venice* (also known as *Vampires in Venice*). As the title indicates, this follow-up (never released theatrically in the U.S.) is an Italian film, not a German one, written and directed by Augusto Caminito. The story begins with a Van Helsing-like character named Catalano (Christopher Plummer) summoned to modern-day Venice on a mission. He is to help rid a noble family of their one-man family curse whose evil memory still haunts their villa.

The long-dead miscreant is named Nosferatu (the name of Dracula is never used); his origins were in Transylvania, Catalano says, "ten centuries ago" (!). Seems he made his way to Venice in 1786, afflicted the family in question, and vanished at the time of the carnival during an outbreak of plague. We see in flashback some of his earlier atrocities, including an attempted exorcism which ends with three clerics being hurled out a window to be impaled (Vlad Tepes style) on the spikes of an iron fence below.

Over the objections of the household priest (Donald Pleasence), a seance is held to try to determine whether Nosferatu ever left town or is buried somewhere in the hidden family crypt. The seance, of course, revives the vampire, played again by Klaus Kinski, this time with a full shock of long white hair *a la* Stoker's description.

Freshly resurrected, the vampire tramples the head of a snake. This image brings to mind a prophecy from the book of Genesis, in which God, after the Eden debacle, says to the serpent: "I will put enmity between thee and the woman, and between thy seed and her seed; it shall bruise thy head, and thou shalt bruise his heel." Biblical scholars interpret this passage to be a prefiguration of Christ's costly and painful victory over Satan. It seems odd that the vampire, referred to as the "enemy of Christ," should be associated with this image, until Catalano, confronting him, says he is such an outcast that both good *and* evil reject him.

The vampire goes about town during the current carnival, his 18th-century clothing enabling him to blend right in with the costumed throng. Caminito may have drawn inspiration for this episode from a passage in Lawrence Durrell's 1958 novel *Balthazar*, concerning a vampiress lurking in the midst of the Venetian carnival: "... you know of course that carnival is the one time of the year when vampires walk freely abroad," Durrell's narrator, Pursewarden, relates. (Durrell later has a doctor say that the marks of the vampire's bite remind him of something he'd seen "during the plague at Naples when the rats had been at the bodies.") Here Nosferatu's immediate concern is to find out who has summoned him; his long-range plan is to discover some way to die.

It won't be easy: this is one tough vampire, against whom both Catalano and the priest prove to be ineffectual. He has the superhuman strength Stoker describes, and he can transform himself into a bat, as well as appear to be someone else in order to deceive his trackers. Crucifixes don't impress him. Daylight doesn't faze him. Gunshots don't harm him. Catalano oddly remarks that mercury is "the only natural element capable of killing a vampire," but even mercury-laced shotgun shells ultimately fail.

"Only love can kill him now," Catalano asserts, "the love of a consenting virgin"—a scenario reminiscent of the sacrificial seductions of Nina/Lucy in both versions of *Nosferatu*. The vampire also realizes that the love of a young woman is his only exit, and he goes about the business of finding her. His quest seems again to involve a "reincarnation romance," this time centered on a young princess (Barbara De Rossi), the latest in the afflicted family's line, and on another young member of the household (Anne Knecht). But the story is so slow and incoherent it's hard to tell.

Nosferatu in Venice (89 minutes; available on video mainly from sources on the Internet) is atmospheric and visually strong. Kinski, as the taciturn vampire, even though his dated dress and fright wig would make him look right at home at the ball in *The Fearless Vampire Killers*, successfully evinces menace and extreme danger. The rest of the cast are less effective: Plummer speaks mostly in halting whispers, and Pleasence is given almost nothing to do.

The story doesn't work as a sequel: if the vampire has been entombed below Venice from 1786 to the present day, then how could he have invaded Wismar in the early 19th century? Still, some research has been put into the screenplay. Asked how someone can become a vampire, Catalano

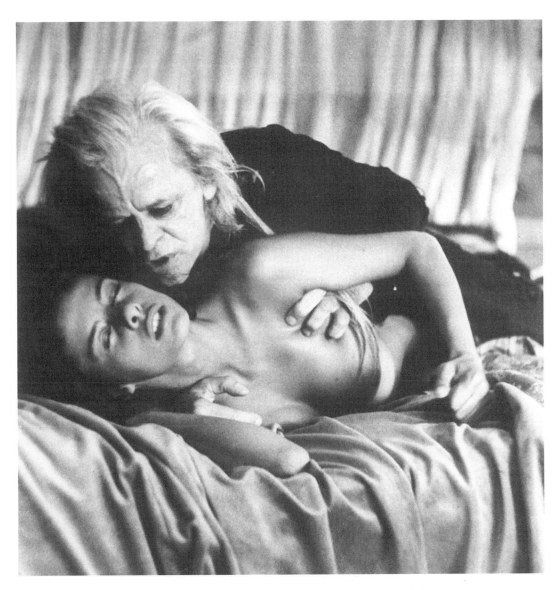

*"I am no longer young; and my heart, through weary years of
mourning over the dead, is not attuned to mirth."*—Count Dracula

**Klaus Kinski as the vampire Nosferatu and Anne Knecht as his victim in *Nosferatu
in Venice* (1988) (courtesy Ronald V. Borst of Hollywood Movie Posters)**

correctly answers with a comprehensive list: vampires can be the illegitimate children of illegitimate parents, children of witches and warlocks, suicides, hanged criminals, impenitent blasphemers, unpunished murderers, and descendants of vampires.

Odd moments linger in memory. Fac-ing a blank mirror (despite his having reflected in water earlier), the vampire glares at it until his reflection slowly comes into view, as though he is willing his image into being. Perhaps it is a symptom of returning mortality, suggesting that he may soon find death. In any case, early on, a mirror helps Catalano explore the nature of the family's ancient curse: In an 18th-century painting, a young woman (the image of the young princess, of course) points to an open book on whose page is seen the cryptic word UTAREFSON. Not until Catalano holds a mirror up to the canvas does the meaning of the word become plain.

The soundtrack features music "based on" Vangelis's album "Mask," and original music by Luigi Ceccarelli.

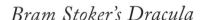

Bram Stoker's Dracula

Columbia Pictures (1992)
Directed by Francis Ford Coppola
Screenplay by James V. Hart, based on *Dracula* by Bram Stoker
Running time: 2 hours 8 minutes
Available on video

Cast

COUNT DRACULA . . . . Gary Oldman
MINA . . . . Winona Ryder
VAN HELSING . . . . Anthony Hopkins
JONATHAN HARKER . . . . Keanu Reeves
JOHN SEWARD . . . . Richard E. Grant
ARTHUR HOLMWOOD . . . . Cary Elwes
QUINCEY P. MORRIS . . . . Bill Campbell
LUCY WESTENRA . . . . Sadie Frost
RENFIELD . . . . Tom Waits
BRIDES OF DRACULA . . . . Monica Belucci
Michaela Bercu
Florina Kendrick
MR. HAWKINS . . . . Jay Robinson

Synopsis

In a 1462 prologue, Dracula is identified as Vlad the Impaler, who turns against God when his wife commits suicide.

In 1897, Renfield is a patient in an insane asylum run by Dr. Seward. Renfield catches and eats insects. He is linked to Dracula because he traveled to Transylvania and returned insane, having preceded Jonathan in Mr. Hawkins' employ.

On behalf of his employer, Mr. Hawkins, Jonathan Harker travels to Transylvania to close a real estate deal with Count Dracula. Jonathan keeps a written daily journal.

A letter from Dracula reaches him on the way. Jonathan's fiancée, Mina, also keeps a diary.

The coach to Bukovina, which is drawn by four horses harnessed abreast, only takes him as far as the Borgo Pass. A woman on the coach gives him a crucifix and says, "For the dead travel fast." Dracula's own carriage picks him up.

En route to the castle, the carriage is pursued by wolves, and mysterious blue flames flicker by the roadside.

At the castle, Jonathan is greeted by the Count, who is white-haired and very pale. The Count carries a lamp. He has pointed nails and hair in the palms of his hands. He casts a shadow whose movements are independent of his own.

Jonathan enjoys a supper in which the Count does not join him. Dracula says, "I never drink ... wine."

Dracula tells Jonathan about Transylvanian history.

They discuss the sale of an old house in London, which is called Carfax Abbey.

Dracula sees and asks about a picture of Mina. Mina looks exactly like Dracula's long-lost 15th-century love, so he assumes she has been reincarnated.

Dracula tells Jonathan he must stay at the castle for a month in order to help the Count perfect his knowledge of English customs. He tells Jonathan to write terse, uninformative letters home.

*"Take care ... take care how you cut yourself. It is more
dangerous than you think in this country."*—Count Dracula

**Keanu Reeves as Jonathan Harker and Gary Oldman as Dracula
(in one of many bizarre incarnations) in *Bram Stoker's Dracula* (1992)
(courtesy Ronald V. Borst of Hollywood Movie Posters)**

In England, Mina is visiting her friend Lucy at her London estate of Hillingham.

Dr. Seward keeps a phonograph journal.

Renfield eats insects in the belief that he can thereby absorb their souls and prolong his own life. Renfield now eats birds as well, and he asks Dr. Seward for a kitten. He attacks Dr. Seward. "The blood is the life!" he cries.

Jonathan cuts himself shaving. In his shaving mirror, he notices that the Count has no reflection. The sight of blood excites the Count, but he is repulsed, first by the mirror, which he breaks with a glance, then by the crucifix.

Wolves howl outside, and Dracula remarks, "Listen to them—the children of the night. What sweet music they make!"

Looking out a window, Jonathan sees Dracula climb headfirst down an outer wall.

Jonathan realizes he is a prisoner in the castle.

Jonathan is attacked by three vampire women, two brunettes and a blonde. The attack is stopped by the Count, who gives them a child to feed on.

Jonathan waits helplessly as Dracula's final travel preparations are made. He finds a vault in which the Count reposes in a sarcophagus. Dracula is in a death-like trance, but leaps up when discovered.

Dracula soon departs, leaving Jonathan at the castle at the mercy of the three women.

Back in England, Lucy becomes

engaged to Arthur Holmwood, a young nobleman, having also been courted by Dr. Seward and by Quincey Morris, a Texan.

Dr. Seward's asylum is next door to Carfax.

Along with an unspecified number of boxes of earth, Dracula travels by ship, the *Demeter*, to England. En route, he terrorizes and kills members of the crew, as is recorded in the ship's log. The ship weathers a storm.

Dr. Seward, upset over having his proposal to Lucy rejected, shoots drugs intravenously.

The ship drifts into port in London. As it nears shore, a wolf, evidently Dracula in metamorphosis, leaps ashore and runs away. As revealed later in newspaper clippings, the ship's crew are missing.

Lucy walks in her sleep. Mina follows her to a cemetery and sees her, at a distance, being preyed upon by Dracula, who disappears. Mina walks Lucy back to her room.

Dracula's boxes are moved to Carfax by a moving company. Renfield becomes excited as Dracula moves in.

Dracula, who can and does come out into sunlight, turns his attention to Mina. He seeks her out and introduces himself to her. They start an awkward friendship that soon blossoms into an awkward romance.

Lucy suffers from a mysterious illness that leaves her pale and weak. Her illness baffles Dr. Seward, who sends for Van Helsing, his former professor, to come from Amsterdam and have a look at her. Lucy has two tiny wounds on her throat.

Dracula and Mina go to the cinematograph, where they encounter a wolf which has escaped from the zoo, under the Count's control.

Lucy continues to waste away, despite blood transfusions from Arthur and Dr. Seward.

Jonathan climbs out his window and makes a desperate leap to escape. He is subsequently nursed back to health in a convent hospital in Europe.

Van Helsing has placed garlic in Lucy's room and made a wreath of it for her to wear in her sleep. It has done no good.

On her deathbed, Lucy speaks with strange seductiveness to Quincey. Her teeth seem to be longer and sharper. Van Helsing prevents her from biting him.

Van Helsing reads a book about vampires.

Mina goes abroad to fetch Jonathan. Dracula is heartbroken.

Jonathan and Mina are married abroad shortly after their reunion. Jonathan's hair has turned gray.

Quincey takes a shot at a wolf, the Count incognito. The wolf is not harmed.

The window to Lucy's room is broken by the Count in the form of a wolf.

Shortly afterward, Lucy dies and is buried.

Jonathan and Mina return from Europe. Jonathan is shocked to see the Count on the streets of London, looking younger.

Van Helsing leads Dr. Seward, Arthur, and Quincey to the graveyard. Inside the tomb, Lucy's coffin is empty.

Lucy returns to the tomb carrying a child, whom she carelessly drops when confronted by Van Helsing and the others. After trying to sweet-talk Arthur, she retreats from a crucifix and returns to her coffin, vomiting blood into Van Helsing's face. She is then staked by Arthur and decapitated by Van Helsing.

Van Helsing, Jonathan, Quincey, Arthur, and Dr. Seward infiltrate Carfax, where Dracula rests by day in a box of his native soil.

Mina, who, along with Jonathan, is a guest in the residential wing of the asylum, pays Renfield a visit. He tries to warn her about Dracula.

Van Helsing and the others burn the boxes. Dracula, transforming into a bat, sees them at work.

In the form of a mist, Dracula enters the asylum via Renfield's window and kills Renfield for having tried to warn Mina. Still in the form of a mist, he enters Mina's bedroom.

Mina willingly drinks some of Dracula's blood from a cut on his chest. Drinking Dracula's blood will create a psychic link between her and the Count, and will cause Mina to become a vampire. Van Helsing and the others burst in on this scene and are attacked by rats.

Dracula flees. Van Helsing must rely on Mina's psychic link to Dracula to learn where he is. Dracula is on board a ship bound for the Black Sea port of Varna.

Van Helsing and the others travel by rail to Varna to await the arrival of Dracula's ship. But the Count outwits them, and the ship goes on to Galatz.

Mina is showing increasing signs of becoming a vampire, and the party realize that the Count can likewise use her to learn their whereabouts.

Continuing on to Transylvania, the pursuers split up: Mina and Van Helsing travel by carriage, the others separately.

Near Dracula's castle, Mina and Van Helsing are approached by the three vampire women. Mina's "taint" is shown by a scar on her forehead, made by a communion wafer. Van Helsing encloses Mina in a circle of fire, a barrier neither she nor the women can cross. He holds them at bay until they leave. Before they go, they kill the horses.

The next day, Van Helsing goes alone into the castle and kills the women, beheading them.

Just before sunset, Dracula approaches the castle. He is in a box which is loaded onto a wagon driven and guarded by peasants. A violent confrontation ensues, in which Quincey is mortally wounded.

Quincey stabs Dracula in the heart with a Bowie knife, and Jonathan slashes the Count's throat with a kukri. Quincey dies.

As Dracula dies, he shares a tearful farewell with Mina. He becomes young and handsome again. God forgives him, and a look of peace is seen on his face. Mina drives the Bowie home, and then decapitates him with it.

After Dracula's death, the scar fades from Mina's forehead.

Commentary

In the summer of 1992, the first of the posters went up advertising the upcoming release of the latest adaptation of *Dracula*. Other than the film's title, the poster simply read BEWARE. Finally, it seemed that someone had gotten it right. Someone had gone back and read the novel and rediscovered that the title character is an irredeemable villain.

But in fact no such discovery had been made. The next poster read LOVE NEVER DIES. What could such a line have to do with Dracula—unless the film were another "reincarnation romance" interpretation? This threat was realized, and then some.

Bram Stoker's Dracula is a wretched movie truly deserving of everyone's contempt. It is a deeply frustrating film because, despite its close adherence to the novel in most of its particulars (as the above synopsis, compared with that of the novel, reveals), and despite the large budget and the enormous amount of talent that were invested in the project, the result is an overlong, confusing film in which virtually nothing works from beginning to end.

Several days before the opening of *Bram Stoker's Dracula* on Friday the 13th of November, 1992, a friend of mine attended a sneak preview. She tells me that a publicity person read to the audience a letter from Francis Ford Coppola—always a bad sign when a director does anything other than let his film speak for itself. (For purposes of researching this book, I asked Columbia Pictures for a copy of the letter, but they declined to respond.) My friend tells me that, in the letter, Coppola said that *Bram Stoker's Dracula* was the first faithful film adaptation of the novel, a claim which is false both coming and going: not only is the BBC's 1977 version faithful to both the letter and spirit of the book, as has been demonstrated, but Coppola's film is, in important ways, not very faithful at all.

The letter reportedly went on to claim that Stoker's novel was a love story, not a horror story. Anyone having read the book won't be fooled by this nonsensical claim; it explains a lot, though, about why so much of this film goes so wrong. Coppola, in a behind-the-scenes HBO program about the making of his film, refers to Van Helsing as being "as evil as Dracula." This outrageous, insupportable claim, demolished by even the most casual glance at the novel, gives us further insight into how badly Coppola misunderstands his source material, and why the resulting film is so totally wrongheaded. (Coppola went on to be executive producer of the equally wild-eyed and mistitled *Mary Shelley's Frankenstein* in 1994. With that film, director Kenneth Branagh achieved something one might not have thought possible: he made an even worse film than *Bram Stoker's Dracula*.)

Even the title is a problem. Bram Stoker was a novelist, not a filmmaker, so the only object which can accurately be called "Bram Stoker's *Dracula*" is his book. As anyone knows who has seen virtually any film adaptation of virtually any novel, or who knows the differences between written works on a page and works intended to be performed or shown (plays, films,

etc.), a book is not a movie, and never can be.

But even taking the title as what it is meant to be—a claim that this film is, within the limits of adaptation, the story that Bram Stoker wrote—it is misleading. Anyone familiar with the novel won't make it past the first few minutes before noticing that Stoker didn't write *this*.

We start with a 1462 episode from the life of Vlad the Impaler, defender of the faith against the Turks, who becomes a vampire when he rebels against God after the suicide of his wife. In no way is this sequence related to anything Bram Stoker ever set down on paper. While it is true that, as Florescu and McNally and any number of subsequent authors have written, Vlad the Impaler was the probable inspiration for Stoker's character, Stoker gives us no such flashback. The suicide—indeed, the very existence—of Vlad's wife Elisabeta, while based on local peasant legend, is pure fiction, but not Stoker's.

The battle scenes are cheesily and unconvincingly done, looking like something from a film with a fraction of this one's budget and it is questionable whether any research into late medieval armor was actually conducted: Vlad's armor is designed to resemble external musculature. One is given to wonder why. This suit of armor serves as the best example of the problem with Eiko Ishioka's overrated (in fact, Oscar-winning) costumes: they *look like costumes*, like something for the opera stage, instead of like actual clothing.

Everything about *Bram Stoker's Dracula* is overwrought and overblown. Wretched excess is the only esthetic. It is filmed in a frenzied, would-be-fever-dream style replete with gimmicky dissolves and rapid-fire editing. This visual style is wildly inappropriate for an adaptation of a 19th-century novel.

Yet the awfulness of *Bram Stoker's Dracula* is not totally Coppola's fault.

Much of the blame must go to screenwriter James V. Hart, who had earlier adapted the Peter Pan story into his screenplay for *Hook* (1991), another overlong, confusing, boring exercise in "revisionism." Making a revisionist version of *Dracula*, or of any other well-known literary property, is not the unforgivable sin; sometimes, as we have seen with both versions of *Nosferatu* as well as with *Horror of Dracula*, the results can be quite good. But the claims that this is exactly what Stoker wrote fall short here. (Even the BBC's *Count Dracula* makes no such claim for itself. Indeed, the makers of the BBC production differentiate their product from the novel, first by giving it a different title, and then, in the opening credits, by describing their version as being "by Gerald Savory" and as "A Gothic Romance based on Bram Stoker's *Dracula*.")

To give credit where it's due, Hart's screenplay includes a number of details from the novel not seen in any other version. These range from major themes such as Dracula's ability (per both Stoker and folklore) to come out in broad daylight, to such trivia as the harnessing four-abreast of the horses pulling the coach to Bukovina in the film's early scenes. (Leonard Wolf, in *The Annotated Dracula*, remarks, "In no *Dracula* film yet made has anyone ever depicted the horses harnessed in this way." In 1975, when Mr. Wolf made this observation, it was true. Mr. Wolf served as historical consultant for *Bram Stoker's Dracula*.) This is the only version to depict Lucy callously dropping the little child she brings to her tomb; the only other adaptation in which Lucy brings a child to her tomb at all is *Horror of Dracula*. And in no other version does Quincey die. Indeed, this is the only version that features Quincey Morris, Texan. (Two of the other adaptations include Quincey, but in *El Conde Dracula*, Quincey Morris is English; and in the BBC version, the Texan is named Quincey Holmwood.)

Hart's screenplay also includes some never-before-filmed details only to turn right around and ruin them. The mysterious blue flames are seen flickering by the roadside en route to Dracula's castle for the first time ever—only to return near the end of the film as part of some sort of New Age-feminist-witchcraft-Gaia-goddess nonsense apparently involving Mina's past-life karma. Dracula is, for the first time ever, stabbed in the heart with Quincey's Bowie knife—but Jonathan's kukri, leveled at his neck, only slashes his throat instead of decapitating him as per the novel. True, Stoker doesn't specifically state that the Count is decapitated; but his use of Mina's words, "I saw [the blade] shear through the throat," plus the very nature of the kukri, designed for dismemberment and decapitation, leave little room for any other conclusion than that the Count is beheaded. Merely slashing Dracula's throat instead of lopping off his head unfortunately allows him to live long enough for the lugubrious—and very non-Stoker—farewell that he and Mina share afterward.

Gratuitous miscues abound on all sides, some springing from corruptions or exaggerations of Stoker, some purely home-grown by Coppola, Hart, *et al.* What, exactly, are the mousetrap-looking contraptions Renfield wears on his hands? Why do the attendants in Dr. Seward's asylum wear square cages on their heads as though begging some 19th-century madman to invent what is known in the NFL as "facemasking?" Why is the Count's inverted wall-crawl taken as a cue to turn Castle Dracula into an anti-gravity funhouse, with fluids dripping upward and rats running across the ceiling? Why does the castle resemble a person sitting on a throne? And why does Dracula's shroud

"I believe it is the Count, but he has grown young. My God, if this be so! Oh, my God! my God! If I only knew!"—Jonathan Harker

Gary Oldman as another weird version of Dracula in *Bram Stoker's Dracula* (1992). Winona Ryder as Mina is in the background (courtesy Ronald V. Borst of Hollywood Movie Posters)

look like it was designed by Gustav Klimt? (In a making-of-the-movie book, the source of inspiration for these last two decisions is acknowledged to be the late-19th-century Symbolist school of painting. But this explanation is unsatisfactory: Symbolism, like other artistic movements, took place inside museums and galleries. The whole Victorian world didn't look like its pre-Surrealist images.)

To continue: Why does none of this "most faithful" version take place in Whitby? Why does Dracula take Mina on a "first date" to the *movies*? And what is the point of their encountering the escaped wolf there? Why is the wolf, once introduced into the story, *not* used to break Lucy's window as per the novel, a task instead taken on by Dracula himself in metamorphosis? Why does the garlic placed in Lucy's room do no good at all? How is it that Jonathan recognizes Dracula in the streets of London, seeing as how the Count has not only grown younger, but has totally changed in appearance? (In Stoker's novel, Dracula's increasing youthfulness is revealed only insofar as his hair changes from white, to gray, to black, as is seen in *El Conde Dracula*. His appearance otherwise does not change—not even his clothes—and he certainly doesn't become more attractive: "His face," Mina writes, "was not a good face; it was hard, and cruel, and sensual ... he looked ... fierce and nasty.") Why the nonsensical claim, contrary to both Stoker and folklore, that vampirism is contagious only if the *victim* drinks the blood of the *vampire*?

Why the general contempt for the religious content of the novel? Specifically, why does Jonathan's crucifix melt when a vampiress hisses at it, and why does a cross burst into flames when Dracula snarls at it? Why do Van Helsing *et al.* burn Dracula's boxes instead of sterilizing them with communion wafers, and why does Van Helsing enclose Mina inside a circle of fire

instead of the crumbled Host? And how, pray, does he draw a circle of fire *in the snow*?

Finally, why does Hart's screenplay fall back yet again on the gimmick of the "reincarnation romance?" The horror of Stoker's novel lies largely in the fact that the women of the story fall under the spell, not of an attractive young man who loves one or the other of them, but of a repulsive old man of boundless, timeless malevolence. The hoary cliché of the "reincarnation romance" was already old by the time it was spoofed in *Love at First Bite* (1979), and even *Fright Night* (1984), that museum of vampire-movie clichés, gives the idea no more than a passing glance. With indications like these, it's safe to say that the "reincarnation romance" is an idea whose time has come and gone. And it never was Stoker's idea.

It's not hard to understand why this adaptation of an English novel is peopled with a mostly American cast. The explanation is box office, always a hard consideration to argue with in commercial filmmaking. Still, it's jarring to hear young Americans struggling with *faux* British accents, while two of the only actual Brits in the cast, Gary Oldman and Anthony Hopkins, ironically fake Continental accents.

Gary Oldman is, like many other actors before him, miscast in the role of Dracula. In no way does his soft-cheeked, weak-jawed countenance resemble the hatchet-faced warlord who glares at us from the woodcut prints. Putting a fright wig and a pair of shades on him doesn't help. And his initial appearance at the castle, in that grandmotherly hairdo, is—in a word—hilarious. White hair or not, this conception of Dracula is, in its own way, as different from Stoker's description as any other version's. And Oldman's delivery of his lines is so heavily accented, mumbled, and lisped that someone who hasn't read the novel likely won't understand a word he says.

Still, it's hard to tell what to make of Oldman's interpretation of the role, since the performance belongs less to Oldman than it does to the makeup and mask and prop and special-effects departments. The film's numerous transitional forms—half-man, half-wolf, etc.—are found neither in the novel nor in folklore. Montague Summers, in *The Werewolf*, quotes at length from classical theologians who opine that transformations of men and women into animals were false miracles performed by Satan by means of a "glamour" or illusion, and were not actual metamorphoses. This is an opinion at odds, not only with the skin-stretching, bone-crunching shape-shifts of such films as *The Howling* and *An American Werewolf in London* (both 1981), but with the literal, physical transformations of *Bram Stoker's Dracula*. Whatever other problems the Langella version had, its instantaneous transformations are more in keeping with the concept of a false miracle, as opposed to an actual physical phenomenon.

Anthony Hopkins clearly enjoys himself as Van Helsing, although it's the mugging, hammy sort of fun Vincent Price used to have in similarly Gothic roles. Having seen Hopkins at his sinister, bloodthirsty best as Dr. Hannibal Lecter in *The Silence of the Lambs* (1991), one wonders what the results would have been if *he* had played Dracula instead. (Gary Oldman, for that matter, would have made a terrific Renfield!) As it is, Hopkins's turn as Van Helsing reminds one of a star player on a losing team who decides he might as well enjoy himself, since a solo effort on his part won't be enough to prevent the rest of the team from blowing the big game badly.

And blow it they do. Winona Ryder just is not convincing as a young Englishwoman, coming off as a California girl in a costume. (Unfortunately, but unavoidably, her Victorian hairstyle makes her ears look unflatteringly prominent.) Certainly, though, Ms. Ryder comes off much better than the unfortunate Keanu Reeves, whose Jonathan Harker looks and sounds like a refugee from one of Reeves' *Bill and Ted* movies. One expects him at any moment to say to Dracula, "Yo, royal Transylvanian ugly dude! Bodacious castle, man!"

The other cast members fare no better, thanks to Coppola and Hart, whose interpretation treats the characters with absolute contempt. Sadie Frost (whose English accent, at least, isn't faked), far from embodying what is described in the novel as "Lucy's sweet purity," is the sort of girl who wears an off-the-shoulders red dress while deliberately provoking all three of her suitors at a party, and who delights in scandalizing Mina by frankly sharing her sexual fantasies with her. Per Stoker, Lucy's undead state is characterized by "voluptuous wantonness"; with *this* Lucy, who would notice the change? And what can be said about the scenes in which she and Mina giggle over *Kama Sutra*-esque book illustrations and share wet kisses in the rain, other than that Stoker would likely have found them appalling?

As for Lucy's three suitors: Cary Elwes, as Arthur Holmwood, comes across as an upper-class twit. Bill Campbell's Quincey Morris is a crude, vulgar lout, a trailer-park Texan. Richard E. Grant's Dr. John Seward, for some unfathomable reason, falls flat on his face the first time we lay eyes on him, and later yields to the temptation (resisted by the Dr. Seward of the novel) to shoot drugs intravenously. And the film's insistence on including *all* these characters serves as a bit of unintended literary criticism, to wit: Stoker's novel has too many do-nothing characters.

But as usual, the biggest misfire is the

script's handling of Renfield. Once more, there is a bogus "explanation" for Renfield's involvement with the Count: as Jonathan's predecessor in the attempt to sell Carfax to Dracula, Renfield (yet again!) went to Transylvania and returned insane. But while Hart's script takes the trouble to explain how Renfield *got* into the story, it fails to tell us why he's *still* in the story. Renfield is not the key to Dracula's admittance to the asylum; no mention is made of the vampire's need for an invitation to enter. Nor is Renfield given anything else to do other than hang around like a piece of furniture. We get an indication of how little the makers of this version "get" Renfield when we see one of his identification documents ... and his name is misspelled! Worse, when the Fox Network gave *Bram Stoker's Dracula* its broadcast television premiere, in order to fit the running time of the film, plus commercials, into a two-and-a-half-hour time slot, they cut out every scene with Renfield in it ... and the story didn't suffer for his absence at all!

Yes, there are multitudinous problems with *Bram Stoker's Dracula*, any number of which could be considered fatal flaws. But the ultimate question concerning us here is: Does the "gist" of Stoker's novel survive? It does not. Despite the script's often slavish adherence to the letter of the novel, one can hardly expect its spirit to make it onscreen under the guidance of a director who thinks the world's most famous horror story is a love story. *Bram Stoker's Dracula* would be bad enough if it were just another misguided adaptation, but, as noted earlier, what rankles is its makers' claim, implied by the title and made overt in their self-congratulatory hype, that this is *the* definitive version—not simply the most faithful ever filmed, but the most faithful possible.

So, does *anything* work in this version? Actually, yes; a couple of things come to mind:

Jonathan and Mina's wedding, performed with Eastern Orthodox splendor, is beautifully done.

And Dracula sports a pair of very sharp blue sunglasses. Enough said.

Musical Notes

Wojciech Kilar's soundtrack music for *Bram Stoker's Dracula* is available on CD from Columbia Records (53165). The film's main title is a dark, spooky theme in A minor, in 4/4 time at a moderate tempo. Its instrumentation is strings only, with the melody switching back and forth from the high and low strings throughout.

Also on the CD, Annie Lennox, formerly of Eurhythmics, warbles a schlocky pop concoction titled "Love Song for a Vampire." This tune accompanies the film's end credits, as though enough hadn't already gone wrong in the previous couple of hours.

Dracula: Dead and Loving It

A Columbia Pictures release (1995)
Directed by Mel Brooks
Screenplay by Mel Brooks, Rudy De Luca, and Steve Haberman
Based on characters created by Bram Stoker
Running time: 1 hour 30 minutes
Available on video

Cast

COUNT DRACULA	Leslie Nielsen
RENFIELD	Peter MacNicol
JONATHAN HARKER	Steven Weber
MINA	Amy Yasbeck
LUCY WESTENRA	Lysette Anthony
DR. SEWARD	Harvey Korman
VAN HELSING	Mel Brooks
VAMPIRE WOMEN	Darla Haun
	Karen Roe
MARTIN	Mark Blankfield

Synopsis

The year is 1893. Renfield travels to Transylvania to close a real estate deal with Count Dracula.

En route, he meets fearful, superstitious people on a coach who are frightened because the sun is about to set. The coach refuses to go to the Borgo Pass, and so he must walk.

He then meets people at an inn who are frightened at the mention of Dracula's name. A woman sells him a crucifix.

At the castle, Renfield is greeted by Dracula, who is tall, pale, and white-haired. The Count dresses in a tux and a full cape. He casts a shadow whose movements are independent of his own.

A bat flutters by, and Dracula says of bats and their guano: "Children of the night—what a mess they make!"

Dracula helps Renfield with his bags and shows him to his room.

Renfield and Dracula discuss the sale of an old house in England, which is called Carfax Abbey.

Renfield suffers a terrible paper cut. The sight of blood excites the Count.

Later, in his room, Renfield is attacked by two vampire women, a blonde and a brunette. The attack is stopped by the Count, who places Renfield under his power. He tells Renfield they will set sail for England the following evening.

Dracula travels by ship, the *Demeter*, to England. En route, abetted by Renfield, he preys on members of the crew.

The ship weathers a storm and drifts into port at Whitby. The ship's captain is dead, and the rest of the crew are missing. The only living person on board is Renfield, who has gone mad. A newspaper account tells the story. Renfield is subsequently linked to the Count as a result of his experiences in Transylvania.

Renfield is committed to an insane asylum run by Dr. Seward.

Dracula goes to the opera in London and introduces himself to Dr. Seward, whose asylum is in Whitby, next door to Carfax Abbey. Along with his new neighbor, Dracula meets Dr. Seward's daughter

Mina, her fiancé, Jonathan Harker, who is also Dr. Seward's assistant, and Mina's friend Lucy Westenra.

In order to get to Lucy in her bedroom that night, Dracula turns into a bat.

Renfield catches and eats insects.

Lucy suffers from a mysterious illness which leaves her pale and weak. She also has two tiny wounds on her throat.

Lucy's illness baffles Dr. Seward, so he sends for Professor Van Helsing, who teaches in London, to come and have a look at her.

Dracula rests by day in a coffin inscribed with the single word: DRAC-ULA. He suddenly finds he can come out in the sunlight. At a picnic, he says, "I never drink ... wine." The sun suddenly starts to burn him, and he awakens from a "daymare."

Van Helsing reads a book on vampires, which reveals that garlic repels them. He places garlic in Lucy's room.

Looking out a window, Renfield sees Dracula climbing headfirst down an outer wall of the asylum. During an indignant rant about the garlic in Lucy's room, Dracula reveals that he is centuries old. Dracula bends the bars on Renfield's window, and Renfield escapes. He goes straight to Lucy's room to remove the garlic, but he is caught.

Later that night, Mina goes out onto the terrace and sees Lucy, at a distance, being preyed upon by Dracula, who disappears.

Lucy dies and is buried.

Count Dracula is identified as Vlad the Impaler.

Van Helsing tells the others of his suspicion that Dracula is the vampire they seek. Dr. Seward thinks it may be Renfield, based on his eating live insects and his apparently having bent the bars on his window. Lucy, now a vampire, attacks and kills a graveyard attendant.

Jonathan and Van Helsing go inde-pendently to the graveyard. Lucy encounters Jonathan outside her tomb. After trying to sweet-talk him, she retreats from Van Helsing's crucifix and returns to her tomb. Jonathan stakes her, and is drenched by an enormous gush of blood.

Dracula turns his attention to Mina. In order to get to her, he casts a trance over her and her maid. He abducts Mina and takes her to Carfax Abbey for the night.

Back in her room, Mina speaks with strange seductiveness to Jonathan, aggres-sively putting the moves on him. She has two tiny wounds on her throat, which she tries to pass off by saying she pricked her-self while pinning on a shawl. Her "taint" is shown by a scar in the palm of her hand, made by a cross.

Dracula accepts an invitation to a ball. A large mirror on the wall shows that he has no reflection, removing all doubt as to the identity of the vampire. Dracula breaks the mirror and flees, leaping out a window. Abducting Mina as he goes, he again takes her to Carfax Abbey.

Van Helsing and the others must then rely on Renfield's link with the Count to determine where he goes next. They release Renfield and follow him to see where he will go.

Van Helsing, Jonathan, and Dr. Seward pursue Renfield to an abandoned chapel on top of a cliff, where they fran-tically search for both Dracula and Mina.

Renfield pleads with the Count to punish him for having led their enemies straight to the hideout, but Dracula says there's no time for that. He instead tells Renfield to distract them.

When Dracula is found, a violent confrontation ensues. Dracula is killed when Renfield, trying to help him escape, opens a hatch in the ceiling and admits the morning sunlight.

After Dracula's death, his body crum-bles to dust. Jonathan and Mina are restored to each other, and Renfield mourns.

"'I don't see where the joke comes in there either!' I said; and I did not feel particularly pleased with him for saying such things."—John Seward

Leslie Nielsen as Dracula and Amy Yasbeck as Mina in *Dracula: Dead and Loving It* (1995) (courtesy Ronald V. Borst of Hollywood Movie Posters)

Commentary

Following the lukewarm reception of his 1991 social satire *Life Stinks*, Mel Brooks returned to the style that had served him so well twenty years earlier: genre parodies. *Spaceballs* (1987) had come too soon after the *Star Wars* saga to have the nostalgia-spoof appeal of *Blazing Saddles* (1973) and *Young Frankenstein* (1974), which had parodied *Destry Rides Again* (1939) and the Boris Karloff *Frankenstein* films of the 1930s. This time around, Brooks followed in the footsteps of big-name, big-budget remakes of well-known properties, following Kevin Costner's *Robin Hood: Prince of Thieves* (1991) with *Robin Hood: Men in Tights* (1993; Brooks's second take on the Robin Hood legend,

including the short-lived 1970s TV series *When Things Were Rotten*), and following *Bram Stoker's Dracula* with *Dracula: Dead and Loving It*.

In no way does Brooks recapture the "glory days" of *Young Frankenstein* with *Dracula: Dead and Loving It*, an appallingly unfunny film, full of lame gags and stale, predictable jokes. What's missing? Gene Wilder, for one, who co-wrote *Young Frankenstein*; the memorable "Puttin' On the Ritz" number was his idea. Sorely missed, too, are Madeline Kahn, Cloris Leachman, Kenneth Mars, and, of course, the late Marty Feldman, who would have made the ultimate comic Renfield. Of Brooks's former standard troupe, the only returnee (other than Brooks himself) is Harvey Korman as Dr. Seward. (Amy

Yasbeck and Mark Blankfield return after *Robin Hood: Men in Tights*, the title role of which was played by Cary Elwes, late of *Bram Stoker's Dracula*.)

But it is beside the point how *Dracula: Dead and Loving It* fails as a comedy. What is interesting to note is that, even with *Bram Stoker's Dracula* fairly fresh in the public's mind, Brooks chooses instead to spoof the Lugosi version. Even after more than sixty years, and any number of intervening adaptations, Brooks correctly observes that the Dracula most people remember is the one who sports a tux and speaks with a Hungarian accent. (Brooks takes only a couple of pokes at the newer film, sight gags having to do with Dracula's twin-peaked hairstyle and his detachable shadow.)

While the screenplay for *Dracula: Dead and Loving It* is described as being "based on characters created by Bram Stoker," implying the very loosest of associations, it is actually, in several ways, more faithful to the novel than the 1931 version it spoofs. For one thing, the year is once more in Stoker's Victorian era, not the 1920s. While it is still Renfield who makes the trip to Transylvania, at least Jonathan Harker is Jonathan again, instead of John; similarly, Lucy Westenra has her proper last name back (as opposed to Weston). And Lucy's episode of vampirism is given fuller play than either of the 1931 versions gave it, though she doesn't victimize children: Brooks apparently decided there was no way to make that a laughing matter. (Two words: Eddie Munster.)

In fact, there are several instances where the story turns serious in spite of itself. When Lucy dies, and Van Helsing laments that she has not stayed in the safety of her garlic-filled room, we wait for the other, comic shoe to drop ... and it doesn't. Lucy attacks a graveyard attendant, a stock and often comic character in horror movies, but again there is no joke

attached to the incident. And the branding of Mina's hand with the cross is played seriously as well. It may be simply that Brooks and his co-writers Rudy De Luca and Steve Haberman have too much "respect" for the material to spoof it at these points, but it plays more like someone's inability to think of a punch line. By contrast, the script manages to make light of Vlad the Impaler's atrocities. And the staking of Lucy, with its attendant eruption of blood, not only is the closest thing this film has to offer in the way of a comic highlight, but, as noted in the chapter about *El Conde Dracula*, is rooted in the folkloric realities of the messy hazards of staking vampires.

Peter MacNicol—who played the young hero in *Dragonslayer* (1979) but who went on to play such unpleasant characters as the malevolent ghost's catspaw in *Ghostbusters II* (1989) and the smarmy camp counselor in *Addams Family Values* (1993)—here does a serviceable spoof of Dwight Frye's Renfield. His performance suffers only by comparison with Arte Johnson's in *Love at First Bite*. Renfield's participation in the story is more clearly defined than in the 1931 versions: we see exactly how and when it is that he comes under Dracula's control; the bars of his window are clearly bent to allow him to get out, and not to let Dracula enter; and he is called upon to remove the garlic from Lucy's room, a use to which he is not put in either the novel or the 1931 films, but which makes perfect sense. This being a comedy and not a tragedy, Renfield survives the story.

Leslie Nielsen, still enjoying his second career as a comic actor (which makes it hard for audiences to watch his earlier work with a straight face; 1956's *Forbidden Planet*, for example, comes off as *Police Squad Goes to Mars*), is appropriately cast—white hair and all!—as Dracula, as is Mel Brooks himself as Van Helsing. If only they'd been given better, funnier lines to say with their bogus accents.

On a second viewing, once one has gotten past the moment-by-moment realization of how numbingly unfunny the movie is, one can enjoy the high production values of *Dracula: Dead and Loving It*. In this age of ever-more-affordable digital effects, we've probably seen our last rubber bat on a string. Dracula's transformations into a bat are not only smoothly and startlingly done, they are also funny: the bat retains Nielsen's face, topped with gigantic bat ears. In this guise he can react to slapstick situations like having Lucy's window closed in his face. Later, Dracula's image is seamlessly erased from a large ballroom mirror, in a scene that pulls the switcheroo on the ballroom scene in *The Fearless Vampire Killers*.

The film is, in general, lavish; nothing about it looks cheap. The aforementioned ball is sumptuous; the opening credits—which unfold across the turning pages of a horrifically illustrated book—would have done a straight vampire movie proud; and a shot near the film's end, of Renfield scaling a seaside slope by moonlight to meet Dracula at a chapel at the top of the cliff, is a thing of beauty.

The movie's just not funny, for the most part. Which is a pity, but not surprising: for whatever reason, vampire humor, especially in the movies, tends to be lame. There are a few exceptions: *Abbott and Costello Meet Frankenstein* works because the horror elements, including Bela Lugosi as Dracula, are generally played straight. *The Fearless Vampire Killers*, a spoof of the distinctive Hammer style, works because it evokes that style so atmospherically that even the presence of a garrulous Jewish vampire, or of a gay vampire (a novelty at the time), doesn't disrupt it; the humor is dark and absurd, and the ending an ironic nightmare. *Love at First Bite* works partly in the way *Young Frankenstein* does—by evoking the familiar characters, if not the entire look and feel, of the 1930s films, and doing so with a great deal of affection. *Fright Night* works because its humor, such as it is, centers around the protagonists instead of the vampire; the same is generally true of 1992's *Buffy the Vampire Slayer*, although Paul ("Pee Wee Herman") Reubens does a memorable turn as a comic vampire. (The TV series that grew out of the movie is much darker, and its cruel, ugly, ill-tempered vampires are no laughing matter at all.) But *The Lost Boys* (1987), *From Dusk Till Dawn*, and *Bordello of Blood* (both 1996) are more like spoofs of action pictures than of horror films; in these movies, both the vampires and the heroes are caricatures. Speak not to me of *Once Bitten* (1985), an early Jim Carrey outing; nor of the only film debatably as bad, *Transylvania 6-5000* (1985). The latter film, a total waste of a good cast (and Geena Davis), was directed by Rudy De Luca. De Luca was one of Brooks' co-writers for *Dracula: Dead and Loving It*, which probably explains a lot.

There is, of course, really no question as to whether the spirit of Stoker's novel survives here. It isn't intended to; *Dracula: Dead and Loving It*, while structurally quite true to the familiar story—and, more especially, to earlier film adaptations of it—is a spoof. Though the movie generally fails to amuse, at least Mel Brooks doesn't insult his audience by claiming Bram Stoker wrote a comedy, not a horror story.

Musical Notes

The soundtrack music for *Dracula: Dead and Loving It* was composed by Hummie Mann. The main title theme is a fully-orchestrated John Williams-esque piece in 4/4 time at a moderate tempo. After a chromatic introduction, the main body proceeds in C minor, goes through another chromatic stage, then returns to C minor. The melody alternates between the brass and string sections.

Mann's original compositions are complemented by excerpts from Brahms's *Hungarian Dances*. Apparently Mel Brooks, like many before him, labors under the misapprehension that the historical Vlad the Impaler was Hungarian.

No CD soundtrack album for *Dracula: Dead and Loving It* appears to have been released.

Afterword to the Adaptations

As we head into the novel's second century, have we seen the end of film adaptations of Bram Stoker's *Dracula*? Not likely. As long as Hollywood remains out of new ideas, it will continue to recycle older, preferably box-office-proven ones. As we have seen before, this tendency will consist not only of cannibalizing earlier films (not to mention every single TV series ever produced in the 1960s), but of turning again and again to the classics and near-classics of literature and pseudo-literature, which has a lot to do with why two of the most popular screenwriters, so to speak, of the 1990s have been William Shakespeare and Jane Austen.

As a novelist, Stoker was more prolific than Austen, but let's face it: he was a hack writer who got lucky and touched a nerve with *Dracula*. Two of his other novels have also been filmed: *The Jewel of Seven Stars* (twice, though neither time under that title), and *Lair of the White Worm* (1988). Is anybody really in a hurry to see either of them remade? It's a safe bet, then, that when Stoker is again pressed into service as source material, it'll be another incarnation of the Count who graces the screen, say in another ten or fifteen years ... and another after that. As always, new technology yields interesting possibilities. As digital imagery is perfected and made more affordable, it will be possible to generate new "footage"— footage that was never actually filmed, but computer-generated—even of actors long dead. Films of generations ago can be recast, even as a hobby or a recreational lark. (As a commercial endeavor, imagine the legal entanglements.) A young John Wayne can be buddy-cop to an aging Clint Eastwood ... or, for that matter, an aging actor can play father-and-son with the image of his younger self, which might throw a damper on the Sheen family's uniqueness.

For our purposes, think of Klaus Kinski as Dracula, opposite Klaus Kinski as Renfield. Or imagine a formidable young Christopher Lee, grafted whole into the BBC's 1977 version, gleefully transforming into a digitized bat. Perhaps Gary Oldman could be recast after all, as Renfield, in the 1973 version where the character is omitted. That would free up the role of Dracula for Anthony Hopkins, versus Vincent Price as Van Helsing. And so forth.

It could happen. Something will, because Dracula is, as we've seen, harder to kill than a cockroach in a corner when you're wearing round-toed shoes.

II. The Universal Dracula Series

By the mid-1930s, the success and notoriety of such early '30s horror movies as *Dracula, Frankenstein*, and *Dr. Jekyll and Mr. Hyde*, as well as even more disturbing projects such as *Murders in the Rue Morgue, Island of Lost Souls*, and Tod Browning's *Freaks*, had led to such a public outcry that the film industry felt compelled to police itself. To that end, the Production Code Administration was empowered to be Hollywood's in-house censorship authority. In order to produce sequels to its lucrative horror twins *Dracula* and *Frankenstein*, Universal had to proceed with caution, toning down much of the emphasis on sadism and torment characteristic of the films of the early '30s.

As a result, many of the Universal sequels, while atmospheric, lack the manic edge of the earlier films. By the 1940s, they had become standard studio product, mostly familiar and formulaic. Bela Lugosi, whose performance had indelibly stamped Dracula onto the map of the American consciousness, wouldn't be invited to return to the series until long after the studio had stopped even pretending to take its horror output seriously.

For our purposes, amid all the revisions, rewrites, and diminishing returns of Universal's Dracula series, the search for the "gist" of Stoker's novel continues, in the form of the question: How true is the depiction of the Dracula character, and the situations surrounding him, to the way Bram Stoker originally envisioned him in the novel?

Dracula's Daughter

(1936)

In *Dracula's Daughter*, the first of the Universal sequels, the question, as it applies to the character of Dracula himself, is moot, since the Count is dead. As the title indicates, the problem of how to continue the story is solved by dragging in the main character's relatives. While Stoker never specifically mentions a daughter or any other close relatives, he does have Van Helsing inform us: "There have been from the loins of this very one great men and good women...." Dracula himself says to the three women in his castle, "I too can love; you yourselves can tell it from the past." This is an ambiguous utterance, to be sure, but it admits at least the possibility of children and family.

Certain folklores allow for the siring of children by vampires, so the daughter in this film may have been conceived before or after Dracula's "death"—in 1476, history tells us. As for the historical Vlad the Impaler, Professors Florescu and McNally, in *Dracula, Prince of Many Faces*, provide family trees for Vlad's descendants in Romania and Hungary, both of which lines died out in the 17th century.

Dracula's Daughter begins where the 1931 film left off: in Carfax Abbey, with Professor Van Helsing (again played by Edward Van Sloan) discovered by the police in the company of two dead bodies. One of the two unfortunates—Renfield—is dead of a broken neck, possibly suffered in a fall from the stairs. But the other has clearly been murdered, since he has a stake driven through his heart; this time, we actually get a brief glimpse of the sight. Van Helsing freely admits to having staked the well-dressed gentleman, as a result of which he is promptly arrested.

The police are comic-relief constables who have no idea what to make of Van Helsing. He is lucid, he is erudite, his credentials prove to be impeccable, and he offers them no resistance or trouble. Yet he calmly admits to having spiked a man through the heart, and he further claims that the victim has been dead "about five hundred years" (making this fictional Dracula slightly older than the historical one). He tells the police the Count was a vampire, responsible for "many mysterious attacks" in London (evidently not just the three—Lucy, Mina, and the flower girl—we saw in the 1931 film). The stake is, Van Helsing says, "the only way a vampire can be destroyed." As we have seen elsewhere in this book, this claim is untrue, but it is already being woven into "Hollywood folklore."

When the police, of course, disbelieve Van Helsing's story, he informs them, "The strength of the vampire lies in the fact that he *is* unbelievable." This statement, an echo of a line from the earlier film, is built upon Stoker's assertion, again in Van Helsing's words, that "in this enlightened age, when men believe not even what they see, the doubting of wise men would be his greatest strength. It would be at once his sheath and his armor...."

Van Helsing and the two corpses are transferred from Carfax to the *Whitby* jail, continuing the geographic confusion of the first film. The error persists, no doubt, because both films were written by the same screenwriter, Garrett Fort. According to the opening credits, Fort's screenplay was "Based on a story by Bram Stoker." That story would have to be "Dracula's Guest," which originally was the novel's first chapter; deleted at the request of the publisher, who considered the book too long, the chapter was published as a separate story after Stoker's death. The "guest" of the title is Jonathan Harker, who, en route to Transylvania, has a harrowing experience in a German graveyard, a misadventure in which he is trapped between a snowstorm (with lightning!) and a vampiress whose tomb affords him the only shelter.

"Dracula's Guest" has yet to be filmed as written. The presence of the female vampire is the only element of the story that makes it onto the screen in *Dracula's Daughter*. An Austrian suicide, "Countess Dolingen of Gratz in Styria" (as her tombstone identifies her), a briefly-seen potential threat in the story, becomes the title character of the film: Hungarian countess Marya Zaleska, played by Gloria Holden.

As a wolf howls like a herald announcing her arrival, the Countess turns up at the Whitby jail. Relying on the standard vampiric power of hypnotism (or something like it: she later refers to her power as "something older and more powerful" than hypnotism), she puts the guard on duty into a trance, using her large, dark eyes and a ring with a glowing jewel to fascinate him. She then steals her father's body, which, contrary to Stoker, has not crumbled to dust. (The Count's body, far from being played by Bela Lugosi, is a tuxedo-clad wax-dummy prop that bears no particular resemblance to him.)

With the help of her brooding manservant Sandor (Irving Pichel), the Countess burns the body, which, as we've seen, may be easier said than done but is one of the few sure ways to be rid of a vampire. In this case, what the Countess seeks to destroy is Dracula's "influence" from beyond the grave: she wishes to be freed from her own "life" of vampirism. She performs an exorcism over the pyre, an odd rite combining both pagan and Christian elements. She flings handfuls of salt into the fire (which flares up as though she's dispensing gunpowder); the use of salt may be related to an old European practice (per Matthew Bunson in *The Vampire Encyclopedia*) of tossing salt into coffins to ward off evil spirits. Finally she holds up a cross from which she must avert her own eyes. Sandor, too, is unable (or unwilling) to look at the cross, which is strange, since he is not a vampire.

On the other hand, Sandor is no ray of sunlight, either. As the Countess plays some relaxing music on the piano, jubilant that "the spell is broken" so she can now "live a normal life," Sandor dourly—and correctly, it turns out—insists that she's not out of the primordial woods yet. The music, against the Countess's will, turns unpleasantly compelling and minor-key. "That music doesn't speak of release," Sandor observes. (This is an early, and chilling, scene linking vampirism with the sometimes mesmeric power of music. As will be seen, Universal makes use of the motif again in 1945's *House of Dracula*; and Hammer puts it to effective use in 1964's *Kiss of the Vampire*.)

As Sandor's behavior indicates, he does, of course, have his own agenda. But for the time being, when the Countess inevitably continues her vampiric career, he dutifully tends to her as she whiles away the daylight hours in her coffin. He also sees to the dry-cleaning needs peculiar to such a lifestyle: "There's blood on it again," the Countess says, handing him her cloak at the end of an evening out.

The gentleman who had until recently owned the blood in question, having suffered a fatal loss of it, undergoes a post-mortem in an operating theater. This scene is similar to Lucy's autopsy in the 1931 film, right down to a line which tells us the victim received his last transfusion "four hours before he died." We do not see him again: vampirism as a haphazard contagion is not a factor in this film.

*"She was ... so radiantly beautiful ... that the very instinct of man in me,
which calls some of my sex to love and protect one of hers, made my
head swirl with new emotion."*—Van Helsing

**Irving Pichel as Sandor and Gloria Holden as Hungarian countess Marya Zaleska
in *Dracula's Daughter* (1936) (courtesy Ronald V. Borst of Hollywood Movie Posters)**

Good thing, too, since Van Helsing is in the hands of Scotland Yard, facing execution if he's found sane, and the madhouse if otherwise. He calls upon a former student, Dr. Jeffrey Garth (Otto Kruger), as a character witness ("John" Harker, Mina, and Dr. Seward all having mysteriously vanished from the story with the end of the first film). Garth, we're told, studied under Van Helsing in Vienna, whereas Dr. John Seward, according to Stoker, had been his student in Amsterdam. Having placed Van Helsing in Switzerland in the script for the 1931 film, Garrett Fort seems to be having trouble determining the professor's country of origin. When Garth, unaware of Van Helsing's arrest, is asked about the professor, he replies, "He's in Budapest." One wonders why.

Dr. Garth and his gal Friday, Janet Blake (Marguerite Churchill), drop what they're doing to come to Van Helsing's aid. While in London, Garth meets the Countess at a party, where she turns down the offer of a drink with the familiar non-Stoker line, "I never drink ... wine." Garth rivets the Countess's attention when he says he uses psychiatry as a means to help his patients attain "release" from their compulsions. Hoping to combat her vampirism with psychiatry, but unable to keep a daytime appointment, she arranges for Garth to come to her home. "You know," he indiscreetly notes upon arrival, "this is the first woman's flat I've been in that didn't have at least twenty mirrors in it." Ironically, the treatment he ultimately plans to use involves hypnotism. The Countess balks, since Garth's hypnotic regimen makes use of a machine that includes mirrors.

The Countess's vampiric depredations continue. Under an alias, she has rented a loft above a bookshop and set up an artist's studio therein, creating an early example of the link, extant to this day, between vampires and the bohemian world of artists and writers. Sandor recruits a street waif to model for the Countess, bringing to mind the servants who procured girls for the cruel pleasures of Countess Erszebet Bathory, Hungary's sixteenth-century "Blood Countess." One wonders whether Garrett Fort knew of Countess Bathory at the time and was deliberately drawing a parallel. In any case, the girl, Lili (Nan Grey), is victimized in a scene that was considered provocative at the time because of its lesbian overtones. But she survives the encounter long enough to tell Garth, who also hypnotizes her, something of her experience … and her attacker.

Scotland Yard, initially a haven for

"Come, sister. Come to us. Come! Come!"—Dracula's brides

Nan Grey as Lili is seduced by Gloria Holden as the Countess in *Dracula's Daughter* (1936) (courtesy Ronald V. Borst of Hollywood Movie Posters)

skeptics, becomes convinced that the recent attacks are the work of Dracula himself: his body has disappeared (which ultimately frees Van Helsing from the murder rap), and the m.o. is the same. Van Helsing tells them that another vampire must be the culprit, since, as he insists, "No vampire can survive the stake." (Again, as we will see elsewhere, he is in error. But since the Count's body has been burned, the point is moot here.) Van Helsing points out that Dracula was able to make his "many victims" into "creatures like himself," although the only one such that we've seen—Lucy "Weston," in the earlier film—has presumably been dealt with.

The investigator protests what he takes to be Van Helsing's suggestion that London is "hag-ridden" with vampires …an interesting term, since it refers to the sort of nocturnal nightmarish "visitations" that helped give rise to vampire folklore in the first place (and to "alien abduction" delusions in more recent times). Even today, the term "night hag" refers to a type of sleep disorder characterized by a sense of suffocation and paralysis, which once would have been interpreted as the "hag" (vampire, incubus, malefic ghost, etc.) sitting on (or "riding") the sufferer's chest.

The Countess, frustrated at her inability to conquer her vampiric habit, and incriminated by Lili's deathbed revelations, decides it's time to skip town. Garth's therapeutic ideas are of no use to her, but she decides Garth himself will do nicely for other purposes: as often happens in real life, she has developed a crush on her therapist. To lure him into her trap, she abducts Janet and flees to Transylvania. She travels by plane, as we're told Dracula himself arrived in England in the Balderston/Deane play. Garth's pursuit of the Countess back to her Carpathian homeland parallels the pursuit back to Transylvania at the end of the novel, a chase which goes only as far as Carfax in the 1931 film.

TRANSYLVANIA, a superimposed title tells us. The locals are celebrating a wedding; all is music and colorful folk costumes. The party, looking like the one disrupted in *Frankenstein* (1931) by the arrival of the bereaved father carrying the body of his drowned little girl, is doomed to suffer just as abrupt an ending. Again the "heraldic" howl of the wolf is heard, whereupon the villagers notice a light in one of the windows of the old Dracula place. Needless to say, the party breaks up.

The castle itself seems to be bigger, more intact, and (if our first look at it is meant to be from the POV of the villagers) much closer to town than was the case in the earlier film. Inside, as the Countess rises from her coffin, director Lambert Hillyer follows Tod Browning's lead and pans away from the sight, as though giving her her privacy. Granted, it must be awkward to climb out of a box while wearing a floor-length formal dress. This was in the days when horror films regularly included in the closing credits a listing for "Gowns" (in dire contrast to some of today's credits, such as "Creature Effects Coordinator" or "Bug Wrangler").

Dr. Garth, meantime, must bribe a coachman to take him to Borgo Pass. "He must be mad," a local old woman grumbles. Evidently the villagers, so helpful and concerned in Stoker's novel, are getting tired of having their warnings go unheeded by intrusive foreigners. As Garth arrives at the castle, Sandor, jealous that the Countess has passed him by in order to share the gift of immortality with Garth, lets fly with an arrow in what must be history's last such defense of a medieval castle. He narrowly misses.

Indoors, we find ourselves in a familiar huge hallway with its broad flight of cobweb-festooned stairs. As Garth confronts the Countess and demands Janet's release, she coolly warns him, "You're not in London, Dr. Garth, with your police. You're in Transylvania, in my castle." This line brings to mind Dracula's similarly-worded caution to Jonathan in the novel: "We are in Transylvania; and Transylvania is not England. Our ways are not your ways...."

A second arrow from Sandor strikes home—killing the Countess! She and Garth are standing so close together, as she tries to hypnotize him, that it is impossible to tell whether the arrow that finds the Countess's heart was meant for Garth's back. Sandor's disillusionment with the Countess, and his earlier warning to her that "there is ... destruction for you" if Garth comes to the castle, make it plausible that he has revolted against her, striking her down rather than allow her to grant someone else the immortality he seeks for himself. Sandor joins her in death, gunned down by a Scotland Yard officer before he can get off a third arrow. Van Helsing and the police have followed Garth in an effort to rescue him from the danger he faces by going to Transylvania alone.

The arrow, a wooden shaft, serves as a stake, and proves fatal to the Countess.

Her body doesn't turn to dust any more than her father's did; she could be just another exotically beautiful woman murdered with an arrow. "She was beautiful when she died," observes Van Helsing, "a hundred years ago." Evidently the professor knows more about her personal history than he's let on up to this point.

In sum, *Dracula's Daughter* features a few of Stoker's ideas and themes—from the novel itself, if not from "Dracula's Guest"—and ignores others, generally following through on Universal's handling (or mishandling) of these ideas in the earlier film. Two notable changes: the Countess's seeming inability to transform into a bat or wolf, and her poor-me-I'm-a-vampire attitude (later given fuller treatment in *Dark Shadows* and the novels of Anne Rice). Like many horror films of the time, it is marred by "comic relief," mostly in the form of cutesy banter between Garth and Janet.

Dracula's Daughter (running time 70 minutes; available on video) is the only film of the Universal series that can be considered in any way a sequel to *Dracula*. As shall be seen, the rest of the films in the "series" represent a total departure from anything that has gone before.

Son of Dracula

(1943)

If *Dracula's Daughter*, five years after *Dracula*, was a somewhat belated sequel, *Son of Dracula* was even later in arriving. The title is misleading: whereas it gives the impression that we're about to see further exploits of yet another member of the Count's immediate family, the vampire of this movie is, in fact, the Count himself. One gets the impression that Curt Siod-

mak, who wrote the original story (from which Eric Taylor then wrote the screenplay), was given a "high-concept" title by a production head and instructed to write a story to go with it. This is a not-uncommon sequence of events in Hollywood, especially when dealing with exploitation films, which is what the Universal horror series had become by the mid-1940s.

In *Son of Dracula*, we find the Count (Lon Chaney, Jr.), in the words of Van Helsing in the novel, again "leaving his own barren land—barren of peoples—and coming to a new land where life of man teems till they are like the multitude of standing corn." This time his travels take him further afield than England, all the way to America, to seek, as the Count puts it, the blood of "a young and vital race." To some, his choice of relocation sites may not seem promising: a mossy, foggy swamp in the deep South. But this desolate ambiance satisfies the Count—possibly because (contrary to what he says) it is similar to the way Transylvania is often depicted in the movies.

What's more, this time the Count has been *invited* (though, unlike the novel, there is no supernatural significance attached to the question of whether a vampire has been invited to enter a home). A certain Katherine "Kay" Caldwell (Louise Albritton), an heiress of Dark Oaks Plantation, has been corresponding with Dracula and has asked him to come stay awhile. As a student of the occult, she is at least as much of an early Goth-punk as Sandor was, and with motives just as ulterior. The death of her father, Colonel Caldwell, on the very night of the Count's arrival, is hardly coincidental. Dracula has come in on a train, but the people sent to greet him at the station fail to find him. He is, of course, in a crate, and he misses (or avoids) the gala reception Kay throws in his honor, an affair which Stoker's reclusive Count would have had little inclination to attend.

Dracula instead goes about pursuing his own ends by means of a couple of strategic killings, which he carries out in the form of a bat. The first victim is swamp-dwelling Queen Zimba (Adeline de Walt Reynolds; listed in the credits as "Madame" Zimba), a muttering Gypsy woman who is Kay's mentor in the ways of metaphysics. She is, in fact, another of Kay's imported Hungarians; and her warnings to Kay, which prompt the Count to kill her, also establish her as the equivalent of one of Stoker's frightened villagers. ("That sort of news travels fast," Kay's fiancé says of the Gypsy's death a short while later, in a distinct echo of a line from Stoker.)

The second victim is Colonel Caldwell himself, and his demise sets the stage for Kay to inherit Dark Oaks, while her sister Claire (Evelyn Ankers) gets the cash and investments. (Neither of the Count's victims returns as a vampire.) Kay then throws over her fiancé, Frank Stanley (Robert Paige), with whom she has been involved since childhood—in favor of the Count! Frank, friends, and family are stunned.

Who is this mysterious Count, anyway? The family physician, Dr. Harry Brewster (Frank Crane), has his suspicions: he has noticed that the Count's given name, "Alucard," is "Dracula" spelled backwards—a particularly cheesy alias. Dr. Brewster checks with the story's Van Helsing surrogate, a Professor Laszlo from Hungary (J. Edward Bromberg); the professor confirms that while the name "Alucard" is not Hungarian, as the Count claims to be, anyone calling himself by such an obvious anagram bears watching. "In Transylvania," Laszlo explains, "that name [Dracula] is associated only with evil." (This is untrue, by the way: because of his successful military actions against the Ottoman Turks, Dracula is to this day regarded by the Romanians as a national hero. There was even a 1976 postage stamp commemorating the 500th anniversary of his death.)

The professor says that "the last Count Dracula became one of the undead —a vampire—and was finally destroyed in the nineteenth century." This recap is at odds with Universal's adaptation of *Drac-*

"... he can live for centuries, and you are but mortal woman. Time is now to be dreaded..."—Van Helsing

Lon Chaney, Jr., as the Count and Louise Albritton as Kay in *Son of Dracula* (1943) (courtesy Ronald V. Borst of Hollywood Movie Posters)

ula, since it was set in modern times, but is in agreement with Stoker's novel. It is as though Siodmak wrote a sequel to the novel, with no reference to the two earlier films in the series. But in either case, we are left with no explanation of how the Count has turned up again, "alive" and whole, since the novel reduced him to dust and *Dracula's Daughter* reduced him to ashes. Is he, after all, a descendant—a

"son"—of Dracula, as Laszlo suggests? That would mean that there were at least two vampire Count Draculas on the loose in Europe simultaneously, and apparently for quite some time. The mind boggles at the thought, which this film fortunately doesn't ask us to accept; instead, we are left with the original question: Why that title?

And why, it has been asked over the

years, that actor? Lon Chaney, Jr., (listed in the credits without the "Jr."), who could politely be described as "stout" at this stage of his career, has only one thing in common with Stoker's physical description of the cadaverously thin Count: a mustache. It appears that Universal was taking advantage of Chaney's famous name (i.e., his father's; "Junior's" real first name was Creighton), and in more ways than one. Not only had the elder Chaney been the studio's first choice to play the Count before throat cancer felled him in 1930, he had also been a renowned make-up artist known as "The Man of a Thousand Faces." Universal was able to cash in on this protean legacy: the younger Chaney *appeared* to follow in his father's shape-shifting

footsteps by being the first (and indeed, the only) actor to play the entire Universal monster lineup. Having played the title role in *The Wolf Man* (1941), the monster in *The Ghost of Frankenstein* (1942), and Kharis the mummy in *The Mummy's Tomb* (1942), Chaney, in *Son of Dracula*, completes the Mount Rushmore of horror.

So Chaney's miscasting is a publicist's dream. The obvious question is: How is he in the role? Surprisingly good, as it happens. He plays the role much as Stoker conceived the character, with the unapologetic arrogance of ancient nobility accustomed to having its way. His performance is therefore totally (and refreshingly) unlike his sniveling outings as Larry Talbot, the cry-baby werewolf. Both before he

"You think to baffle me, you—with your pale faces all in a row, like sheep in a butcher's! You shall be sorry yet, each one of you!"—Count Dracula

Lon Chaney, Jr., as Count Alucard and J. Edward Bromberg as Professor Laszlo in *Son of Dracula* (1943) (courtesy Ronald V. Borst of Hollywood Movie Posters)

marries the heiress of Dark Oaks ("Announce me!" he demands of an intimidated black butler who has meekly told him that the bereaved Caldwell family are not receiving visitors, and certainly not in the middle of the night), and afterwards ("I am now master of this house," he warns a snooping Dr. Brewster; "... anyone who enters here without my permission will be considered a trespasser"), this Dracula leaves no doubt as to who is in charge. (How surprised he will be to learn how wrong he is.) He settles into the antebellum plantation as though he were born there: "I like old houses," he tells Kay. Stoker's Count similarly (if not as tersely) approves of Carfax largely on the basis of its age: "I am glad that it is old and big. I myself am of an old family, and to live in a new house would kill me. A house cannot be made habitable in a day; and, after all, how few days go to make up a century."

The Count here also has the full range of supernatural powers—and limitations—Stoker describes. His transformations into a bat, accomplished by shadowy animation, are sudden and startling, even if the technique is dated to the modern eye. He can appear as a swirling cloud of vapor: in one justifiably famous scene, his coffin, hidden in the swamp prior to his acquisition of Dark Oaks, bobs to the surface of the murky waters (bringing to mind Paul Barber's assertion that the problems of *keeping* the dead buried, despite pesky things like subterranean water tables, contributed to the lore of the restless dead); a mist emerges from the coffin and congeals into the Count, who glides slowly to the shore and into the waiting arms of Kay. (Apparently he is "surfing" the coffin, and not just floating along above the water's surface; we aren't shown his feet, but the box—filled, as always, with his "native soil"—later turns up on dry land.) He has great physical strength,

at one point flinging the jilted Frank across the room. He has the usual aversions to crosses, the stake, and (alas) the sun. But bullets do him no harm, as Frank finds out the hard way: appalled at the news that Kay and the Count have been married in secret, Frank shoots Dracula twice ... and kills Kay, who is hiding behind the Count.

A nightmarish sequence follows, in which Frank, pursued by Dracula (in the form of a bat), flees through the swamp and turns up at Dr. Brewster's place in a state of shock. At the time of Frank's arrival, Brewster is reading a book, the title of which we see at the top of the page: *Dracula*!

Viewed in close-up, the page features a close paraphrase of an excerpt from Jonathan Harker's diary, found in Chapter 3 of the novel: "What manner of man is this Count Dracula, or what manner of creature is it in human form? I feel the dread of this horrible place overpowering me. I am in awful fear and there is no escape for me. I am encompassed with fears I dare not think of." In the novel, Jonathan writes these words after seeing Count Dracula climb head-first down the outer wall of the castle. Here, the passage seems to be commenting on Frank's experiences with the shooting and his subsequent flight. (A second paragraph begins, now a departure from Jonathan's words: "Terrors that are numbing in their effect on me. The first impressions were a quickening of my faculties, but repetitions seem to stun me." Repetitions, indeed: the magic of freeze-frame reveals that the rest of the text on this briefly-glimpsed page is a threefold repeat of these same two paragraphs!) While underscoring Dracula's terrifying strangeness, this page also makes it clear that Curt Siodmak looked to the novel for inspiration. This appearance of a copy of the novel in the context of a film about Dracula is, as far as can be ascertained, unique. But it is a variation on the commonly-used plot device of the use of a book as a "mentoring tool"—or indeed, as a surrogate mentor—in vampire films. As we have seen, Jonathan is given a book about vampires in both versions of *Nosferatu*. In *Horror of Dracula*, Jonathan's diary is the book that informs Van Helsing and convinces the Holmwoods. In *Bram Stoker's Dracula*, Van Helsing consults a huge, all-encompassing tome that includes images of Vlad the Impaler. And *Dracula: Dead and Loving It*, as noted earlier, features the book and its chilling illustrations in the opening credits, rooting the film, although a comedy, in the lore of ancient dreads. Nor is the use of the book limited to adaptations of the novel; it will turn up again, for example, as we consider the Hammer series in the next chapter. (Universal's use of the book spilled over into its Frankenstein series in the form of Dr. Frankenstein's coveted notes about "the secrets of life and death," spoofed years later in *Young Frankenstein* with a book smugly titled "How I Did It.")

Non-Dracula vampire films make use of the book motif as well; Professor Zimmer (Clifford Evans) in *Kiss of the Vampire*, for instance, finds his vampire-killing spell in an ancient volume. And in *The Fearless Vampire Killers*, Professor Abronsius (Jack MacGowran), with his pile of papers, seems to be composing the book himself. In later years the book has been modernized in various ways: as a comic book in *The Lost Boys*, and as a TV show (with its has-been host) in *Fright Night*. Finally, in the TV series *Buffy the Vampire Slayer*, the mentor is the high-school librarian; the information in his host of quaint and curious volumes is being formatted onto CD-ROM by a computer wonkette who is one of the band of teen vampire hunters.

When Dr. Brewster goes to Dark Oaks to check out Frank's story, the Count, with the soft-spoken, menacing politeness

of a gangster, leads him to Kay ... who is alive! The two of them make it clear to Brewster that they are effectively cutting themselves off from the land of the living. They have already dismissed all the plantation's staff, leaving Dark Oaks as free of servants as the castle is in the novel. Their claim that they will be conducting "scientific research" that will occupy "all of our daylight hours" and leave them "no time for social life" brings to mind Dracula's vague explanations, in the novel, of his lengthy absences from the castle: "I trust you will forgive me, but I have much work to do in private this evening." In brief, they are becoming the sort of reclusive, secretive living dead Stoker describes. One wonders how long it will take the Count to complete his harem of three (or more) wives.

How is it that Kay has returned from the dead? Obviously the Count is involved somehow, but we do not see him plant the vampire's kiss on her prior to her apparent death at Frank's hands; indeed, the Count is homing in on her welcoming neck, the newlyweds having just returned from the J.P.'s office after their midnight nuptials, when Frank's knock at the door interrupts. Professor Laszlo, who has come to town at Dr. Brewster's request, speculates that Kay may have become undead owing to her "morbid" streak: her "fear of death"—and this is the only film that comes to mind which uses the word "thanatophobia" in its dialogue—may have created such a spiritual kinship with the Count that vampirism seeped into her as if by osmosis.

Certainly this is an unusual, perhaps unique, means for someone to become a vampire in a movie, but it has a certain plausibility, partly rooted in Stoker. Kay can be compared to Renfield: though she doesn't develop his appetite for bugs, he too is motivated by an overpowering fear of death that leads to the development, first of his vampiric habits, and then of what Dr. Richard Noll, as we have seen, describes as a telepathic attraction between him and Dracula. Significantly, Dr. Brewster attempts to have Kay committed to an asylum when he learns of her marriage to the Count.

Also, in certain folklores, witches become vampires after death; and while Kay is more of a dabbler than a sorceress, she does open the door to the occult. She goes so far as to seek Dracula out, invite him into her home, and marry him. She then dies violently, a frequent precursor of restless death. How could she *not* become a vampire?

Frank, meanwhile, turns himself over to the sheriff, still claiming to have killed Kay. Obliged to investigate, the sheriff goes with Frank and Dr. Brewster to Dark Oaks. The place is standing wide open, much as the castle in *Horror of Dracula* is found by Jonathan: as the new guy in town, the Count hasn't yet learned that Americans aren't intimidated by titled nobility like the peasants in the old country are, and that telling commoners to get lost isn't sufficient home security. The sheriff's party find Kay dead in her coffin in a tomb! Frank is locked up, Kay is transferred to the county morgue, and Brewster is eyed with suspicion for saying he'd spoken with her after Frank claimed to have shot her.

In another of the story's nods to Stoker, a child victim of the vampire's bite turns up. Dr. Brewster applies topical medication in a cruciform pattern, a gesture worthy of Van Helsing's adherence to both science and faith.

Frank, in jail, receives an after-hours visit from Kay, whose body has disappeared from the morgue. As a mist, she infiltrates his cell and finally tells him what her plan has been all along. She wants to be with Frank forever; she doesn't want death to interfere with their togetherness; she has attained immortality and is now in a position to share it with him. It

has been Dracula's secret of eternal life that she has coveted, and not the portly, ill-tempered foreigner himself. All Frank has to do now, since he can move about in the daylight, is kill Count Dracula! Kay even tells him how to do so: either with the stake, or by burning his coffin before dawn, leaving him no haven against the sunlight.

After Kay springs Frank from jail, he gets to work, not waiting for dawn. Ahead of a manhunt, he makes it to Dark Oaks and burns Dracula's coffin after dragging it out of its hiding place in a drainage tunnel. The Count arrives on the scene and attacks him, realizing too late what a fix he's in: the sun comes up and reduces him to a skeleton.

Frank then enters the plantation house, where Kay has secluded herself in her room and succumbed to the catatonia brought on by the day. In an absolute reversal of the expected Hollywood ending, in which Kay, after Dracula's death, would awaken as if from an awful dream and fall into Frank's arms, the two young lovers reunited like Jonathan and Mina, the evil threat destroyed, and oh-my-darling-can-you-ever forgive-me … Frank torches her where she lies. Like Arthur in the novel, he loves this woman too much to allow her to continue in this state. She has become part of the problem and must be destroyed. As the sheriff and Dr. Brewster arrive, we see in Frank's haunted eyes that, while the danger is past and the story is over, he will never be the same again. And to that extent, the bad guy has won.

Son of Dracula (78 minutes; available on video), despite its inappropriate title and the less-than-ideal casting of Chaney, is one of the best of the Universal Dracula series—indeed, one of the best of the studio's entire horror cycle—and certainly better than the non-sequels that were soon to follow. Part of its effectiveness arises from Curt Siodmak's evident return to

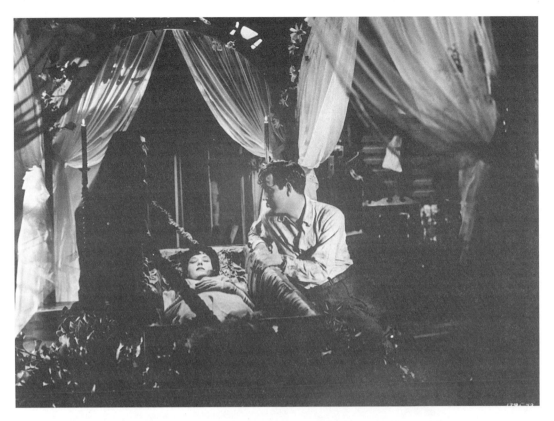

"Were death, or the fear of death, the only thing that stood in the way I would not shrink to die here, now, amidst the friends who love me."—Mina Harker

Louise Albritton as Kay and Robert Paige as Frank in *Son of Dracula* **(1943)**
(courtesy Ronald V. Borst of Hollywood Movie Posters)

Stoker for ideas. It is also visually strong: director Robert Siodmak (Curt's brother) takes full advantage of a southern-Gothic milieu—shadowy, weedy, and moss-hung —that would have done Faulkner proud. The musical score, by H. J. Salter, is enjoyable, loaded with "chilling" organ riffs.

As a sequel to no film prior to it, and a precursor of no film that follows, related to Universal's horror series only by general subject matter, *Son of Dracula* is as much a stand-alone film as, say, *The Return of Dracula* in 1958 (which, despite its title, is also not a sequel).

House of Frankenstein

(1944)

As the title of *House of Frankenstein* indicates, it is one of Universal's Frankenstein series; it is included here because

Dracula puts in a guest appearance. *Frankenstein Meets the Wolf Man* (1943), the sequel to both *The Wolf Man* (1941)

"Euthanasia' is an excellent and a comforting word! I am grateful to whoever invented it."—John Seward

Boris Karloff (left) as Dr. Niemann and John Carradine as Count Dracula in *House of Frankenstein* (1944) (courtesy Ronald V. Borst of Hollywood Movie Posters)

and *The Ghost of Frankenstein* (1942), established the primacy of the Frankenstein series as Universal's dominant horror franchise. With *House of Frankenstein* and its sequel, *House of Dracula*, the series absorbs Universal's version of the further adventures of Dracula as well. *House of Frankenstein* is a total monster rally, also featuring a (but not "the," i.e. not Victor Hugo's) hunchback, and a mad scientist played by Boris Karloff, returning to the series for the first time since his third and final appearance as the monster in *Son of Frankenstein* (1939).

The episodic story (again by Curt Siodmak, adapted to the screen by Edward T. Lowe) starts with Karloff's Dr. Niemann (cf. German *niemand* = "nobody") in prison for having conducted Frankensteinesque transplantation experiments, frowned upon at the time. After Niemann makes clear to us, via diagrams and anatomical sketches on the walls of his cell, that time and incarceration haven't cooled his enthusiasm for his unorthodox work, he and his hunchbacked cellmate, Daniel (J. Carrol Naish) are sprung from prison by a convenient blast of lightning.

The fugitives thumb a ride with the traveling "Chamber of Horrors" of a Professor Lampini (George Zucco), whose collection of oddities includes a display breathlessly advertised as "The Actual Skeleton of Count Dracula!" Seeing an ideal opportunity for traveling under cover, Niemann has Daniel kill Lampini and his only employee, the driver. The pair then revise the show's itinerary, making for the village of Reigelberg, where Niemann has scores to settle.

Lampini's show is apparently one of the few such entertainments whose exhibits are actually what they claim to be. Dracula's perfect, store-bought skeleton is neatly arrayed in a coffin, a stake through the rib cage in the place where his heart once was. This situation takes us back to the end of the 1931 film, when Lugosi's Count was staked; perhaps we are to believe, despite our glimpse of his intact body at the beginning of *Dracula's Daughter*, that his skeletal condition is the result of that stake. Or perhaps his daughter reduced him to bones when she burned his body, which begs the question as to why the wooden stake was not consumed as well. As we have seen, he is reduced to a skeleton at the end of *Son of Dracula*, but that is the result of sunlight, not staking. Perhaps Lampini inserted the stake for its dramatic visual value. Perhaps, and most likely, Count Dracula has been so trivialized by this series that he is no longer a character deemed worthy of continuity.

The Universal monsters were as unkillable in their day as Jason and Freddy in later years (and for the same reason: box office). What makes this series the Frankenstein series is the continuity given the monster: whatever befalls him at the end of one movie, the scripters are careful, in the next installment, to pick up with the monster where we left off, no matter how far-fetched a contrivance it takes to do so. For example, at the finale of *Son of Frankenstein*, the monster is toppled into a subterranean pool of molten sulfur; in *The Ghost of Frankenstein*, he is discovered inside the now cooled and dried sulfur bed, comatose but still alive.

Count Dracula, by contrast, has become a bit player in the series, a stock archetype to be written into (and out of) a plotline as needed, with no reference to anything that has gone before. When Niemann pulls the stake out of the skeleton's chest, Dracula quickly reappears—clothes and all—from thin air (via a succession of *Gray's Anatomy*-type transparencies), in total contradiction of Van Helsing's claim, in *Dracula's Daughter*, that "no vampire can survive the stake." While Van Helsing's claim, as we will see, has little basis in folklore, Universal nonetheless includes the statement in its own mythos as fact, only to turn around and ignore it as soon as playing by a consistent set of internal rules becomes inconvenient.

Count Dracula, this time around, is played by John Carradine, whose gauntness, gray-white hair and mustache, fierce eyes, and rich voice make him a natural for the role, if only it had been better written. (Still, Carradine was to see worse, playing the Count in *Billy the Kid vs. Dracula* in 1966, plus a Mexican potboiler or two.) Here he is a dapper Count, looking relaxed in his evening clothes, full cape, and top hat. His manner is suave and polite, rather like the Count's behavior early in the novel, before he shows Jonathan his true colors. He agrees to a deal with Professor Niemann (who has assumed Lampini's identity): In exchange for safe haven in Lampini's mini-caravan, with Niemann looking after his coffin during the daylight hours, Dracula will bump off an enemy of Niemann's. Stoker's Count, with his own deadly agenda, no doubt would have sneered at the "opportunity" to be anyone's hired killer under any circumstances.

Dracula picks up the target of his "hit"—the buergermeister of Reigelberg, who had a hand in sending Niemann to jail fifteen years earlier—in a hired carriage, along with the buergermeister's grandson and the younger man's American bride, as the party stroll home from an evening at Lampini's show. As in *Son of Dracula*, the Count is again traveling incognito, introducing himself as "Baron Latos, from Transylvania." Whereas the derivation of "Alucard" is only too obvious, the significance (if any) of "Latos" escapes me; the name seems to be an arbitrary invention.

Would Stoker's proud Count have used an alias, or otherwise disguised his identity? In the novel, he does so at least twice. Early on, he goes so far as to sport a fake beard in order to pass himself off as his own (non-existent) driver: Jonathan describes the driver as "a tall man, with a long brown beard and a great black hat, which seemed to hide his face from us." But the "driver's" red eyes, sharp teeth, and "grip of steel" (when he helps Jonathan aboard the carriage) leave us no doubt, in hindsight, as to his true identity. Much later, in London, Dracula buys a house in Piccadilly under the assumed name of "Count de Ville." Obviously, he has learned English well enough to pun in it.

Dracula may be on a hired-hit mission, but he still has priorities of his own. After delivering his passengers to the buergermeister's home (where, accepting their offer of hospitality, he *drinks wine!*), the Count leaps at the first opportunity to put the moves on Rita (Anne Gwynne), the American newlywed. As usual, he takes unfair advantage of her by using hypnosis, employing a dazzling ring as Gloria Holden did in *Dracula's Daughter*. He puts the ring on her finger, and as it magically changes its size to fit her, he creates an implied marriage by telling her that it is "the bond that links us together."

To kill the buergermeister, the Count turns into a bat, a transformation seen by his shadow on the wall (a shadow which he shouldn't have, according to Stoker. But as we've seen since 1922, it's easier, in films of this nature, to use the shadows than to lose them). Since the buergermeister doesn't return as a vampire, it would seem that vampirism isn't contagious by the bite in this film, or indeed in most of the Universal series. Apparently Dracula's creation of "creatures like himself" is a matter of selective recruitment and initiation, as he is doing with Rita. After killing the buergermeister, the Count abducts Rita, making off with her in the carriage. (He does the driving himself, leaving behind the hired driver, last seen accepting the offer of a cup of coffee.)

The police get word of the abduction almost immediately and give chase. When Niemann and Daniel see the police approaching Lampini's tandem-wagon rig, they panic and take off. Soon it occurs to them that the police are pursuing Dracula, and the solution to their problem becomes clear: Niemann reneges on his arrangement with the Count by having Daniel jettison Dracula's coffin from the trailing wagon.

It's just the beginning of a short, bad day for Dracula. The horses come unhitched from the carriage, which runs off the road and rolls over. He struggles to make it to his coffin, but the sun is just rising; and, since we were told earlier, as part of Lampini's pitch, that "one single ray of sunlight falling upon a vampire will destroy him," the Count is again quickly reduced to a skeleton. (The image of his bony, clutching hand is similar to the one seen at the end of *Son of Dracula*.) As Rita is rescued from the overturned carriage, Dracula's ring returns to its former, larger size and falls from her finger, an incident reminiscent of the fading of the scar from Mina's forehead in the novel.

Niemann and Daniel move on to the village of Frankenstein, where they encounter further misadventures concerning the monster, the Wolf Man, and a love triangle involving a Gypsy girl (Elena Verdugo). This part of the story is irrelevant to us here, since Count Dracula has been destroyed ... less than half an hour into the movie.

One of the main values of *House of Frankenstein* (71 minutes; available on video; directed by Erle C. Kenton) is nostalgia. Another is its strong cast: In addition to Karloff, Carradine, and Chaney, and frequently-seen Universal co-stars Naish and Zucco, Lionell Atwill plays his usual martinet Inspector, and the aptly-named Glenn Strange debuts as the monster. H. J. Salter again provides the musical score.

House of Dracula

(1945)

The title character of *House of Dracula* turns up immediately in the form of a large bat, infiltrating the home of a Dr. Edlemann (Onslow Stevens). The Count's ability to do so, despite his not having been invited, indicates the usual measure of disregard shown Stoker's novel by the movies, and by the Universal series particularly. His reappearance with no explanation, after his apparent destruction in *House of Frankenstein*, shows Universal's ongoing cavalier attitude toward the character ... and their growing contempt for their audience.

Once more identifying himself as Baron Latos, the Count (John Carradine again) nonetheless promptly reveals a secret that he has hidden in Dr. Edlemann's cellar: a black coffin on which Edlemann recognizes the "Dracula crest." (This heraldic ornament includes a bat and a huge Gothic "D", unlike the "Alucard" crest, which featured a raven and several crowns. The mantling, and the coronet surmounting all, correctly identify Dracula as nobility.) The Count tells Dr. Edlemann that he has sought him out in hopes of finding a medical cure for vampirism.

Edlemann is not afraid of Dracula, and doesn't even seem surprised at his visit; if anything, he seems mildly annoyed (possibly because the Count has turned up at 5 a.m.), but is sufficiently curious to take on the medical and scientific challenge Dracula has presented him. He agrees to keep the Count's secret, acknowledging the need to stash the coffin in the cellar: he recites the line about how "a single ray of sunlight falling on a vampire would destroy him" matter-of-factly, without conviction, as though quoting a verse from someone else's Scriptures.

Working from a blood sample, Dr. Edlemann shortly has a preliminary finding to report to Dracula. Vampirism, Edlemann believes, is caused by a previously unknown parasite he has discovered in the Count's blood; a lengthy series of treatments will be required to bring the parasite under control. This diagnosis and prognosis are totally foreign to both folklore and Stoker, in which vampirism is seen as spiritual in nature, evil by definition, and often self-incurred, the ultimate in "bad karma."

By contrast, the medical explanation is similar to the conclusion reached years later by Dr. Julia Hoffman (Grayson Hall) in Dan Curtis's *House of Dark Shadows*. Barnabas Collins (Jonathan Frid), the vampire of that film and the TV series from which it arose, was, more so than Stoker's Count, presented as an unwilling victim of his own vampirism. One sees a

"Notwithstanding his brave words, he fears us; he fears time ..."—Van Helsing

**Onslow Stevens (left) as Dr. Edlemann and John Carradine as Count Dracula in
House of Dracula (1945) (courtesy Ronald V. Borst of Hollywood Movie Posters)**

parallel with the ongoing modern debate as to whether violent criminality is a behavior to be punished or a syndrome to be treated; a full discussion of this question, important though it is, is beyond the scope of this book.

Meantime, Dracula has renewed his acquaintance with one of the doctor's assistants, Miliza (Martha O'Driscoll), whom he has recently met at "Schonheim," wherever that may be. We are not told under what circumstances they met, although she is pleasantly surprised to see him again. He, too, feigns surprise, but we know that he is lying: we have seen that the first thing he did on arrival at Edlemann's home (which also houses his laboratory and his staff) was to pause and look in through Miliza's window, seeing her asleep.

So what is he up to this time? Has he really come to Dr. Edlemann for help, only to be tempted and distracted by the coincidental presence of an attractive young woman of his acquaintance? Or has he followed her to her new place of employment in order to finish whatever plan he had for her before? Bearing in mind that Dracula, in the novel, targets Whitby as his port of call simply because he knows Lucy and Mina will be there, we know what Stoker's answer to this question would be.

At this point, *House of Dracula* takes a lengthy hiatus from the questions of Dracula's problems and motives, in order to introduce the rest of the film's monster menagerie. Larry Talbot, shot with a silver bullet at the end of *House of Frankenstein*, somehow turns up alive again, still suffering from lycanthropy and pleading for Edlemann's help. And the Frankenstein monster, last seen sinking in quicksand, is discovered—comatose, but still alive—in a cavern, where he has been deposited (alongside the bones of Dr. Niemann) by a subterranean mud flow. This film's version of the hunchback has already been introduced, in the person of Nina (Jane Adams), Edlemann's other assistant.

When Dracula reappears, it is a finely atmospheric moment: Entering Edlemann's front door amid stark contrasts of light and shadow created by the light of the full moon, he makes his way along the front hall to the sound of Beethoven's "Moonlight Sonata." We soon learn that Miliza is playing the music. She isn't surprised to see the "Baron," since he's there for a scheduled appointment; they chat briefly, remembering Schonheim. Of the sonata, the "Baron" says, "They played it the night we met, at the concert." So, not only is the piece "their song," but this Count is one who enjoys a social life and an appreciation for the arts, contrary to Stoker's Count, but consonant with Lugosi's.

Then, in a scene reminiscent of the similar one in *Dracula's Daughter*, the music starts to change: under the Count's influence, Miliza finds herself playing music she says she's never heard before. In terms almost identical to what Rita said about Dracula's ring in the previous film, she says the music "makes me see strange things—people who are dead, yet they're alive." "Mine is a world without material needs," Dracula replies, without explaining whether this is the case because he's

dead, or because he's rich. Miliza succumbs further to the spell of the music, and of Dracula's staring eyes. Suddenly her crucifix breaks his concentration; he recoils, and Beethoven is restored.

But, as though a post-hypnotic command has been put into effect, Miliza is not yet free of the spell. Later, noticing Miliza's strange, dreamy behavior, Nina follows her, like Mina tailing a sleepwalking Lucy, and is shocked not simply because Miliza meets the "Baron" in another part of Edlemann's palatial house, but because he casts no reflection in a huge mirror before them. When Nina reports her discovery to Edlemann, he reveals the truth to her about the "Baron," whom he regrets having taken on as a patient.

Edlemann interrupts Dracula and Miliza in the garden—just in time, since she has just tossed away her crucifix—and, in a confusing bit of plotting, says he wants to give the Count another transfusion immediately. But the Count, apparently suspecting that the jig is up, turns the tables once the operation starts: casting an hypnotic stupor over both Edlemann and Nina, he reverses the stopcock and transfuses his own blood into the doctor. Having seen, both in Stoker's novel and in the 1931 films (English and Spanish), the sort of unsavory effects that can result from an ingestion of Dracula's blood, we know there's trouble ahead; but having also seen that the Universal series doesn't tend to pay much mind to Stoker, we don't quite know what to expect.

Just before dawn, Dracula makes one last grab for Miliza. In a well-executed scene, he makes his way to her room in the form of a bat, with the reawakened Dr. Edlemann and Nina in pursuit. While Nina wakes Larry Talbot—needlessly, it turns out—Edlemann, a man of both science and faith *a la* Van Helsing, confronts Dracula with a crucifix, forcing him to flee without Miliza. Moments after Dracula re-enters his coffin, Edlemann drags it into the light of the rising sun and opens the lid. Dracula yet again fades to a skeleton—neatly, painlessly, and without waking. In the Universal series, this is the last we'll see of Carradine's Dracula.

But while the character has been eliminated, less than two-thirds of the way into the movie, his influence lingers because of the tainted blood he has placed into Edlemann's veins. With the coming of the following night, in a truly nightmarish, hallucinatory moment, Edlemann watches as his reflection in a mirror grows transparent, then disappears completely. He does not become a vampire, though, as this scene would lead us to expect.

Instead, scripter Edward T. Lowe weaves yet another monster into the mix by making the rest of the plot a Jekyl-and-Hyde story by another name. We can tell when Edlemann is having one of his "Hyde" moments: he grins unpleasantly, he is harshly lit from below, he throws enormous shadows on the walls, and he puts enough juice into the Frankenstein monster to light Manhattan for a month. He also kills, casting suspicion on Larry Talbot, since the moon is full.

Fortunately, and ironically, Dr. Edlemann, in one of his remaining "Jekyll" moments (cf. German *edel* = "noble"; Jekyll is often depicted as altruistic and idealistic in scripts that have little to do with Robert Louis Stevenson's vision of the character, but that's another book), has managed, at long last, to find a medical cure for lycanthropy. Talbot stands in the light of the full moon, staring at it blissfully and without consequence. Larry Talbot is finally freed from the curse that caused him to kill like an animal. He can now kill like a

"Oh, what a strange meeting, and how it all makes my head whirl round! Can it all be possible, or even a part of it?"—Mina Harker

John Carradine as Count Dracula and Martha O'Driscoll as Miliza in *House of Dracula* (1945) (courtesy Ronald V. Borst of Hollywood Movie Posters)

man—with a gun—which he does, when Edlemann/Hyde threatens again. Dracula's curse is finally ended, along with that of the werewolf. For now.

House of Dracula (67 minutes; available on video; directed by Erle C. Kenton) maintains the same few crumbs of Stoker that were found in its immediate predecessor: the Count's powers and limitations, his general appearance, and his eye for the ladies, plus the occasional accident of Stokeresque plotting. By this point in the Universal series, though, ideas were getting scarce; and while the special effects, the technology of sound and music, and the overall *mise-en-scene* of these films had become more sophisticated since the early 1930s, so had the audiences.

Nothing left to do now but poke fun.

Abbott and Costello Meet Frankenstein
(1948)

"And then some pillowhead decided that since it was such a thin line between horror & hilarity, why not erase the line altogether?"
—Robert Bloch

Either the above quote, or the very title of *Abbott and Costello Meet Frankenstein*, could have served as the studio pitch for this, the last of Universal's Frankenstein/Dracula films of the 1940s. Light-years removed from Stoker or Shelley, the film is notable as only the second and final time Bela Lugosi played the role of Dracula on the screen. In the interval between the 1931 film and the 1948 farce, Lugosi had not only played a wide variety of other parts (most memorably Ygor in *Son of Frankenstein* and zombie master Murder Legendre in 1932's *White Zombie*), he had also maintained an identification with the role of Dracula by playing similar cape-clad roles (the phony Count Mora in MGM's *Mark of the Vampire* in 1935; the vampire Janos Tesla in Columbia's *Return of the Vampire* in 1943). So, despite the intervening Universal films, with Lon Chaney acting and John Carradine looking the way Stoker describes the Count, Lugosi, doing neither, steps back into the role of Dracula as though he's never been away.

The plot, such as it is, revolves around a couple of blue-collar mugs who, working at a freight company, take delivery of two crates containing newly-acquired exhibits for a house of horrors: the actual bodies of Count Dracula and Frankenstein's monster. There is no attempt at continuity with any earlier film—even Larry Talbot, cured of his lycanthropy at the end of *House of Dracula*, has suffered a relapse—nor any effort made to explain how the two monsters, both very much "alive," have been packed into crates. Glenn Strange matches Boris Karloff's record by playing the monster a third time; for the first time since *The Bride of Frankenstein* (1935), the monster *speaks*, although his lines are limited mostly to "Yes, Master" (i.e., Dracula).

Again establishing himself under an alias, Dracula assists foxy Dr. Sandra Mornay (Lenore Aubert), on the lam for illegal experiments, in an effort to secure a new brain for the monster. They decide Lou Costello's brain will suit their purposes,

"Oh, friend …, it is a strange world, a sad world, a world full of miseries, and woes, and troubles; and yet when King Laugh come he make them all dance to the tune he play."—Van Helsing

Bela Lugosi as Dracula meets Lou Costello in *Abbott and Costello Meet Frankenstein* **(1948) (courtesy Ronald V. Borst of Hollywood Movie Posters)**

since it seems never to have been used. Dracula has the usual assortment of well-known powers: he can hypnotize, again using a ring as a prop; he transforms into a bat by way of peculiar-looking animation (unlike those of the earlier Universal films, in which the brief transitional form is simply a black blot of shadow, Lugosi's transformations here include such details as the folds of his cape). But director Charles Barton commits one directoral flub: when Dracula puts the bite on "Sandy" in order to enhance her cooperation, his reflection is seen in a background mirror.

Abbott and Costello's comic style plays like the Three Stooges with Larry on a lunch break: Bud is short-tempered and bossy *a la* Moe, and Lou is plump, sweetly stupid, and—importantly, in this film's context—easily frightened, *a la* Curly. Amid the farce, a couple of familiar situations present themselves, borrowed from Stoker and filtered through Universal's earlier outings: Lou pricks his finger as Renfield once did; Sandy puts the moves on him as Mina once approached "John" Harker. In this scene, he looks into her eyes and sees bats on the wing, a startling image worthy of a serious vampire film.

At the climax, the Wolf Man leaps

*"He ... insisted that it was only his sense of humour asserting
itself under very terrible circumstances."*—John Seward

**Bela Lugosi as the Count and Lenore Aubert as Sandra Mornay in *Abbott and Costello
Meet Frankenstein* (1948) (courtesy Ronald V. Borst of Hollywood Movie Posters)**

out a window and grabs Dracula-as-bat by both wings, and the two plummet to their deaths in the pounding surf ("running" water; of which, more later) below Sandy's island castle (a fine set which would have done a straight horror movie proud). While falling to their apparent deaths, particularly in water or otherwise out of sight, ordinarily would be a setup for yet another sequel for these resilient creatures, this time they won't be back. Comedy has finally killed them.

To be sure, there were sequels aplenty: Bud Abbott and Lou Costello went on to "meet" the Invisible Man (1951), Captain Kidd (1952), Jekyll and Hyde (1953), the Mummy (1955), the Keystone Kops (1955), even "the Killer Boris Karloff" (1949). But the stake had been driven through the heart of Universal's Dracula, and the Frankenstein monster and the Wolf Man along with him. After *Abbott and Costello Meet Frankenstein* (83 minutes; available on video), the next Universal Dracula wouldn't be along until Frank Langella's version in 1979.

Sadly, it was all over for Bela Lugosi, too. Succumbing to drug addiction, he was in only a few more films—with titles like *Bela Lugosi Meets a Brooklyn Gorilla* and *Old Mother Riley Meets the Vampire* (both 1952)—before his death in poverty in

1956. Ed Wood's legendarily awful *Plan 9 from Outer Space*, released in 1959, was Lugosi's last film appearance, consisting of footage shot shortly before his death. The "tortured-artist" aspect of Lugosi's later years has helped make him something of a cult figure in the ensuing decades. The "Gothic" band Bauhaus memorialized him in their 1979 song, "Bela Lugosi's Dead" (featured in the soundtrack of 1983's *The Hunger*). And Martin Landau received the Academy Award for Best Supporting Actor for his performance as the aged, ill Lugosi in Tim Burton's 1994 biopic, *Ed Wood*.

To recap: The Universal Dracula series can be split up into discrete sections. The first two films, *Dracula* and *Dracula's Daughter*, are a matched set, with the latter being the further adventures of Van Helsing. The Spanish *Dracula* is an interesting and excellent alternate-universe view of the same story told in the first film. *Son of Dracula* stands alone, with no connection to the films before or after it.

The next two films, *House of Frankenstein* and *House of Dracula* (the John Carradine Draculas), are actually part of the Frankenstein series, and are quite similar to each other in a number of ways, as we have seen. (These are the only two entries in this wildly uneven "series" that were helmed by the same director.) And the final film, *Abbott and Costello Meet Frankenstein*, which features the return of Bela Lugosi as Count Dracula, in addition to being the last of the Frankenstein monster-rally series, is the first of the Abbott and Costello Meet This or That Monster series, which lasted into the years when Gothic horrors in the movies had made way for space aliens and giant radioactive mutants.

"… the glories of the great races," Stoker's Dracula said to Jonathan, "are as a tale that is told." And retold: less than two years after Lugosi's death, Dracula was back on the screen in Hammer's 1958 adaptation. As will be seen in the next section, this Count, too, proved difficult to kill.

III.   The Hammer Dracula Series

By the late 1950s, Hammer Films had been producing low-budget movies in a variety of genres for about a decade, with middling success. With *The Quatermass Xperiment* (1955) and *X The Unknown* (1956), Hammer successfully tapped into the contemporary popularity of science fiction films.

But it was in 1957 that the studio hit its stride, and found its niche, with *The Curse of Frankenstein*. While not as true to Mary Shelley's novel as originally conceived, the film was the first treatment of the Frankenstein story in color, and it was far more visceral and graphic than anything Universal had attempted. It launched the series of Hammer Gothics that would continue for nearly twenty years, revisiting much of the same haunted territory that Universal had mapped: not only Frankenstein's lab, but the tomb of the mummy, the lair of the werewolf, and the crypt of the vampire, including, of course, Count Dracula.

Whereas Universal had followed up its success with *Dracula* by producing *Frankenstein,* Hammer reversed the order, releasing *Horror of Dracula* (British title simply *Dracula*) in 1958. That same year, Universal packaged dozens of its horror classics, near-classics, and also-rans into a bundle called *Shock Theater*, sold to TV outlets nationwide. The rediscovery of the Universal movies by a young mass audience helped fuel a hunger for Hammer's continued treatment of the same horrific themes. Together, the recycled Universals and the proliferating Hammers contributed to the creation of a pop-culture phenomenon of monster-movie fandom that expressed itself in toys, games, comics, costumes, and other merchandise. (This fan culture, in turn, may have partially prefigured the so-called "Gothic" scene of more recent years.)

Though mindful of the British censor's office, Hammer was unfettered by the Production Code Administration, and the studio's product became more graphically blood-soaked and explicitly erotic as time went by. In Hammer's ongoing annals of the further exploits of Dracula, we resume the search for the "gist"—or the ghost—of Bram Stoker's novel.

The Brides of Dracula
(1960)

Hammer Films' series of Dracula sequels begins robustly with *The Brides of Dracula*, also directed, as were many other Hammer efforts, by Terence Fisher. Like Universal's first Dracula sequel, this one lacks the Count himself; as a somber voice-over tells us, the "monarch of all vampires is dead." Again, then, instead of considering how this film depicts the character of the Count, we will examine how well it presents what might be called Stokeresque situations, as well as folkloric elements.

In a promising start, the first word of the introduction is "Transylvania," which, unlike *Horror of Dracula*, places the action into its (in name, at least) familiar setting. The introduction goes on to tell us that Dracula's "cult" has survived him; while Van Helsing referred to vampirism as a "cult" in the previous film, here the theme is expanded on.

The story begins with a familiar-enough setting for a vampire film: a passenger coach, traveling along a muddy road through a misty wood. This could be Harker's journey we're seeing, and is not too dissimilar, insofar as it involves a young foreigner heading into Transylvania on a job assignment: Marianne Danielle (Yvonne Monlaur), a young French woman, is en route to her first job as a teacher's assistant at a finishing school for girls.

Marianne's troubles begin immediately. Tailed by a sinister stowaway, she is stranded in a village inn when the coach takes off without her. The mysterious stranger briefly looks in at the front door, eyeing her with satisfaction, then disappears. Even this fleeting appearance is enough to empty the place of the locals, who seem to anticipate something they'd rather not see or know about.

The innkeeper and his wife behave like Stoker's frightened, helpful peasants: their claim not to have a place for Marianne to stay the night is a transparent excuse to put her back on the road somehow and out of the way of some unknown danger. Before they can figure out what to do with her, the real trouble arrives in the person of Baroness Meinster (Martita Hunt).

Putting two and two together, we realize that the elderly Baroness has been alerted to Marianne's presence in town by the stranger of a few moments earlier. We do not see this character again, but he reminds us (as Sandor did in *Dracula's Daughter*) of the servants who procured girls to be tortured and murdered by Countess Erszebet Bathory. (Hammer made a fictionalized version of the story of Countess Bathory in 1970. *Countess Dracula* starred Ingrid Pitt in the "title role," so to speak, although that wasn't the character's name. The film, directed by Peter Sasdy, is blessed with well-researched period atmosphere: unlike most of Hammer's films, it is set in Hungary c. 1600, not the Victorian era. *Countess Dracula* is not given fuller treatment in this book because, despite its title, it has nothing to do with Bram Stoker's novel or with the rest of the Hammer series.)

Baroness Meinster, the local nobility, is a *grande dame* who conducts herself with an arrogance worthy of Stoker's Count. She invites Marianne to join her for some tokay (a golden Hungarian wine served to

*"He was deathly pale, just like a waxen image, and the red eyes glared with
the horrible vindictive look which I knew too well."*—Mina Harker

**David Peel as the Baron Meinster, the vampire in *The Brides of Dracula*
(1960) (courtesy Ronald V. Borst of Hollywood Movie Posters)**

Jonathan Harker by the Count in the novel); learning of Marianne's plight, she says, in front of the innkeeper and his wife, "You cannot stay in a poor place like this." She welcomes Marianne's company because "breeding" is such "a rare thing in these parts."

Of course, a skull-faced, high-handed Baroness, clad in black and red, issuing an invitation to spend a thunder-filled night in her castle "in the hills" nearby, is a situation flapping with red flags; in the visual and situational language of films of this nature, it is an ominous invitation by definition. Marianne, a nineteenth-century ingenue oblivious to these twentieth-century cues, cheerfully accepts the Baroness's offer of hospitality.

At the castle, Marianne looks out the window of her room into an interior courtyard, where she sees a young man standing on a balcony on a lower floor. She is puzzled by the sight, having been told that the Baroness and her dour only servant, Greta, live alone (the sinister procurer must have been a free-lancer). Greta (Freda Jackson) sheds no light on the mystery, but at dinner, the Baroness reveals that the young man is her son. She says he is "ill," by which she means insane, and that she must keep him locked away in the castle, allowing the locals to believe rumors of his death.

After dinner, Marianne's curiosity naturally gets the better of her, and she seeks the young man out. He is a handsome young Byronic blond, evidently in his mid-twenties (although the actor, David Peel, was 40 at the time). Marianne is horrified to see that he that he is imprisoned by means of a leg-iron and chain. He identifies himself as the Baron Meinster (we never learn his first name!) and claims that his mother has imprisoned him and told all the tenants of the Meinster estate that he is dead, in order to keep his inheritance from him. A pretty face and a

silver tongue work their magic: Marianne seeks out the key and frees him.

Emerging from his rooms in a sharp gray cape, the Baron asks Marianne to wait for him, then takes his mother aside for a *tete-a-tete*. Shortly later, Marianne follows the sound of manic laughter to find Greta, who has lost her mind at the sight of the Baron's empty shackle. Greta shows Marianne the Baroness'-body, slumped in a chair with two punctures in her throat, whereupon Marianne flees into the night.

Greta then launches into a backstory apostrophe directed at the dead Baroness, whereby we learn the extent to which the story thus far has been driven by what today would be called "bad parenting" or "family dysfunction." The young Baron, Greta says, was "always self-willed and cruel … and you encouraged him … and the bad company he kept…. You laughed at their wicked games … till one of them took him, and made him what he is." Afterward the Baroness locked him up, and has spent the intervening years "bringing these young girls to him, keeping him alive with their blood." This is definitely, as noted earlier, a Bathory-type situation. It is unclear exactly when the Baroness and Greta planned to hand Marianne over to the Baron, but in any case, she has unwittingly turned the tables on them, not only escaping herself, but freeing him as well. But, Greta notes, he'll be back. "He's got to come back here before cockcrow," she says, drawing back a curtain to reveal his coffin.

Some reviewers have commented on the "Oedipal" aspect of the Baron's attacking his mother. In fact, it would have been surprising if he *hadn't* attacked her; in doing so, he again follows the traditional vampiric pattern of attacking a family member first. Of course, he has a purely human bone to pick with his mother as well, since she has kept him chained up for no telling how many years. But, as Van

Helsing himself asks in the Balderston/ Deane play, "What bars or chains can hold a creature who can turn into a wolf or a bat?" (Of which, more later.) If the chain is made of steel, the principal ingredient of which is iron, then it is worth noting that iron, according to ancient belief, is the enemy of demons. Certain folklores say a vampire should be killed with a stake or spike, not of one type of wood or another, but of iron.

We return to the road through the woods. Marianne is found unconscious by the roadside and given assistance by a kindly passenger in a passing coach. The Good Samaritan is none other than Professor Van Helsing (Peter Cushing again); like *Dracula's Daughter*, *The Brides of Dracula* turns out to be the further adventures of Van Helsing. Although he doesn't first appear until half an hour into the story, he is a more active participant in the proceedings than was the case in *Dracula's Daughter*. One could hardly expect less from a "doctor of philosophy, a doctor of theology, a professor of metaphysics," as he is described later (although he always introduces himself more modestly with, "I am a doctor"). The professor's erudition is, if anything, understated here; according to Stoker, he was "Abraham Van Helsing, M.D., D.Ph., D.Lit., etc., etc."

Van Helsing takes Marianne back to the same inn where she met the Baroness. The innkeeper's wife is pleasantly surprised to see her, and equally surprised when she hears that the Baron lives as well. Meantime, a wake is going on in an adjoining room for a local girl who died of unknown causes during the night. Van Helsing investigates and notices that a wreath of wild garlic has been placed around her pale neck, on which he finds the two familiar puncture wounds. Baron Meinster has wasted no time.

As Van Helsing sees Marianne to her destination at the girls' academy, just a few kilometers further on, we learn that he is already on the trail of the Meinster clan. He advises Marianne that he has been asked to come to the area to study "a sickness partly physical, partly spiritual"; he then mixes metaphors by referring to the "cult of the undead." Hammer's uncertainty about, or ambiguous double definition of, vampirism as both a physical and spiritual malady is given fuller voice in *Kiss of the Vampire*. The film's Van Helsing surrogate, Professor Zimmer, tells the hero, Harcourt (cf. "Harker"), that vampirism is a "foul disease" visited upon human beings by "the Devil," and that someone who is so afflicted can follow one of two paths: he can either "pray for absolution, or he can persuade himself that his filthy perversion is some kind of new and wonderful experience to be shared by the favored few. Then he tries to persuade others to join his new cult." Whether vampirism is approached from the "disease" or "cult" model, Van Helsing, the good doctor of medicine *and* of faith, is unusually, and perhaps uniquely, qualified to combat it.

Meanwhile, the dead girl has been buried in the churchyard in the absence, and without the blessing, of the village priest, who has summoned Van Helsing to the area. Vampirism, Van Helsing explains to him, is "a survival of one of the ancient pagan religions"—he doesn't say which one—"in their struggle against Christianity." Van Helsing tells the priest the standard elements of vampire lore, which would seem to indicate that we are in some part of Catholic (Saxon) Transylvania that is apparently coming into contact with Eastern Orthodox (Romanian) superstitions for the first time.

If so, then this town is a backwater indeed: Austria took possession of Transylvania in 1699, and by the 1730s and 1740s, a vampire panic gripped parts of central Europe, including territories in or controlled by Austria and Hungary. It was this "importation" of Eastern European superstition that first called the vampire phenomenon to the attention of the West, as far away as France and England: the word "vampyre" entered the English language in 1734. Since the voice-over introduction of *The Brides of Dracula* tells us that the story takes place "as the nineteenth century draws to its close" (the era of Stoker's story, of course), we can assume that the character of the priest exists for the sole purpose of having Van Helsing spell out to him—and to the audience—the rules of the game this time around.

Good thing, too, since some of them have changed since *Horror of Dracula*. Vampirism is still contagious, spread by the vampire's "kiss." "The cult grows," Van Helsing says; "infinitely slowly, but it grows." This is a puzzling statement. A cult would grow "infinitely slowly" if it involved lengthy, difficult, and/or expensive initiations; but a disease, and a disease infectious by the bite, would be expected to spread quickly under the right circumstances, such as ignorance of its existence, causes, prevention, and cure, all of which Van Helsing has been called upon to address here.

A vampire, he continues, must sleep by day in a tomb, "issuing forth as a living form only at night." He must be protected by a living person—a relative or a servant, say—or he could be "tracked down during the day and destroyed." This destruction can be affected "by driving a wooden stake through the heart or by burning." Vampires can be identified by their tendency to be "repelled by holy things and Christian images," and to "cast no reflection." So far so good.

"And some," Van Helsing says, "have the power to transform themselves into bats." Here he totally contradicts the position he took in *Horror of Dracula*. This curious backtrack—possibly a caving-in to

convention on the part of the Hammer team—can fortunately be accounted for insofar as Van Helsing is the type of man who's not afraid to admit when he's wrong, or to absorb new and contrary information. The word "some" is important in this context, too, since, as noted earlier, Dracula himself never acquires the power of transformation throughout the entire Hammer series.

One may wonder how it is that a vampire such as Dracula, much more "senior" to a relative pup like the Baron Meinster, lacks comparable powers. The "external" reason—having to do with decisions affecting the making of these films—is simply that Hammer, for whatever reason, dropped the ball in the first film of the series, then decided afterwards in favor of consistency with regard to the Count. The "internal" reason—having to do with the folklore of vampires as internalized by these films—would have to be that powers such as transformation aren't necessarily badges of rank among vampires, or the acquisition of centuries of "experience"; but that the difference in these powers from one cinematic vampire to the next can be compared to differences in vampire lore from one locality to the next. Transformation into bats is not universal in vampire folklore; neither is, say, contagion; neither is the lack of reflection. One of the protagonists of the later Hammer effort, *Captain Kronos: Vampire Hunter* (in which vampires reflect in mirrors, come out in broad daylight, and aren't affected by stakes), goes so far as to assert that there are "many species" of vampire.

Before abandoning the topic of metamorphosis altogether, a few words about fangs. The prominent canines of cinematic and literary vampires are unknown in vampire folklore. So are the two telltale puncture marks on the throat: since the vampire of folklore tended to prefer heart's blood, it usually attacked the breast of its sleeping victim—again, the "night hag" phenomenon of suffocation. Stoker (who wrote fiction, not folklore) refers to Dracula's "peculiarly sharp white teeth [which] protruded over the lips," ascribing the same feature to Dracula's three wives and later to Lucy. Though Max Schreck sported rat-like front teeth in *Nosferatu*, and Lon Chaney appeared in *London After Midnight* with a whole mouthful of shark-like teeth—in the role of a *fake* vampire, ironically—not one of the vampires in Universal's series of the 1930s and '40s bared a single fang. By contrast, Hammer's Count, and his various saber-toothed minions, brandish their bloody teeth with abandon. In the case of a "social" vampire such as Baron Meinster—who, with his now-you-see-them-now-you-don't fangs, is able to pass for human to the extent that he has Marianne and her employers totally fooled—the question arises: where do his fangs go when they're not in use? Sometimes the suggestion arises that the vampire has retractable fangs, like a viper's. This "naturalistic" "explanation" overlooks the vampire's power of transformation, which is found in both folklore and fiction, and which is adequate to explain "disappearing" fangs.

When Van Helsing suggests staking the buried girl, the priest responds simply, "Sacrilege!" This laconic reply accurately reflects the church's overall attitude towards the practice of disinterring, staking, dismembering, or burning the bodies of suspected vampires. Such activities were against both church and secular law, and could legally only be carried out with proper permission. (In those parts of the Balkans and the Greek Archipelago that came under the rule of the Ottoman Empire, the Turks took just as dim a view of vampire-hunting activities.) In Stoker's novel, the illegality of the entry into Lucy's tomb is addressed: "I realised distinctly," Dr. Seward writes, "the perils of the law which we were incurring in our unhallowed work." While Van Helsing is adamant about the need to deal with the dead village girl, he is at least game to let her exhume herself.

Sunset. As Van Helsing and the priest watch from hiding, Greta acts as a hellish midwife attending the "birth" of the vampire girl. Greta has become this story's Renfield: though lacking that character's tortured ambivalence, her madness, and her long association with a vampire in the household, have given her a spiritual kinship with vampires that enables her to attend this resurrection as though she's an old hand at it. As the girl (Marie Devereux) sits up, Greta removes the garlic wreath as though cutting an umbilical.

The girl's grave is incredibly shallow, her coffin barely covered with a thin layer of soil, which tumbles off as she opens the lid. As Paul Barber notes, shallow burial is frequently associated with vampirism in folklore. A corpse considered "dangerous," as this girl's is because of her mysterious death, is often hastily and inadequately buried, only to be dug up by scavenging carnivores (wolves, etc.) that can smell the ripening flesh. A corpse dragged halfway out of its shallow grave was often mistakenly thought to be trying to rise of its own accord. Of course, in the context of this movie, there is no mistake; the girl *is* a vampire. So her skin-deep interment is either the result of fearful haste, or else her coffin has somehow supernaturally "surfaced."

As the girl rises, the priest mixes in. Greta runs interference, and the girl runs off with Van Helsing in pursuit. He is immediately beset by a huge bat—adequately done, as fake rubber bats on wires go. This bat could be the girl herself, but is more likely the Baron covering her escape.

Van Helsing goes to the Chateau Meinster, where he finds that the Baron has removed his coffin. The Baroness appears, a reluctant vampiress who evidently hasn't yet mastered the trick of "disappearing fangs" mentioned earlier: she hides hers behind a veil in shame. The initial dialogue between her and Van Helsing is like the riddle of an oracle. "Who is it that is not afraid?" she asks. "Only God has no fear," he replies. The Baron bursts onto the scene; he and Van Helsing briefly slug it out (in classic Hammer Gothic-swashbuckler style: throwing candelabra, overturning tables), after which he flees Van Helsing's cross and escapes in the baronial carriage.

The Baroness is consumed with regrets over the way things have turned out: "When this monstrous thing took possession of him"—a telling phrase—"I didn't take him to a priest or a doctor"—again, both the medical *and* spiritual interpretations. Van Helsing assures her that he can release her from "this life which isn't life or death." Later, at dawn, he stakes her; oddly, she is not in a coffin or a tomb, but in a dormer window. Wanting to see her last sunrise, perhaps?

The Baron, meanwhile, has gone to the girls' academy, where he proposes to Marianne. Naturally, she accepts; the Baron not only has a pretty face and a silver tongue, but a title, a chateau, a vast estate, and lots of old money.

"I wish it had been me," her roommate Gina (Andree Melly) mopes. Careful what you wish for: the Baron immediately pulls the old Bela Lugosi trick of flapping in through an open window in the form of a bat. After failing to reflect in a mirror, he hypnotizes Gina and kills her.

Back at the inn, Van Helsing and the priest compare notes. A new guest has arrived: the garrulous, overbearing Dr. Tobler (cf. German *toben* = "bluster" or "clamor"), summoned to determine Gina's cause of death. Van Helsing, joining him, identifies the bite wounds on her throat as "the mark of the vampire, sometimes called the seal of Dracula." Dr. Tobler (Miles Malleson) guffaws at this diagnosis. "I'm a scientist," he says; "I always laugh at these ridiculous legends." Van Helsing's response is totally unlike the long-winded "list of nature's eccentricities and possible impossibilities" that he recites in the novel in an effort, he says, to help Dr. Seward to "believe in things you cannot." He simply counsels Dr. Tobler, "I shouldn't, if I were you."

Van Helsing has Gina's body quarantined to the stable—an unpopular decision with the horses. Marianne takes the opportunity to tell him of her engagement. Van Helsing is aghast, of course, but thinks better of alarming her with the truth about the Baron.

As Marianne and a stable hand take a shift watching over the coffin, one of its locks uncannily falls off. At Marianne's request, the man goes for help, and is promptly killed by the bat. The other lock then drops off, and Gina rises.

Gina's vampiric resurrection is simply horrifying, and is one of Hammer's (and Terence Fisher's) finest moments. As the horses scream in the background, she slowly advances on Marianne, her pale skin and white shroud sharply contrasting with her black hair and her huge, dark, staring, *unblinking* eyes. True to Stoker's description of Lucy's vampiric behavior, Gina has cast off her prim schoolteacher's persona in favor of a slinky, unnerving lasciviousness. Grinning with fangs as prominent as tusks, speaking in a voice not much louder than a whisper, she invites Marianne to embrace her, to kiss her, and to join her and the Baron at the old windmill for a threesome.

Having found the murdered stable hand, Van Helsing arrives just in time, and Gina flees. Van Helsing breaks the news to Marianne about the Baron. She is unwilling to believe him at first, but finally tells him what she learned from Gina.

It all wraps up quickly. At the mill, Van Helsing encounters the vampire women and Greta; the madwoman snatches his cross and plummets to her death. The Baron turns up, throttles Van Helsing into unconsciousness, and puts the bite on him as the two women look on approvingly. He then sets out to fetch Marianne.

Van Helsing comes to, realizes he has been infected, and cauterizes the bite with a red-hot iron (heated in a fire likely built by Greta, who was, prior to her fall, the only living person holed up in the mill ... not to mention the only domestic). He then bathes the raw wound in holy water, a flask of which he has obtained from the priest, whereupon he is miraculously healed. All the while, the two women look on *dis*approvingly, but oddly take no action. If the Baron has given them a hands-off directive similar to the Count's orders to his wives concerning Jonathan in the novel, we don't know of it. More likely, the women fear Van Helsing, his resourcefulness, and his holy water. In any case, the women are disappointingly underutilized from this point on.

The Baron returns with Marianne, who is to be the third member of his rapidly-growing harem. Van Helsing splashes him in the face with the holy water, making the sign of the cross with it

"... her eyes blazed with unholy light, and the face became wreathed with a voluptuous smile."—John Seward

Andree Melly as the resurrected vampire Gina in *The Brides of Dracula* (1960) (courtesy Ronald V. Borst of Hollywood Movie Posters)

*"… abhorred by all; a blot on God's sunshine; an arrow in
the side of Him who died for man."*—Van Helsing

Yvonne Monlaur as Marianne and David Peel as the Baron in *The Brides of Dracula* **(1960)
(courtesy Ronald V. Borst of Hollywood Movie Posters)**

for good measure; it burns him like acid. (The women, seeing what is about to happen, look at the Baron in alarm, but say nothing!) The Baron kicks over the brazier and starts a rapidly-spreading fire.

After helping Marianne escape the burning building, Van Helsing turns the windmill's blades so that they cast a cross-shaped shadow in the full moonlight; this shadow falls across the fleeing Baron, killing him. The two women are not seen again, presumably having been destroyed by the fire. The final image of the burning windmill takes us all the way back to the finale of Universal's 1931 *Frankenstein*— appropriately enough, since *The Brides of*

Dracula was released outside Britain by Universal-International.

The credits of *The Brides of Dracula* list three screenwriters (Jimmy Sangster, Peter Bryan, and Edward Percy)—often a sign of trouble, in the form of extensive rewrites. In fact, the original script had a much different ending, in which Van Helsing used black magic to summon up a legion of hellish bats to destroy the vampires. (For more details, see the synopsis in Leslie Halliwell's book, *The Dead That Walk*; oddly, Mr. Halliwell seems unaware that he's describing the version *not* filmed.) Peter Cushing reportedly balked at such a turn of events, pointing out how inappropriate it would be to depict Van Helsing as a sorcerer; certainly Bram Stoker would have disapproved. This bizarre ending can instead be seen in *Kiss of the Vampire*. That film's Professor Zimmer, while as purposeful in his own way as Van Helsing, also has a dark streak a mile wide: bereaved, brooding, embittered, and alcoholic, he is not above using any means whatsoever to destroy the vampires, again depicted as a cult.

The Brides of Dracula (85 minutes; available on video) is one of the best of Hammer's entire body of work, not just its Dracula series. It is fast-paced, atmospheric, and handsomely produced, and includes several truly (and stylishly) frightening moments. The music, by Malcolm Williamson, features broad, "religious-sounding" organ themes that are appropriate here. The film benefits from several wonderful performances, most memorably those of Freda Jackson, Martita Hunt, and, of course, Peter Cushing.

Dracula, Prince of Darkness

(1965)

Christopher Lee returned to play the title role in *Dracula, Prince of Darkness*, seven years after his success in the original film. There have been differing explanations for the delay—reasons ranging from salary disputes, to a fear of typecasting on Mr. Lee's part, to the inability of Hammer's scripters to figure out a way to revive a character reduced to ashes. This demise—referred to as "final and absolute destruction" in a voice-over—turns out to be neither final nor absolute. Thanks to the box office, Hammer took Stoker's term "Un-Dead" to mean "nine lives," and were to invent, over the next few sequels, an entire catalog of ways to do Dracula in, and a short list of ways to bring him back. (The latter may be summarized: "Just add blood.")

In any case, the first two and a half minutes or so of *Dracula, Prince of Darkness* are a reprise of the finale of *Horror of Dracula*, wherein Van Helsing chases the Count back into the castle and destroys him with sunlight. Whatever sense of continuity the encore of this scene is intended to establish with the earlier film is immediately undercut by the voice-over introduction, which tells us we're witnessing the conclusion of "a reign of hideous terror spanning more than a century." "*A*" century? From a character who, we were told in *Horror of Dracula*, may be five or six centuries old? This glitch is the first of many troubling aspects of this movie.

We cut to a burial procession: led by a priest, several locals are carrying the body of a dead teenage girl as her distraught mother tags along. We know something is terribly wrong here because the procession is heading down a road in the dark woods—long held to be the home of magic and evil spirits—and not to a cemetery or a church. When we see the hammer and stake carried by one of the men, their intentions become obvious.

The staking is broken up by a huge, bearded monk on horseback. Father Sandor (whose name, though spelled the same as that of the valet of Dracula's daughter, is pronounced "Shandor") calls the villagers "barbarians" and their priest an "idiot," threatening to report him to the Bishop for trying to commit "an act of blasphemy." This threat is consistent with the church's attitude toward unauthorized vampire-hunting activities, as noted earlier. Father Sandor (Andrew Keir) comes across as a sort of two-fisted, gun-toting Dom Augustin Calmet: a churchman determined to get to the truth of the matter about vampires while being intolerant of superstition. Examining the girl's body (or, more to the point, her throat), he announces that he himself will bury her in the churchyard, where she belongs.

Father Sandor stops at a country inn, where he meets two English couples traveling in the area, brothers Charles and Alan Kent (Francis Matthews and Charles Tigwell) and their wives Diana and Helen (Suzan Farmer and Barbara Shelley). We learn from their conversation that we are in the Carpathians; once again, Transylvania is never mentioned in this film, although the Carpathian Mountains form one of its borders. Father Sandor sneers at the locals for their practice of hanging "garlic flowers to keep out the bogey man," reminding them that he's been dead for ten years. But when he learns that the English tourists are planning to go to Carlsbad (not the Klausenburg of *Horror of Dracula*, in another rupture in continuity), he warns them to stay away, and especially not to go near the castle.

The following evening, the travelers have trouble with their coachman, who sullenly refuses to go any closer to Carlsbad, since night is coming. This situation compares to various adaptations of Stoker's novel (if not the novel itself) wherein Jonathan is unable to find transport to, or beyond, Borgo Pass. After the driver abandons them, having refused even to look at a nearby castle, the stranded Kents are approached by a carriage with no driver. Despite Helen's fretful misgivings, they decide to take the carriage the rest of the way to Carlsbad. But the horses have other plans: taking the bits in their teeth, they

make straight for the castle. The particulars differ, but again this scene is parallel to Jonathan's uncanny ride to Castle Dracula. The castle, seen from a distance, is a bit of stock footage glimpsed through the trees. On arrival, we see that it is quite a different castle from the one in *Horror of Dracula*; a back-to-back screening of the Hammer series reveals that the Count never inhabits the same castle twice. The one feature these two castles have in common is a narrow mountain stream that flows under a bridge outside the front door. Here, the rivulet is frozen.

The Kents enter the unlocked door and find, again contrary to Stoker, a castle in good shape and well-kept. Moreover, candles are lit, four places are set at table, and their bags have already made it from the carriage to a couple of bedrooms. There is every sign of habitation except inhabitants, and every sign that the Kents are being welcomed. Helen suffers an anxiety attack at the strangeness of it all.

Soon the party are approached by Klove (Philip Latham), the sole servant Stoker tells us the Count does not have, and a man of unknown origin. Klove is stiffly, unsmilingly polite as he advises the party that dinner will soon be served. Over dinner, he explains that his master, Count Dracula, is dead, but that he arranged to have his castle always ready to receive guests, having left no heirs. "My master died without issue … in the accepted sense of the term," Klove explains, a line hinting at armies of bastard children, but more likely referring to the "cult" of vampirism. (The Dracula family's armorial bearing, briefly seen, is innocuous-looking enough; on a quartered field, it includes such "harmless" elements as a tree and a couple of fish, and is flanked by a pair of supporters that appear to be a dragon and an eagle. A medieval helmet crest again identifies the bearer of these arms as nobility. There is an unreadable motto below; the

"... he pulled open his shirt, and with his long sharp nails opened a vein in his breast.
When the blood began to spurt out, he ..."—Mina Harker

Christopher Lee as Dracula and Suzan Farmer as Diana Kent in *Dracula,*
Prince of Darkness **(1965) (courtesy Ronald V. Borst of Hollywood Movie Posters)**

Count's arms in *Horror of Dracula*—even more briefly seen, and completely different —bore the motto *FIDELIS ET MORTEM,* evidently somebody's bungled attempt at "faithful unto death.")Throughout this entire part of the story, there is a great deal of time wasted. The sad fact is that the Kents are tedious company. Charles' lame attempts at humor are annoying, and Helen's constant observations of how "frightening" everything is are unrelieved in their tiresomeness by our realization that her fears are well-founded.

Late that night, Helen and Alan hear footsteps. Alan goes to investigate, and

probably to get away from Helen's fretting for a while. Discovering a passageway hidden behind a tapestry, Alan descends a staircase and finds a sarcophagus, draped in black and red, and bearing the nameplate DRACULA. He is puzzled by the sight of a black suit and red-lined black cape that Klove has neatly laid out nearby. As Alan steps into an adjoining room, Klove fatally back-stabs him.

With a demon-clustered picture of the Temptation of St. Anthony in the background, Klove suspends Alan by the heels over the tomb. He then dumps into it the contents of a small casket he retrieves from nearby: ashes—presumably, and improbably, the same ashes we saw blowing away at the end of the previous film, and again at the beginning of this one. In a controversial scene often cut from commercial TV, Klove slits Alan's throat and lets the blood gush into the ashes below. The results are "instant vampire": Dracula materializes layer by anatomical layer, similar to John Carradine's fade-ins in the later Universal series, except messier and unclothed. As the Count's bare arm emerges from the thick mist that forms in the tomb, only the large ring on his finger —a ring last seen on a rapidly-fading finger of ashes behind this film's title—underscores his identity.

Klove rouses Helen, cruelly letting her find Alan's body herself. Dracula immediately attacks her. It is nearly fifty minutes into the movie before he makes his first appearance, but Hammer knows how its bread is buttered: Christopher Lee is top-billed this time around.

The next morning, Charles and Diana, unable to find Alan and Helen, flee the castle. Leaving Diana in an abandoned hut, Charles goes back to look for the others. Later, Klove pulls up at the hut in a one-horse trap and tells Diana that her husband wants her to get in and ride back to the castle. Idiotically, she does.

Night has fallen by this time. Charles has found Alan's mutilated body, and

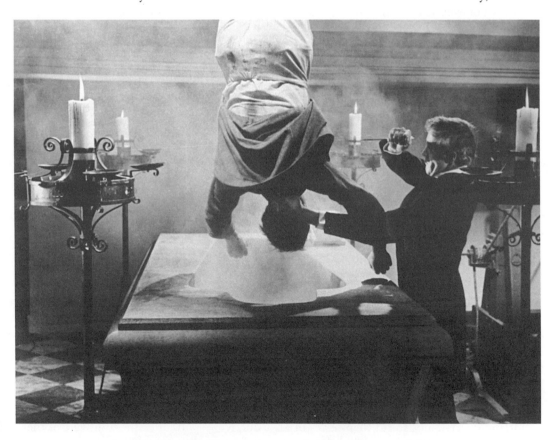

"... they cannot die, but must go on age after age adding new victims and multiplying the evils of the world."—Van Helsing

The servant Klove (Philip Latham) murders Alan Kent (Charles Tigwell) in
***Dracula, Prince of Darkness* (1965) (courtesy Ronald V. Borst of Hollywood Movie Posters)**

Count Dracula is afoot. Helen, now a vampire, is enjoying herself for the first time, wearing a couple of things she's probably never worn before: a diaphanous nightie and a smile. As she tries to seduce Diana, the Count bursts into the room and intervenes, since he wants Diana for himself. Charles then shows up, and Helen turns her attention to him with the Stokeresque invitation: "Dear Charles! Let me kiss you!"

A broader parallel with Stoker's storyline can be seen in what could be referred to as the Lucy-and-Mina syndrome: having vampirized one woman, analogous to Lucy in the novel, Dracula then goes after a second, analogous to Mina (this time not even having the courtesy to wait until the first woman has been staked). *Dracula, Prince of Darkness* is not the last time we will see this plot structure at work.

Charles and Dracula fight; the Count breaks in two a sword Charles grabs off the wall. Diana accidentally finds that the cross around her neck will keep Helen away. (Look for an error in film editing: Diana is glimpsed holding her cross up at Helen, and then, in the next shot, she reaches down and lifts up the cross for what is supposed to be the first time.) Charles makes a cross out of the two parts of the sword, a move reminiscent of Van Helsing's improvised cross at the end of *Horror of Dracula.*

As it happens, such a move is unnecessary: had Charles known a bit of history, he'd have known that the Crusaders and other Christian soldiers used the cruciform hilts of their swords as crosses. In fact, in Pitton de Tournefort's account of the efforts of the inhabitants of the Greek island of Mykonos to rid themselves of a revenant in their midst, we find that they thrust "I don't know how many naked swords into the grave of the corpse." Then an Albanian happens by with his own

local version of the folklore: "Can you not see, you poor blind people, he said, that the guard of these swords, forming a cross with the handle, prevents the devil from leaving this corpse!" In any case, Charles's improvisation works, even though the hilt itself should have sufficed. (In Hammer's *Vampire Circus*, one of the heroes uses a cruciform dagger, and even a crossbow, in such a way!)

Charles and Diana flee in the little carriage, its one horse apparently not programmed with the castle-homing instinct. But they crack up in a road accident and are found shortly by Father Sandor, who makes an embarrassingly bad situation worse by saying, in effect, "I told you so."

Father Sandor takes them into his monastery, where he and Charles decide to send Diana home and destroy Dracula themselves. He tells Charles the ways a vampire can be done in: the stake; sunlight; "running water will drown him." While seldom seen in movies, this is a folklorically valid way to kill a vampire: "Running water in particular," as Montague Summers quotes Petrus Salius in *The Werewolf,* "is known to dissolve spells and evil charms." (Which is why, incidentally, the Wicked Witch of the West in *The Wizard of Oz* melts when hit with a pailful of hurled, i.e. "running," water.) Barber adds, in *Vampires, Burial, and Death,* a reference to the ancient belief that "spirits [of the dead] cannot cross water." Stoker has Van Helsing tell us that the Count "can only pass running water at the slack or the flood of the tide." Screenwriter John Sansom (a.k.a. Jimmy Sangster) builds on such clues as these to posit the possibility of watery doom for a vampire.

Meanwhile, unknown to Father Sandor, Klove pulls up at the front gate of the monastery in a covered wagon containing two black coffins. He is not admitted, but is told he is welcome to stay outside for the night.

Father Sandor tells Charles they will all be safe at the monastery since "a vampire cannot cross a threshold unless he's invited by someone already inside." And right on cue, Renfield appears, with his function per Stoker—as the one who lets the Count in—presented correctly on-screen for the first time ever. Gratuitously renamed Ludwig (we're still, after all, somewhere in the Carpathians), he is a ward of the monks in the monastery. Ludwig is referred to as a "brilliant craftsman"; we see him unconvincingly putting the finishing touches on an ornate book cover he's crafted. The late Thorley Walters, a Hammer veteran, plays Ludwig as a demented Captain Kangaroo. His condition is once again "explained" in terms of his having been found, "unhinged" and amnesiac, near Castle Dracula. A Renfield by any other name still eats flies (here presented as a mere eccentricity, not as a symptom of incipient vampirism), stares out the window as he senses Dracula's approach, escapes from his cell (bending the bars himself with his craftsman's tools; he's probably the only mental patient in film history with a hammer and chisel in his cell), and abets Dracula's attempts to get to Diana.

Her own denseness helps. Helen appears outside Diana's window, begging Diana to let her in. Idiotically, she does, and Helen promptly bites her on the wrist. Dracula elbows his way past Helen, but both vampires do a quick fade when Diana's screams bring help. Father Sandor cauterizes the bite with a lamp.

Helen is captured and staked, kicking and squirming, on a tabletop. Again, as per Stoker, the peace of true death is seen on her face afterwards. For impenetrable reasons, this grisly operation is carried out in Ludwig's cell. Ludwig, meanwhile, having coldcocked the monk who was given charge of him, goes to Diana's room and says Father Sandor wishes to see her. Idi-

otically, she goes! This is, by now, the sort of exasperating behavior we've come to expect of her; but incredibly, even the monk watching over her, who knows how irregular it is for Ludwig to be wandering around unattended, falls for his line and doesn't tag along. This is what's referred to by the technical screenwriting term: "bad writing."

Ludwig, of course, leads Diana to Dracula, who hypnotizes her and makes her remove her cross. Then, in another development from the novel, the Count prompts her to drink his blood from a cut on his chest, as per Stoker, not on his arm, as was the case in both of Universal's 1931 versions. It is the first time this scene is filmed as written. Pity it makes no sense: as noted earlier, the Count has no dialogue at all in this film, so the expository gloating he does in the novel is absent. An audience member who has not read the book would have no idea what's going on. You can almost hear the bewildered plaints of: "But … I thought … *he'd* drink … *her* blood."

Why is it, incidentally, that Dracula has no lines in this film? Why is this "bogey man" not only stalking and staring, but silent? Different sources have it different ways. Some say that the part was written that way, as a follow-through on the Count's silence through most of *Horror of Dracula*. But Bruce Lanier Wright, in his book *Nightwalkers*, quotes Christopher Lee himself as saying that the part had a "great deal of dialogue originally," but that he refused to speak it because it was so badly written. The world may never know.

Interrupted, Dracula abducts Diana and flees, each of them occupying a coffin in the back of the wagon as Klove drives. Once again the story resolves itself into a pursuit of Count Dracula back to his castle *a la* the novel. En route, Charles shoots Klove dead, and the out-of-control wagon

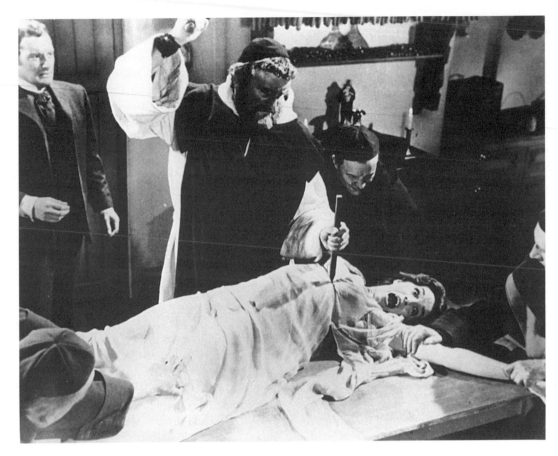

"[He] placed the point over the heart, and as I looked I could see its dint in the white flesh. Then he struck with all his might."—John Seward

The vampire Helen (Barbara Shelley) is staked by Father Sandor (Andrew Keir) while Charles Kent (Francis Matthews) looks on in *Dracula, Prince of Darkness* (1965) (courtesy Ronald V. Borst of Hollywood Movie Posters)

crash-lands at Dracula's front door. The Count's coffin tumbles out and slides onto the ice of the frozen river. Charles advances on it with a hammer and stake, despite Father Sandor's warnings to get away because—again as per the novel—they have arrived at the castle right at sunset.

Dracula bursts out of the box and grapples with Charles. Father Sandor uses his rifle to blast holes in the ice, which cracks open beneath their feet. Charles escapes, but the Count slides off a wobbling floe and goes under the running water to his death. While not as horrifying a finale as that of *Horror of Dracula*, Terence

Fisher does what he can with it, in visual and narrative terms: the Count's hand futilely clawing at the edge of the frozen slab; the contrast of the black and red of his cape sliding over the stark white of the ice; finally, Dracula's ghostly, submerged face behind the closing credits.

Dracula, Prince of Darkness (90 minutes; available on video in a wide-screen format complete with trailers, interviews with the cast, etc.) has its defenders—and hordes of detractors. (For a particularly insightful and none-too-favorable view, see S. S. Prawer's book *Caligari's Children*, in the chapter titled "An Image and its Context.") This is a handsome-looking film, with atmospheric sets and a moody use of rich color. James Bernard's music, mostly recycled from the first film, adds to what sense of continuity there is. But the colorless English protagonists, the interminable wait before Dracula's reappearance, and too much bad writing add up to near-fatal flaws. The best that can be said about the film is that it has its moments, one of them being Klove's "ritual sacrifice" of Alan and the attendant splattery resurrection of Dracula, another the powerful scene of the staking of Helen. Barbara Shelley's before-and-after performance as Helen stands out from the bland remainder of the Kent clan. Andrew Keir's Father Sandor is a bellowing delight; with his knowledge of both folklore and firearms, he's the sort of man you'd want on your side whether facing foes mortal or otherwise. Thorley Walters, bless him, is always fun to watch. And Christopher Lee struggles gamely with the constraints of a role that will not become less constrictive with the rest of the Hammer series.

Dracula Has Risen from the Grave

(1968)

(As we consider Hammer's next Dracula opus, *Dracula Has Risen from the Grave*, I find I must beg the reader's indulgence. I have a bit of a soft spot for this film, the first Dracula movie I ever paid cash money to see. It's not a great movie, and in some ways not even a very good one, but it made quite an impression on me at the time, i.e., summer 1969, to the extent that it helped start me on the path to becoming the sort of adult who'd write a book like this one. It remains a guilty pleasure to this day.)

Dracula Has Risen from the Grave is, broadly speaking, yet another rehash of the basics of Stoker's plot: the ancient vampire Count stirs abroad from his ancestral homeland, visits violent misfortune on a group of sympathetic protagonists, and is pursued in the end back to his castle and his destruction. Harker's journey is here undertaken by a monsignor (Rupert Davies), who wishes to see how things are going in the parish of an unnamed mountain village whose church was once desecrated by Dracula. We see this act of sacrilege in an introductory flashback: the village priest (Ewan Hooper, who looks like Larry the Stooge) discovers the body of a young woman stuffed inside the church bell. We are then told that it has been a year since Dracula's (most recent) death.

After he learns that the villagers, and the priest, have not recovered from the trauma, the monsignor decides to put an end to Dracula's lingering evil presence once and for all. Taking a large golden cross from the church, and with the priest as his guide, he ascends to Dracula's castle and does a full bell-book-and-candle exorcism of the place, leaving the cross on the front door.

The unnerved priest panics and runs away. He trips and falls, gashing his head and cracking the ice on a frozen mountain stream. Under the ice, of course, lies the inert form of Dracula (Christopher Lee); and, of course, some of the priest's spilled blood trickles straight into Dracula's mouth, reviving him. This very long shot can at least be rationalized as being so far beyond the range of mere coincidence that it must be a Satanic miracle. The thunderstorm

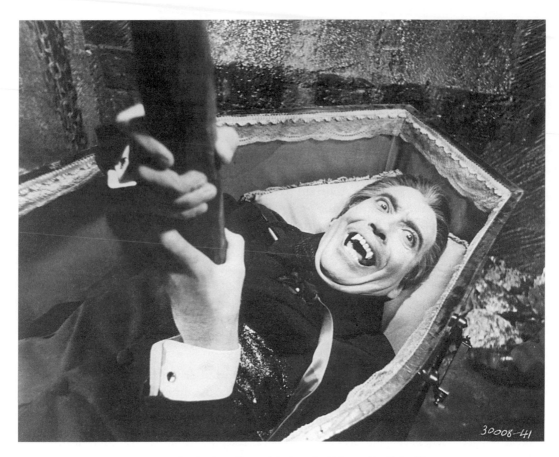

*"The Thing in the coffin writhed; and a hideous, blood-curdling
screech came from the red lips."*—John Seward

**Christopher Lee as Dracula in *Dracula Has Risen from the Grave* (1968)
(courtesy Ronald V. Borst of Hollywood Movie Posters)**

that erupts during the exorcism gives us a hint: medieval superstition, which had a way of lingering into modern times, held that Satan, as "prince of the air," caused thunderstorms. (Compare also this scene with the one in Mario Bava's brilliantly moody *Black Sunday* of 1960 wherein a witch/vampire is revived: Two travelers happen to enter her tomb. A bat which should be hibernating happens to attack them. It happens to light on a stone cross atop the sarcophagus. One of the men happens to strike at the bat with a cane, missing the bat but breaking the cross. Its fragments happen to shatter a glass window in the coffin, over the witch's face,

through which she could "see" the cross and be immobilized by it. One of the men, out of curiosity, happens to reach in through the broken window and remove the spiked mask with which the dead miscreant had been executed. He happens to cut himself on the broken glass. And so on.)

But even if the problematic nature of Dracula's revival can be "explained" in terms of possible supernatural manipulation, the scene still underscores another problem: the film's title, in addition to being overlong, is inaccurate as well. Since Dracula isn't *in* a grave, how can he rise from one? Christopher Lee also found the title unfortunate, saying he thought it should have been *Dracula Arisen*; in France, it was changed to *Dracula et les Femmes* (*Dracula and the Women*), which, as we shall see, is also appropriate.

Exactly how Dracula came to be lying in a frozen mountain stream in the first place is known to anyone who has seen *Dracula, Prince of Darkness*. Anyone who hasn't is left to grope at a hint—the monsignor's reference to Dracula's having been "sent to his doom in the waters of your mountains"—since this film doesn't bring the audience up to speed by recapping the last few minutes of the previous entry, as had been done before. Instead, after the opening credits roll (against a nightmarish "landscape" of shifting, biological-looking forms in garish psychedelic red and blue; this was, after all, the late '60s), we see the bloody incident with the church bell. (Summer 1969: Even though I hadn't seen *Dracula, Prince of Darkness*, I didn't wonder for a minute how Dracula wound up under the ice. Thanks to screenings of the old Universal horrors on a local TV station, I'd seen how the Frankenstein monster—joined on one occasion by the Wolf Man—would turn up from time to time in a mud flow, or in a sulfur bed, or in an ice cave, where he was also discovered in Hammer's own *The Evil of Frankenstein* in 1964. So, before knowing the terminology, I'd come to think of these monsters as elemental spirits of earth or of water, who could vanish into the elements for awhile as a sort of hiding place until their next adventure.)

Dracula, upon reviving, immediately brings the luckless priest under his power, appearing to him first by his reflection in the water! This part of the mythos, though featured in *The Brides of Dracula*, is never strongly enforced in the Hammer series. (The priest, it seems, must have been unconscious for hours, since Dracula's clothes are dry by the time the two of them "meet.")

The monsignor returns to his sister-in-law's home in the nearby town of Kleinenberg (cf. Father Sandor's hometown of Kleinberg). Dracula, meanwhile, embarks on an errand of vengeance: discovering the cross on the door of his castle, he also finds his tongue and demands of the priest, "Who has done this *thing?*" The priest tells him, and the two of them set out for Kleinenberg. Paralleling Stoker, this part of the plot has "Jonathan" temporarily out of harm's way and Dracula en route to "England." Paralleling *Horror of Dracula*, we see that once again it is a vampire hunter's efforts, ironically, that have drawn Dracula out—and even, in this case, revived him.

Locked out of his castle, unable to get to his own coffin, Dracula has the priest rob a grave to obtain one. (Where they get the hearse in which they travel is anybody's guess. It may be stolen as well.) The priest dumps out the rotting body of the young woman in the coffin as the Count looks on approvingly, emblematic of the way Dracula uses and disposes of women. We later get a look at the plaque on the coffin. The name is hard to make out, but the dates are 1885-1905. This woman was very young, obviously; one wonders whether she died of illness, or by accident, or by violence, or by her own hand. Any one of these could have sufficed to make her a vampire herself, but as it happens, the stench of sorrow that hangs over her early death has been enough to attract the vampire's attention. Also, while the just-post-Stoker date is generally correct, it is not in agreement with the particulars of the Hammer series up to this point. We were told that *Horror of Dracula* took place in 1885; that *Dracula, Prince of Darkness* was ten years later; and that *Dracula Has Risen from the Grave* is a year after that. The "present" year should therefore be 1896.

In Kleinenberg, the "Jonathan baton"

is passed to Paul (Barry Andrews), a young student obviously destined to be this story's hero. His "Mina" is Maria (Veronica Carlson), the monsignor's niece. That Paul is an atheist not only sets the stage for friction with Maria's uncle, it also balances the irony that Dracula's flunky is a priest. Paul enjoys a pleasant working relationship with his employer, innkeeper Max (Hammer veteran Michael Ripper, in an endearing role), that recalls Jonathan's friendly terms with Mr. Hawkins in the novel. But if anything, Max's inn is amusingly analogous to Dr. Seward's asylum, partly because of the rowdy parties that go on there, and partly because the place provides lodging for some of the story's principals.

The unfortunate Lucy figure—the first woman attacked by the Count—is Zena (Barbara Ewing), a barmaid at the tavern. One look at her porcelain neck and shoulders and we know she's doomed; soon enough, she is attacked while walking home after work one night, the priest having cased the inn and spied her there. Next day, Zena and the priest form a "composite Renfield": against Max's wishes, she tells the priest that, yes, the inn has a room to rent; and the priest, more than just inviting the Count in, actively smuggles him in. Their respective lodgings are telling: the priest takes a tiny room "right at the top of the house," as Max describes it, symbolic of his tortured attempts, *a la* Renfield, to follow a "higher" path. Dracula, of course, is stashed in a dank, hidden basement. Stoker probably would have approved; so, too, would Freud.

For his part, after making his inevitable bad impression on Maria's uncle, Paul, having been told that the priest is in town on "church business" vaguely involving the monsignor, pulls the Jonathan's-big-mouth move of telling the priest that, while he and the monsignor "have met ... I know his niece better." It is the first the

priest learns that the monsignor *has* a niece, and the news grants Dracula a perfect avenue for his vengeance.

Zena makes an aborted attempt to lure Maria into the basement. After Maria's escape, Dracula blames Zena for failing him. The priest finds Zena's body alongside Dracula's coffin a while later, her eyes staring, her gaping mouth baring fangs. "Destroy her," Dracula laconically commands. This Count prefers to be the only vampire in town, apparently, which makes one wonder how he came to be the "fountainhead" of the "cult" of vampirism, as he was described in *Dracula, Prince of Darkness*. While it is unlike Stoker's Dracula to show such a cavalier disregard for one of his own, it is consistent with the nature of the vampire of folklore. As Paul Barber notes, "I have seen nothing [in folklore] to suggest that, as in the movies, the vampire recruits a small army of vampire-minions intended to take over the world. The folkloric vampire is very much a loner; he creates more like himself without seeking to govern them or even, apparently, deriving satisfaction from their depredations."

In any case, Zena's vampiric career is over before it starts. Since she was a seductive flirt (and a redhead, no less) prior to her death, much unlike Stoker's Lucy (but all too much like Sadie Frost's in *Bram Stoker's Dracula*), the screenwriter, John Elder (a.k.a. Anthony Hinds), must not have been able to think of a way to show that she had been "corrupted" by Dracula. It's up to the miserable priest to dispose of her body, which he does in the time-honored way of burning it, stashing her into the inn's cellar furnace. Along with the grave-robbing episode, it is the second time the priest has desecrated the dead, and we can see that this dark night of his soul is deep, dark, and long.

Dracula takes up making house calls, becoming Maria's window-haunting demon lover. After he learns that Maria has been victimized by a vampire, the monsignor dons Van Helsing's mantle: plunging into a pile of books to find out what to do in these situations, he breaks up the Count's next visit with a crucifix. A rooftop chase ensues, which ends with the priest clobbering the monsignor, who recognizes him, with a roofing tile.

Mortally injured, the monsignor now passes Van Helsing's task of protecting Maria to Paul. He passes along the all-important book of lore: "You will find it all here." Unfortunately, the book this time around is in Latin. To help him read it, Paul enlists the aid of the priest, at the sight of whom the monsignor succumbs.

When the priest tries to sabotage Paul's efforts to protect Maria, his revulsion at being under Dracula's control reaches its crisis, and Paul forces him to reveal the Count's hiding place. Paul arrives just before sunset, with a stake the size of a baseball bat, a two-handed lance similar to the one Stoker describes as having been used on Lucy: "... a round wooden stake, some two and a half or three inches thick and about three feet long." While Dracula is staked from time to time in adaptations of the novel, it's interesting to note how seldom it happens to him in the Hammer series. Here, in his third appearance in a Hammer film, he is finally staked—and it doesn't work! It only provokes a furious response, as Dracula pulls out the stake and throws it at Paul.

This scene has generated considerable controversy and derision over the years. David Pirie, in *The Vampire Cinema*, cavils at what he sees as "a mockery of the original rules," and adds that "Christopher Lee ... protested against the sequence at the time." David J. Hogan, in *Dark Romance*, chides the director, "C'mon, Freddie [Francis], ... vampires can't do that."

In fact, they can. Montague Summers, in *The Vampire, His Kith and Kin*, writes that a "*strigon* (or Istrian vampire) who was transfixed with a sharp thorn cudgel near Laibach in 1672, pulled it out of his body and flung it back contemptuously." This account could just as easily be a description of the scene in question, and it indicates that Anthony Hinds must have done his homework. In *The Vampire in Europe*, Summers continues with an account of a staked vampire who "jeered horribly at those who had thought to have put an end to this plague, and mockingly thanked them for having given him a fine stick with which to drive away the dogs." It could be argued that the "original rules" in these matters are to be found in folklore, not fiction or film. Bottom line: despite whatever you may have seen and heard in the movies, staking a vampire doesn't always work.

Pirie claims that the movie's stake fails "apparently because the staking was not carried out with a proper religious conviction." It fails, we are plainly told, because of the inability of the atheist hero (not to mention the deranged priest) to pray over the proceedings. As Stoker makes clear, staking a vampire isn't merely a type of pest control; it is a form of exorcism and is therefore appropriately, and even necessarily, accompanied by prayer. In the novel, Van Helsing tells Arthur, who is about to stake Lucy, "Then when we begin our prayer for the dead—I shall read [it], I have here the book ...—strike in God's name," something an atheist could hardly do. And in *Dracula, Prince of Darkness*, Father Sandor touchingly performs the last rites for Helen after he stakes her. So in the controversial scene of the failed stake, Hammer is being true to its own "rules," to Stoker's, *and* to those of folklore. Three out of three ain't bad.

His cover blown, fresh out of friends, Dracula abducts Maria and heads for the hills. Once again we find ourselves witness to a frantic pursuit of the Count back to his castle. Paul stops in at a tavern in the village and pleads for help, only to find that Stoker's helpful locals have long since given way to frightened xenophobes: "We're sick of people interfering with our lives," the landlord says, "and if we leave things alone, maybe he'll leave *us* alone!"

At the castle, Dracula has the mesmerized Maria throw the cross off a cliff which has somehow replaced the river that used to be at his front gate. The cross bounces ringingly off several rocky ledges and comes to rest upright, planting itself in a patch of soil. (Summer 1969: a *frisson* runs through the adolescent crowd at the sight of the upright cross, its topmost point bearing the same ornate, wickedly pointed trefoil that adorns the ends of the transept. To this day I remember hearing somebody whisper to a friend: "He's gonna fall on it." Bingo.)

Paul arrives in time to interrupt (anticlimactically) the Count's opening of the castle door; after a brief fight, they both go over the balustrade and off the cliff. Paul grabs hold of a bush and is able to climb back up. The Count is nowhere near as fortunate, of course. (The adolescent audience erupts with cheers and whistles, just as we did for the staking. Not until some time later did I wonder why Dracula didn't just turn into a bat and fly away

"Thus are we ministers of God's own wish: that the world, and men for whom His Son die, will not be given over to monsters…"—Van Helsing

Christopher Lee as Dracula in *Dracula Has Risen from the Grave* (1968) (courtesy Ronald V. Borst of Hollywood Movie Posters)

as he fell. Not until years later did I become aware of Hammer's internal rules for the character.) Blood and irony: the old soldier of the cross done in by one; the Anti-Christ dying on the cross for his own sins; the Impaler impaled.

The cross works where the stake failed, partly, no doubt, because it *is* a cross, and partly because the priest (who appears from out of nowhere!) recites the pater-noster, as he was unable to do earlier. Hammer therefore follows through on the notion that prayer is necessary for this sort of exorcism to work. As Dracula writhes in agony, unable to dislodge the cross from between his shoulder blades, his dying face, weeping blood, fills the screen just as the priest intones, "... *sed libera nos a malo*" ("but deliver us from the evil one"). This juxtaposition of phrase and image forms an interesting and subtle "bookend" with the scene of the bell at the beginning of the film, wherein we see a close-up of the livid punctures in the dead girl's neck as the priest, again off-screen, prays, "Dear God!... When shall we be free of his evil?"

The priest's prayer restores his faith and redeems him. Meanwhile, Paul, watching Dracula dissolve into a puddle of blood and a rumpled cloak, crosses himself. That old-time religion has triumphed, and in more ways than one.

Dracula Has Risen from the Grave (92 minutes; available on video) works on the level of a juvenile fever dream; perhaps those pulsating opening credits are meant to simulate delirium. It has the usual Hammer strengths: atmosphere that can be cut with a knife, aided by excellent set design, James Bernard's moody score, and the occasional arresting image—the monsignor struggling along a mountain ridge, the gleaming cross strapped to his back, with Dracula's gloomy pile of a castle looming in the distance, lingers in mind. A stark palette of color also helps: when Maria looks up from the cellar floor and

gets her first look at Dracula stepping out of the shadows, he appears in silhouette between a slab of black and another of red and yellow. It's as though he's taken up residence in one of Mark Rothko's harsher canvases.

And there are some good performances. Barbara Ewing's Zena is spunky enough, though Veronica Carlson, as Maria, is given little to do other than look good and be in peril. The standout performance is by Rupert Davies as the monsignor. A big, no-nonsense bulldog of a man, the monsignor is no ivory-tower cleric, but one who has spent his life in the trenches. "I am not unacquainted with evil," he tells the priest early on, and we believe him; hardly a young man, he takes it upon himself to scale the mountain and face the evil of Dracula's castle personally—and alone, after the priest deserts him. Though he can be gruff, his face, his words, and his gestures frequently soften with kindness and patience. His niece and sister-in-law dote on him, and it's easy to see why. He can see into people's hearts: while he initially reacts with doctrinaire indignation to the news that his niece is dating an atheist, he knows who to turn to when he can no longer protect Maria himself. "Because he loves her," he wisely observes, "he will help her." Perfect love casteth out fear.

And, of course, there is Christopher Lee's performance as the Count. As usual, he looks terrific, his presence dominates, and he brings to the role more than is found in the script.

The main liability of *Dracula Has Risen from the Grave* is its continuation of Hammer's reduction of Dracula to little more than a stalker and sexual predator. Granted, stalkers and sex fiends are frightening enough, but the horror of the Count, as envisioned by Stoker, is that he is, and was, so much more than that. As Van Helsing says in the novel, the Count "was in life a most wonderful man. Soldier, statesman, and alchemist.... He had a mighty brain, a learning beyond compare, and a heart that knew no fear ... and there was no branch of knowledge of his time that he did not essay." That such a man—da Vinci, Lionheart, and Machiavelli rolled into one—has come to be an immortal force of evil is an incalculable loss, and an inestimable threat.

Hammer's Count hints at no such dimensions—at least, not since the time he tried to hire a librarian. All we know about him is that he thirsts for blood and often hungers for revenge. Fair enough; so does Stoker's Count. But while Stoker's character gloats, "My revenge is just begun! I spread it over centuries, and time is on my side," Hammer's Count, in this most recent episode, goes off half-cocked in pursuit of the monsignor, not bothering to have the priest, who is already in his power, toss away the offending cross so he can re-enter his castle and plot vengeance at his leisure. The arrogant patience of Stoker's Count is thus replaced with an irritable haste and planless anger that, in his destruction of Zena's body, even short-circuit one of vampirism's most horrifying aspects, which is its contagion.

Hammer's Dracula, finally, while having an implacably hostile personality, is not really a person, but a mere menacing image, a character who wouldn't exist apart from the props: the cape, the fangs, the attitude. No wonder his dialogue in *Dracula, Prince of Darkness* was either nonexistent, or so bad as to be unutterable: what could such a character have to say that would be of interest?

We are left, as the Hammer series unfolds (or unravels), with a catalog of missed opportunities, and the frustrating waste of a capable actor. Not surprisingly, it was soon after this time that Mr. Lee jumped at the chance to star in *El Conde Dracula*. As we have seen, that adaptation has its problems, but at least its heart is in the right place.

Taste the Blood of Dracula

(1970)

Taste the Blood of Dracula begins yet again with a coach ride in a dark wood. One of the passengers is Weller, an import-export shopkeeper (the late Roy Kinnear) on his way back to London. He is thrown off the coach by one of the other passengers, a violent half-wit who, in a fit of low frustration tolerance, doesn't want to haggle over a bauble Weller displays.

Weller awakens, hours later, under the same painted, full-moonlit sky that looked down on the end of *Dracula Has Risen from the Grave*. As he pulls himself together and starts to make his way along the road, he suddenly hears several screams of inhuman agony. He panics, runs, falls down a short, rocky slope—and finds himself witness to Dracula's final moments, as grafted in from the finale of the previous entry. As an attempt at series continuity, this segue leaves a great deal to be desired.

For one thing, at the end of the previous film, after a single scream upon being impaled, Dracula afterward lets out only a few croaks and gurgles, a protracted death rattle. Also, we have seen in *Dracula Has Risen from the Grave* that the (latest) castle, in front of which Dracula perishes, is accessible only by foot, and after an arduous hike; here, Weller arrives at the scene after a fairly short flight from a nearby road. But this problem is made moot by a bigger one: the castle itself is gone (as are Paul, Maria, and the priest), so Dracula's gory demise takes place in a vacuum, devoid of both its previous site and context. The Count is now nowhere in particular, with a large golden cross shoved through his midsection for no apparent reason. For both viewers and non-viewers of the previous film, this introductory scene raises more questions than it answers.

Weller, of course, is appalled at what he witnesses. But being the sort of entrepreneur who made the Empire great—the sort for whom the opportunity for profit casteth out fear—he collects some mementos from the scene in hopes of selling them later.

London: Three middle-aged Victorian gentlemen have formed a secret society and together indulge in the pleasures of the double life. But Hargood (Geoffrey Keen), Paxton (Peter Sallis), and Secker (John Carson), bored with the standard whoring and absinthe drinking, approach the mysterious young Lord Courtley (the late Ralph Bates), whom they first encounter at their brothel hideaway. Unsavory rumors of Satanism surround him, and the trio want to see if Courtley can suggest any new vices.

They have come to the right place. We can tell Courtley is as evil as he's reputed to be: he sneers, he is arrogant and rude, he overacts outrageously; worst of all, he wears a cape lined with purple and a lavender ruffled shirt. Without missing a beat, he counsels them, "Sell your souls to the Devil." And off they go to Weller's shop for the accessories they'll need for the Black Mass that Courtley has in mind.

Whereas the Kents in *Dracula, Prince of Darkness* were able to sit in Castle Drac-

ula and drink a toast, in all innocence, to their departed host, this time the Count's reputation precedes him, all the way to England. Secker recognizes Dracula's name; Weller refers to the Count as "the most evil man of all time"; and Courtley reverently refers to him as "the Master." The trio purchase Dracula's cloak, his signet ring, a cloak clasp with his name on it, and a cylindrical vial of his powdered blood. We can already see where this is headed.

The trio undertake the equivalent of Harker's journey to this film's little patch of Transylvania: the desecrated, deep-in-the-woods chapel of the Courtley estate. Courtley has redecorated the place with "Satanic" trappings: a black tapestry (sinister-looking but alchemical in content), black candles, and so forth. Donning the Count's accessories, Courtley distributes Dracula's powdered blood into three chalices for the men and a huge goblet for himself. He then slices open his own palm and mingles a few drops of his blood with the powder in each vessel. To the accompaniment of thunder and lightning—God's warning, or Satan's applause—the vessels fill with Dracula's viscous blood, reconstituted from concentrate. Courtley first invites, then orders, the men to participate in an anticommunion by drinking Dracula's blood. When they balk, he derides them; they challenge him to drink the blood himself, and he gladly does so.

We have seen—from Stoker's novel, through several adaptations, through sequels such as *House of Dracula*—the various consequences that can result from drinking or otherwise ingesting Dracula's blood. This time around, the results are drastic and sudden: Courtley gags, collapses, pleads for help, and dies. The trio flee in panic.

After their departure, Courtley's body is magically transformed into Dracula, "alive" and vengeful. It is more than forty

"Oh, if such an one was to come from God, and not the Devil, what a force for good might he not be in this old world of ours."—Van Helsing

Christopher Lee as Dracula in *Taste the Blood of Dracula* (1970) (courtesy Ronald V. Borst of Hollywood Movie Posters)

minutes into the story before the Count reappears this time—not quite the wait of *Dracula, Prince of Darkness*, but comparable. Here the technique of his resurrection is marginally similar to that of the earlier film, with some significant differences.

First, the blood sacrifice in *Taste the Blood of Dracula* is more literally depicted as a religious ritual (complete with organ music on the soundtrack), as opposed to Klove's abattoir-style massacre of Alan Kent. Second, this ritual involves a *willing* "blood donor"; Courtley's wounding of his own hand can be categorized alongside other instances of false stigmata. Finally, the medium of Dracula's return this time is powdered blood, as opposed to the dust that was used in the earlier film; the dust was a remnant of tissues other than just blood, and was therefore the key to rebuilding the Count's entire body. In *Taste the Blood of Dracula*, only the blood is reconstituted; and recreating Dracula from blood cells alone can be seen as a wedding of sorcery and cloning. The resuscitation of Courtley's corpse *as* Dracula, via an ingestion of his tainted blood, is analogous either to recombinant DNA, or to Dracula-as-virus, a variation on the contagion of vampirism.

Still, the whole premise raises some questions. Is this result what Courtley had in mind? It's hard to believe so; he seems genuinely surprised at the painful distress he experiences after drinking the blood. And what would have happened if all four celebrants had drunk the blood? Would all four have died and returned as Dracula clones?

Also puzzling is the Count's attitude toward all this. "They have destroyed my servant," Christopher Lee says with that inimitable voice; "they shall be destroyed." While this utterance sets the agenda for the rest of the film, it, too, begs questions. In what way have "*they*" killed Courtley? He dies as a result of voluntarily drinking

Dracula's blood. When he pleads for help afterwards and gropes for the men, they deal him a few swift kicks, but nothing that could be fatal. Did their unbelieving, fearful attitudes somehow cause the blood to poison Courtley? All the trio have demonstrably done is foot the bill for the accessories, since Courtley's family cut him off without a shilling. Are the men to be held responsible because they financed the operation? If so, shouldn't the Count pin a medal on each of them, since it is via Courtley's death that Dracula's rebirth is brought about? This is iffy screenwriting at best, but it still manages to underscore the perversity of Dracula's evil: his vengefulness here is more than the opposite of forgiveness; it is the negation of gratitude.

In any case, Count Dracula has—in his fourth appearance in the Hammer series—finally made it to Victorian England, where so much of the action of Stoker's novel takes place. Instead of making a grand entrance via shipwreck, he arrives in a jar. Weller is the equivalent of Harker, the international business traveler who abets Dracula's travels abroad. Lord Courtley is the Renfield surrogate, the societal outcast who greets the Count as "the Master." (Since Dracula refers to Courtley as "my servant," there is an implied link between the two of them—a link which, as in the novel and several of the adaptations, is ill-defined and may, as Noll suggested, be no more than psychic.)

The question may arise as to whether it is appropriate to link Dracula with Satanism, since many aspects of vampire folklore have their roots in pre-Christian times and also, therefore, predated the late-medieval advent of Satanism, a Christian heresy. Overall, this casting into a Christian mold of ancient pagan beliefs concerning vampires is consistent with the tendency of medieval Christianity, in its expansion across Europe, to demonize the various pagan gods. But bearing in mind that, for the purposes of this book, "appropriate" chiefly means "having some basis in Stoker's novel," then the answer to the question is yes, though Stoker touches on it but briefly. "The Draculas," Van Helsing tells us in the novel, were "... a great and noble race, though now and again were scions who were held by their coevals to have had dealings with the Evil One. They learned his secrets in the Scholomance [literally, "school of divination"] ... where the devil claims the tenth scholar as his due."

Meanwhile, we have long since been introduced to the twentyish children of the three men. Hargood's daughter Alice (Linda Hayden) and Paxton's son, another Paul (Anthony Corlan), are in love, but face the stern (and totally gratuitous) disapproval of Hargood. Secker's son Jeremy (Martin Jarvis) and Paul's sister Lucy (Isla Blair) are engaged, also despite parental disapproval, although less harsh than Hargood's. In the development of these characters and their relationships with their elders, we see, as Hammer's Dracula series continues, a more pronounced catering to the youthful audiences who were the studio's bread and butter.

In *Dracula, Prince of Darkness*, the Kents were married couples, and were (with the probable exception of Diana) in their thirties and forties; Father Sandor was in his fifties. In *Dracula Has Risen from the Grave*, while there were sympathetic adult characters, such as the monsignor and his sister-in-law, the bulk of the action had shifted to the younger characters, whom the audiences could "identify with" or "relate to": Paul, the student; Zena, the waitress; Maria, the sorority girl. And part of the function of the adults in the story was to disapprove of Maria's boyfriend.

In *Taste the Blood of Dracula*, Hammer takes the next step: more than just catering to a young audience, the studio

panders to them. All the adults, to one extent or another, are unpleasant: hypocritical, cowardly, greedy (Weller). The hypocrisy of the three men is underscored by our first meeting all these families in church, and by the trio's masking their outings to the brothel as "charity work." And Michael Ripper turns up later as a police investigator who is simply insufferable. All the youth, on the other hand, are attractive young lovers, downtrodden victims of their elders. Lord Courtley is young, though not *as* young; but he, too, has had troubles with his elders, having been disowned by his family. Still, he's a member of the decadent, oppressive aristocracy: leave it to a Lord to side with the Count.

Into this milieu of transgenerational resentment, domestic violence, family dysfunction, and moral hypocrisy wades the Count. He is right in his element. Blood is a mere condiment here; there is enough bad karma in evidence to feed a host of demons. Dracula turns the children against their fathers as instruments of his revenge.

One of them needs only a nudge: Alice is fleeing from her drunken father, who utters such sentimental endearments as, "I haven't beaten you since you were a little girl," when she encounters Dracula lurking in the garden. He sends her back to kill Hargood with a shovel. Since Hargood has been such a brute, to both his wife and his daughter, Dracula ironically appears to be a liberating dark angel.

But his influence also poisons good relationships: Alice lures Lucy aboard a black carriage that takes them on a wild ride to the chapel, where Alice has been hiding out since killing her father. In a nice touch borrowed from the Lugosi adaptation, Lucy hops out of the carriage at the end of the line to berate the driver, only to find that there isn't one. Lucy, true to her Stokeresque name, becomes a vampire; she kills her father, then attacks and mesmerizes Jeremy, causing him to kill *his* father. Alice's bitter relationship with her father is the aperture through which Dracula enters into this circle of friends and family to wreak all this misery.

But we're ahead of ourselves here. After Hargood's death and the disappearances of Alice and Lucy, Secker, the most stable of the three men (being neither a drunken bully like Hargood nor a sniveling coward like Paxton), steps into Van Helsing's shoes. He leads the reluctant Paxton to the chapel to check Paxton's theory that Courtley has somehow returned from the dead. Sure enough, the body is gone; but when they look for it in a recently-disturbed sarcophagus, they find Lucy. Secker has done his homework (we've seen him thoughtfully poking around in his library at home), so he knows the meaning of the wounds on Lucy's neck. Two men, one resolute, the other bewildered, look into a tomb at the body of a beloved young woman named Lucy, who has become a vampire; the resolute man says she must be destroyed with a stake through the heart. For a few fleeting moments, we're in downtown Stokerville.

Paxton, grieving, unprepared for such a drastic action as the stake, pulls a pistol

"Your girls that you all love are mine already ... my creatures, to do my bidding and to be my jackals when I want to feed."—Count Dracula

Linda Hayden as Alice and Christopher Lee as Dracula in *Taste the Blood of Dracula* (1970) (courtesy Ronald V. Borst of Hollywood Movie Posters)

and wounds Secker, running him off. He then lives out a situation hypothetically described in the novel by Van Helsing: "I doubt not that in old time, when such things were, many a man who set forth to do such a task [i.e., staking a vampiress] … found at the last his heart fail him, and then his nerve. So he delay, and delay, and delay, till the mere beauty and fascination of the wanton Un-Dead hypnotize him; and he remain on and on, till sunset come, and the Vampire sleep be over. Then the beautiful eyes of the fair woman open…." And they do, just as Paxton aims the stake at Lucy's breast. But Paxton doesn't "swell the grim and grisly ranks of the Un-Dead," as Van Helsing describes; instead of turning her father into a vampire, Lucy commandeers the stake. She and Alice, under the Count's direction, then stake Paxton in an ironic vengeance for all the vampire girls staked in the Hammer series up to now.

Lucy turns up tapping at the window of the Secker home, recalling Helen in *Dracula, Price of Darkness,* or Lucy Westenra herself in the later Jack Palance adaptation. After victimizing Jeremy, she entices him to stab his father; we later learn from the police inspector that Jeremy has been arrested. Dracula, lurking in the shadows as ever, declares his revenge complete. Having no further use for Lucy, the Count disposes of her; scripter Anthony Hinds, again writing as "John Elder," commits the same lazy-writing sin he committed with Zena in *Dracula Has Risen from the Grave.* This time around, Dracula "kills" Lucy (isn't she already dead?) with another bite to the throat! This is weak writing, in terms of what the Count is doing, how he's doing it, and why.

Fortunately, Secker has left behind a letter for Paul telling him what to do. One wonders why Secker didn't write the note for his own son. "Your love for Alice will act as your strength and your protection," the note reads in part; didn't Secker believe that Jeremy's love for Lucy would give him strength as well, in a desire for vengeance? The note directs Paul to the information he'll need in order to combat Dracula, including a book titled *Vampires and Vampirism* in large letters. (This is a real book, not a movie prop. Written in 1914 by Dudley Wright, it was reissued in 1924 in an expanded version; more recent editions bear the title *The Book of Vampires* or *The History of Vampires.*)

Armed with knowledge and a carpet-bag full of paraphernalia, Paul goes to the chapel. On arrival, he reconsecrates it—or, if that's not something an Anglican layman can do, he at least redecorates it, yanking down the black tapestry, putting a fresh white cloth on the altar, replacing the black candles with white ones. Alice, who has somehow escaped being bitten, is still under Dracula's control, but she snaps out of it when it becomes clear that he intends to dump her, too, and take off for parts unknown. But he is trapped inside the chapel by a cross Paul has placed on the door. As Paul and Alice ("Jonathan" and "Mina" reunited) argue about whether she should get away or stay at his side, Dracula suddenly, dramatically—and anti-climactically—dies.

More weak writing: we are given no clear idea what it is that does Dracula in this time. It may have something to do with Paul's having reacknowledged the chapel as a place of Christian worship. Our only visual clue is that a cross in a stained-glass window glows red as the Count passes close by—like an evil-sensitive motion detector—and that this phenomenon causes him pain. He smashes the window, then lapses into a hallucinatory vision of the chapel in its better days: bright with candles, glowing with stained glass, and glistening with golden crucifixes, with organ music and the Latin liturgy as a backdrop. All that holy light proves too much for the Prince of Darkness, who plummets from the upper floor of the interior and lands on the altar, where he crumbles to red dust. Paul and Alice watch with a bewilderment at least equal to the audience's. "He's having an epiphany," is as good an explanation as any in trying to figure out this sequence.

Taste the Blood of Dracula (95 minutes; available on video) is marred by a contrived beginning, a *deus* (or *Deus*) *ex machina* ending, and the occasional plot misfire such as the disposal of Lucy. Still, the film has several things going for it. As noted, the Count finally makes it to Stoker's England, where effective use is made of locations and costume. There are, as always in a Hammer exercise, some atmospheric sets; the desecrated chapel, with its cobwebby ambiance and its sarcophagi, is a thing of dark beauty that evinces Stoker's descriptions of Carfax Abbey. There are a few crowd scenes—in the church early on, and in the soup kitchen that serves as a front for the brothel—that allow the production a glimpse beyond Hammer's usual narrow confines into the larger world beyond. James Bernard again provides the music; Dracula's three-note theme is heard at times, balanced by a "young-lovers" theme for Paul and Alice.

Good cast, too. Ralph Bates, a Hammer regular in the early '70s, makes the most of his brief but vivid role before disappearing less than halfway into the movie. Linda Hayden is energetic as the conflicted Alice, while Anthony Corlan does what he can with a frustrated but underwritten Paul. To see these two in entirely different roles, check out the unfortunately-titled *The Blood on Satan's Claw* (1971) and Hammer's own *Vampire Circus* of the same year. In the former, Hayden plays a cruelly evil teen witch in rural England of the 17th century; in the latter, Corlan is a vampire/shapeshifter whose effortless, silent transformation into a black panther, in the few seconds it takes him to ascend a flight of stairs, is one of Hammer's more subtly memorable scenes.

Christopher Lee's Count Dracula, this time around, though again motivated by a contrived (and misplaced) revenge, is given more of the presence of a patient plotter/planner/schemer than the hot-headed Count of the previous entry. He is a shadowy conspirator, a low-key, Victorian-era Manson, in his turning the young against their parents.

Some critics have wondered why Dracula is in this film at all, since his role is so small in terms of time spent on-screen. These reviewers need to have another look at the book. After the opening chapters in Transylvania, Dracula is so seldom seen that Leonard Wolf, in *The Annotated Dracula*, provides a chart listing the Count's fleeting appearances, which are sometimes in forms other than human. This man is a recluse, a hermit even "amongst [London's] teeming millions." "I love the shade and the shadow," Stoker's Count confides to Jonathan early on, "and would be alone with my thoughts when I may." Hammer's Count is less poetic, a once-human black hole: if he sees you, he will kill you. For all it lacks, at least Hammer's characterization of the Count is not the sort of man who mingles in polite society or wastes a minute of his limitless time even trying to pass for human.

Scars of Dracula

(1970)

And it finally happened: the plummet in quality that had been threatening the Hammer Dracula series for years came to pass with *Scars of Dracula*, a garish live-action cartoon. Hammer's Frankenstein series was, at the same time, foundering with *Horror of Frankenstein*, an attempted black-comic spoof of the earlier entries. *Scars of Dracula* is such a pastiche of bits and pieces of the Dracula series thus far (and occasionally other Hammer vampire movies as well) that one is tempted at times to wonder whether director Roy Ward Baker meant for this exercise, too, to be an extremely deadpan joke.

We open on a shot of Dracula's mountaintop castle, a cunningly-built model that is the Count's fourth different castle in five films. Inside, we discover Dracula in the same condition he was in at the end of *Taste the Blood of Dracula*: a small pile of red dust heaped atop the familiar red-lined black cape. Of course, how these remains moved from the ruined chapel in England back to the castle in the mittel-European mountains isn't even hinted at. Hammer is now playing the same patronizing game of "don't ask, just play along" that Universal played by having John Carradine's Dracula reappear as inexplicably as Kenny in a *South Park* episode.

Suddenly a bat (about which, more later)—one of those movie bats that can hover in place—flits in through the crypt's small window and spits blood into the dust. The decomposition effects at the end of the previous film are run in reverse, and Dracula is revived yet again. While this scenario doesn't keep us waiting for the

better part of an hour for Dracula to show up, audience members viewing their first Hammer Dracula may wonder whether the Count undergoes this ordeal every sunset.

There follows a sequence similar to the opening of the vastly superior *Vampire Circus* of the following year: led by Michael Ripper, the locals, fed up by one atrocity too many, storm Dracula's castle and burn much of it, while the women of the village take refuge in the church. Afterwards, the men of the expedition learn to their horror that the women have all been killed by a swarm of bats. This development steals from the denouement of *Kiss of the Vampire*, although with the bats on the vampire's side this time, and from the introduction of *Dracula Has Risen from the Grave*, with the Count's desecration of a church, which is shunned afterwards.

By now we have learned that Klove, from *Dracula, Prince of Darkness*, has also mysteriously returned. Not only is he played by a different actor (Patrick Troughton, remembered in certain circles as one of the many actors who played TV's Doctor Who), this Klove seems to be a different character altogether: slovenly, unkempt, ragged, and with eyebrows that could kill a man at twenty paces. He looks more like an embodiment of Renfield's edgier moments.

The story then settles into being mostly an inferior retread of *Horror of Dracula*. Harker's journey to Dracula's castle is undertaken—pointlessly and accidentally—by yet another Paul (Christopher Matthews). On the lam after being

"Don't you know that I am sane and earnest ... that I am no lunatic in a mad fit, but a sane man fighting for his soul?"—Renfield

Christopher Lee as Dracula and Patrick Troughton as Klove in *Scars of Dracula* **(1970) (courtesy Ronald V. Borst of Hollywood Movie Posters)**

caught misbehaving with the buerger-meister's daughter, Paul encounters the usual hazards: a wild coach ride, a border crossing, a road accident, and the Inn of the Frightened Xenophobes, where Ripper is the landlord. After being refused late-night admittance to the inn, Paul curls up for a nap in an unattended carriage—wouldn't anybody?—and wakes up at Castle Dracula. Klove is apparently unaware of the stowaway as he drives back home.

At the castle—whose interior, with its red candles, red drapes, and gold-colored furniture, looks like a whorehouse set from a Wild West movie—Paul is, like Harker before him, met by a mysterious young woman (Anouska Hempel). He then is greeted by the Count, who welcomes him as a guest. Paul, upon learning Dracula's name, seems unpleasantly surprised and starts making excuses as to why he must be going. But Dracula, Klove, and Tania (the young woman, her name swiped from *Horror of Dracula*) insist that he stay the night. "This is not Kleinenberg," Dracula says, somewhat irrelevantly; but the line establishes that we are near the same town where *Dracula Has Risen from the Grave* took place, as well as echoing Dracula's observation in the novel that "Transylvania is not England." As Paul reluctantly follows Klove to his room, the Count, in a brazen bit of petty larceny from *Horror of Dracula*, says, "Sleep well, Mr. Carlson."

The remake of the 1958 film continues: again, the young woman comes to Paul, tells him she is a "prisoner" in the castle, and asks for help—and for sex, this time. Again, she moves to put the bite on him (licking her lips before doing so, as Stoker describes in the novel). Again, Dracula bursts into the room and breaks up her attack, this time by fatally stabbing her in one of the clumsiest-staged assaults in the history of screen violence. Again, there is no telling why he is behaving this way, unless it can be chalked up to jealousy or possessiveness. In any case, his ability to stab her to death, as though she's just another mortal, means that she must not yet have died of his vampiric attentions; in the novel, Stoker says that both Lucy and Mina sprout longer, sharper teeth, like Tania's, while yet alive. Still, there's no need to defend this confusing, badly-directed scene in terms of anything in Stoker's novel. We're basically once more witnessing the outcome of bad screenwriting, and again, "John Elder" is to blame. No wonder Anthony Hinds wouldn't put his real name on these scripts.

Again, Paul is locked into his room; again, he makes Jonathan's out-the-window escape. This time, he ties drapes together and lowers himself down a sheer wall and into the small window of Dracula's crypt, which is accessible no other way. Klove pulls up the "rope," and once more, "Jonathan" doesn't make it out of Castle Dracula alive.

Klove, as we have seen in *Dracula, Prince of Darkness*, is amenable to slaughterhouse chores. He disposes of Tania's body with a hatchet, a saw, and a bath of acid, whistling while he works. He also finds in Paul's room an item seen in *Horror of Dracula*, and in other adaptations as well (though not, as we have seen, in the novel): the picture of the girl. This time around, the girl in the photo is Sarah (Jenny Hanley), a girl caught in a love triangle involving Paul and his brother Simon (Dennis Waterman). And this time, it is not the Count who is distracted by the picture, but Klove.

When Sarah and Simon, having traveled via the Inn of the Frightened Xenophobes, arrive at the castle searching for Paul, Klove recognizes Sarah from the picture. He then takes on Renfield's task, as per the novel, of trying to defend "Mina": he refuses to assist Dracula's attempts on Sarah, disobeying the Count's command to remove her cross pendant as she sleeps. (Simon, meanwhile, is out cold, the Count having slipped him a mickey in a glass of wine. This development is also borrowed from the novel, insofar as Dracula drugs the staff of the Westenra estate of Hillingham, lacing a decanter of sherry with laudanum.) Klove helps Simon and Sarah escape, for which Dracula tortures him with a red-hot sword (whose "glow" is obviously painted on). As Renfield does for Mina, Klove ultimately gives his life trying to save Sarah.

Back at the inn, Simon and Sarah enlist the aid of the priest of the desecrated church (Michael Gwynn). He belatedly takes up Van Helsing's mantle, giving the pair a crash course in Vampirology 101. A surprising bit of news that he tells them is that Dracula "has dominion over some animals," including bats. This is a power never granted to Dracula in the Hammer series before, but it is in keeping with Stoker: as Van Helsing tells the other vampire hunters, "he can command all the meaner things: the rat, and the owl, and the bat—the moth, and the fox, and the wolf." Here he limits himself to bats. In addition to having called in the gruesome air strike at the church early in the movie, the Count is accompanied throughout the story by the large bat that revived him. It acts as his "familiar": it spies on the protagonists, relays information (Dracula apparently can understand "bat speak"), kills the priest, and finally yanks the cross from around Sarah's neck.

In addition to his rapport with the bat, Dracula enjoys a greater range of supernatural powers in this movie than in any other Hammer. Doors open and close for him, untouched. He hypnotizes Simon (who has found the Count in his crypt) while *still asleep*, his eyes glowing red through his eyelids in one of this film's few effective moments. And in an absolutely startling scene, he clambers lizard-like up the sheer outer wall of Castle Dracula above the window of his crypt. This was a full seven years before Louis Jourdan first crawled *down* the wall, as Stoker wrote the scene, but it is groundbreaking nonetheless, for what little it's worth.

But in the end, another act of God, in coordination with an act of dumbness, does Dracula in. On the parapet of the castle, under a sky full of thunder and lightning, the Count stalks Sarah; Klove attempts to come to the rescue and is hurled to his death off the "terrible precipice" described by Stoker in the novel. Simon shows up, wrestles an ornamental spike free from its mount, and hurls it like a spear, impaling the Count through the bread basket ... too low. Dracula pulls the spike out and, as he prepares to throw it at Simon, holds it high over his head ... in the middle of an electrical storm. You'd think a man five hundred years old would know better. Lightning strikes, of course, and (with the help of a stunt double: look for the over-sized, over-the-head "Dracula mask" that doesn't look vaguely like Christopher Lee or any other human being), Count Dracula plummets off the cliff and goes down in flames. So does the Hammer Dracula series.

Scars of Dracula (94 minutes; available on video) is a vile, cheap, lurid, repugnant movie, a collection of scraps of earlier, better Hammers. One or two moments of Stoker-inspired interest come nowhere near saving it. If the earlier films in the Hammer series were bottles of cheap booze, and you drank them one by one until you got violently ill, *Scars of Dracula* is what you'd throw up.

Christopher Lee has more screen time and more dialogue than in some of the previous outings; but he and Michael Ripper, the only two Hammer stalwarts in the cast, look cranky and irritable throughout, even above and beyond the requirements of their respective roles. When the Count tells Paul, "I am Dracula," he then stares the young man down for a few solid seconds, until one almost expects him to add, "You want to make something of it?" Michael Gwynn is earnest enough as the priest, but the other, younger cast members are uniformly pretty, and equally dull.

Once more, James Bernard scores the movie, although the music is mostly recycled from earlier efforts. All told, it's hard to believe this film was directed by the same Roy Ward Baker who gave us the flawless classic *A Night to Remember* (1958; *Titanic* without the soap suds). Unless you're a completist, or desperately curious, this movie can be bypassed.

Dracula A.D. 1972

(1972)

As its title implies, *Dracula A.D. 1972* signals the end of Hammer's Victorian-Gothic Dracula series as the Count invades "modern-day" London. In itself, this idea is not a bad one; in Stoker's novel, Dracula infiltrates contemporary London, the London of Stoker's own era, allowing his enemies to make use of the telegraph, the typewriter, the phonograph, the telephone, and the electric torch (or flashlight, on this side of the Pond) in their efforts against him. It is the execution of this idea, in this film and its sequel, that is troublesome.

We begin with yet another wild ride on yet another driverless carriage. The year, a voice-over tells us, is 1872, and the ancient evil of Dracula has made it to London. Problems already: While Stoker doesn't tell us the exact year of his novel's action, it's generally understood to be in the 1880s or 1890s, contemporary with its publication; several of the adaptations are set in 1897, the very year the novel was published. The Hammer original, *Horror of Dracula*, is set in 1885, so this "sequel" is impossibly opening more than a dozen years *earlier*!

Atop the carriage, two men are locked in a life-or-death struggle. One is Count Dracula, and the other, the voice-over tells us, is the Count's mortal enemy, "Lawrence" (!) Van Helsing! Between the impossible date and the aberrant name of the hero, it would seem that we are actually witnessing a non-sequel: after the "death" of the Hammer series in the awfulness of *Scars of Dracula*, a fresh start is being attempted, and in such a way as to try to fool an inattentive or newly-arrived audience mem-

ber into thinking that this introductory scene is the finale of an earlier entry. But whereas *Scars of Dracula*, as noted, starts with the Count in a heap of dust as last seen at the end of *Taste the Blood of Dracula*, but relocates him from London back to his castle, *Dracula A.D. 1972* leaves the Count in London, but does not pick up where we left off.

Inevitably, the carriage cracks up in yet another road accident. Dracula and Van Helsing (Peter Cushing, too long unseen in this series) are both mortally injured, the Count having suffered a freak-accident impalement on the spoke of a broken wheel. Van Helsing, with his last ounce of strength before dying, sees to it that the Count doesn't dislodge the "stake" that has found him; Dracula's body again crumbles to dust, and Van Helsing dies.

A mysterious young man rides up on horseback, retrieves Dracula's signet ring and the spoke/stake, and collects some of the Count's dust in a vial. Later, at the fringes of Van Helsing's funeral, the young man punches a hole in the ground with the spoke, pours some of the dust into it, and places the spoke back into the hole. Here we go again.

One hundred years later, the young man, or a look-alike descendant, turns up among a group of young party crashers at a posh Chelsea home. The hippie intruders, dressed in laughably dated, oh-so-hip clothes, are so shocking to their tux-clad, strait-laced hosts that somebody calls the "fuzz." The group retreat to their coffee-house hangout, where the young man—whose name, we learn, is Johnny Alucard (!)—invites them to join him for some-

*"It would be impossible to describe the expression of hate and baffled malignity—
of anger and hellish rage—which came over the Count's face."*—John Seward

**Christopher Lee as *Dracula A.D. 1972* (1972)
(courtesy Ronald V. Borst of Hollywood Movie Posters)**

thing "way, way out": a devil worship ceremony.... "Black Mass and all that jazz," as one of them puts it. The place he has in mind is St. Botolph's, a desanctified church scheduled for demolition ... and the site, of course, of the burial place of Van Helsing, and of some of Dracula's dust. Johnny (Christopher Neame), who keeps the ring and the vial of remaining dust at home, obviously enjoys the irony that one of the circle of friends is Jessica Van Helsing, the granddaughter of Professor Lorrimer Van Helsing (Peter Cushing again). As the grandson of Lawrence, he is another look-alike descendant.

The group meet at the church at midnight. Johnny leads them in a ludicrous "ceremony" culminating in the mixing of his blood with some of Dracula's dust in a goblet, which immediately overflows with gore. Outside, in the churchyard, the ground is disturbed in the area around the spoke, which, though made of wood and fully exposed to the elements, has miraculously survived a century. The kids panic and run away—all but Laura, who volunteered to be the living altar in the ceremony when Jessica (Johnny's first choice) balked. Johnny pulls the spoke from the ground, and Dracula issues forth as a gaseous exhalation. The ring turns up on Dracula's finger, to Johnny's surprise, and Dracula quenches his long thirst with Laura's blood. So far this is not so much a sequel to *Taste the Blood of Dracula* as a remake, except that it makes even less sense: subdividing Dracula's dust so that a fountain of his blood gushes forth here, while the man himself pops up there, is a pointless, silly contrivance.

Next day, even as Johnny is telling the others that the whole thing was a joke and that Laura, who was in on it, took a late-night train out of town, her mutilated body is found in the churchyard by some children. A Scotland Yard investigator, Inspector Murray (Michael Coles), thinks he sees occult significance in the manner of her death, referring to "cult murders" in "the States": could he mean Manson? Murray calls upon Van Helsing, occult expert, as a consultant.

Johnny takes a second young woman to the church to be victimized by Dracula, who makes it clear to Johnny that the next girl he brings had better be Jessica Van Helsing. "I have returned," he says, "to destroy the house of Van Helsing forever, the old through the young"—another idea pirated from *Taste the Blood of Dracula*. He continues, "You, and your line, have been chosen." This statement decisively answers the question of whether Johnny is a hundred years older than he looks, or is a look-alike descendant of the young man from 1872. But it raises a host of other questions about the Alucards, such as how they got involved with Dracula in the first place, how long ago their involvement began, and what the Alucard family's real name is. Courtley, maybe? Or Renfield?

Johnny claims it would be easier for him to abduct Jessica if he were "given the power" of immortality that the Count possesses. One wonders how that would make things easier, since he would thereby be sacrificing his access to Jessica during the daylight hours. In any case, Dracula agrees to transform Johnny into a vampire, but the camera discreetly cuts away before the bite is administered; the Hammer series, including this film, has spent too much energy imbuing the Count's bite with heterosexual eroticism to show him swinging both ways.

Van Helsing, explaining to Murray the qualities peculiar to vampires, says, "Like the phoenix, they die only to live again." This characteristic is found neither in folklore nor in Stoker, but it certainly explains why Hammer's Count keeps bouncing back. (Hammer's Carmilla "trilogy," for that matter, ran to *four* films, if you count *Captain Kronos: Vampire Hunter*.) Van Helsing (whose grandfather Lawrence *wrote* the book this time around: *The Legend of Dracula the Vampire*) briefs Murray on the vulnerabilities of the vampire: the cross, the Bible, holy water, running water, and silver, especially a silver-bladed knife. While silver weaponry is more typically associated in fiction with defense against werewolves, its folkloric effectiveness against vampires is also known. "Because of its white, lustrous, and often pure nature," Bunson writes in *The Vampire Encyclopedia*, "silver is considered a formidable bane to evil of all kinds, especially the devil." (Or, one presumes, his kin: one translation of "Dracula" is "son of the devil.") Barber adds that "silver knives, placed under mattresses and cribs, ... keep away both vampires and werewolves."

With the help of Jessica's vampirized boyfriend, Bob, Johnny abducts Jessica. Afterward, Van Helsing goes to Johnny's apartment and confronts him right at dawn. Shut out of his coffin when Van Helsing tosses a Bible into it, Johnny flees into the bathroom, where he is done in by bad writing. He *accidentally* opens a skylight, and as the brightness of day causes him to topple into the bathtub, he *accidentally* turns on the shower and is killed by the running water. Not only is this scene unintentionally funny, but Johnny's back-to-back fatal accidents rob Van Helsing of the appropriate heroics.

The final showdown takes place at

*"It is that we become as him; that we henceforward
become foul things of the night like him..."*—Van Helsing

**Christopher Lee as Dracula and Christopher Neame as Johnny Alucard in
Dracula A.D. 1972 (1972) (courtesy Ronald V. Borst of Hollywood Movie Posters)**

the church. "You would play your brains against mine—against me, who has commanded nations?" Dracula demands of Van Helsing, in a line paraphrased from the novel. In reply, Van Helsing stabs Dracula with a silver knife. Dracula plummets from the upper story to the floor below, where Jessica, in a trance, removes the blade before Van Helsing can get downstairs. Dracula pursues Van Helsing, who leads him outside to the edge of a stake-filled pit the professor spent the day digging. Van Helsing tosses holy water into Dracula's face, causing the Count to fall into the pit and onto the stakes, and then finishes him off by pressing down on him with a shovel to ensure that the stakes do the job.

Dracula A.D. 1972 (100 minutes; available on video) is, by and large, an inferior, minor affair, made frustrating by a few things it has in its favor. Alan Gibson's direction is crisp and fast-paced; his shots are well-composed and the editing is often quite effective. Early in the film, for example, the camera's gaze rises from the churchyard where Lawrence Van Helsing has just been buried, and suddenly a jet airliner roars into view—our first clue that a hundred years have passed. And Laura's dead stare, as she lies half-buried in the rubble of the churchyard, is chillingly matched in the next shot by the stares of the children looking down at her body. The ruined, dusty church and its weedy churchyard comprise an atmospheric set, just the sort of place a vampire would haunt, and Christopher Lee does so with feral delight ... though the filmmakers err in *confining* Dracula to the spot, never having him venture out.

Peter Cushing's return as Van Helsing is a welcome sight, although giving him a granddaughter as an incentive for his involvement is hardly necessary. Since, as he points out, the Van Helsing family have been studying and combating vampires for generations, he would have jumped at the chance to be in this fight even without a gratuitous damsel-in-distress relative to motivate him. It doesn't help that Jessica, as played by Stephanie Beacham, is shallow and lippy.

Christopher Neame, as the unfortunately-named Johnny Alucard, more effectively cuts the figure of a black-clad Goth-punk vampire-wanna-be, though his slim, snake-eyed look seems too obviously modeled after Malcolm McDowell's Alex in *A Clockwork Orange* (1971). The short-lived Laura is played by lovely Caroline Munro, who went on to a career as a "scream queen" in such films as *Captain Kronos: Vampire Hunter*, *The Golden Voyage of Sinbad* (1974), and the repellent *Maniac* (1980).

Ultimately, the movie's most fatal mistake is its self-conscious, embarrassing attempt to depict the youth "scene" of the early '70s, which were, of course, part of the late '60s. "Nothing is so dangerous," Oscar Wilde observed, "as being too modern; one is apt to grow old-fashioned quite suddenly." It happens here. Indeed, while a film set in the "present" will always reflect its times to one extent or another (such as, in this case, the awful pop-rock soundtrack music by Michael Vickers), it's always a mistake to try to recreate the latest thing "the kids" are doing. It not only comes across as a filmmaker's exploitative caricature, but it's likely to be already dated by the time the film hits the screen, and not to improve with the passage of years. In *I Was a Teenage Werewolf* (1957), for example, the story comes to a standstill while one of the kids at a Halloween party sings a pop song to the others, who "spontaneously" jump in and choreograph the number. Granted, the film isn't *Citizen Kane* (1941), but this scene is unwatchable. And even the mohawked, body-pierced, chains-and-leather punks of *The Return of the Living Dead* (1985) are starting to look quaint.

REST IN FINAL PEACE, reads a title superimposed over a shot of Van Helsing escorting the sobbing Jessica from the churchyard. As if.

The Satanic Rites of Dracula

(1973)

The Satanic Rites of Dracula, like its predecessor, was written by Don Houghton and directed by Alan Gibson, and is set in modern-day London. It, too, features Christopher Lee as Count Dracula, Peter Cushing as Lorrimer Van Helsing, and Michael Coles as Inspector Murray; Jessica Van Helsing also returns, though she is no longer a hippychick, and is played by Joanna Lumley this time. The premise of the story is vaguely Stokeresque: Dracula is involved in a conspiracy of world conquest of a sort, but the story is handled in such a way as to make Dracula out to be

*"He that can smile at death, as we know him; who can flourish
in the midst of diseases that can kill off whole peoples."*—Van Helsing

**Christopher Lee in *The Satanic Rites of Dracula* (1973)
(courtesy Ronald V. Borst of Hollywood Movie Posters)**

a James Bond megalomaniac super-villain. (The following year, Mr. Lee was to play such a part, the title role in the Bond entry *The Man with the Golden Gun.*)

Via an infiltrator, a government intelligence agency discovers a sinister cabal being hatched by five powerful men at a guarded estate known as Pelham House. (One of the schemers is named "Lord Carradine." Very funny.) Since Satanic rites are involved, Inspector Murray, assisting with the investigation, once again calls on Van Helsing's expertise. It turns out that Van Helsing is acquainted with one of the men, a Professor Julian Keely (played by veteran character actor Freddie Jones at his twitchiest. Jones had worked for Ham-

mer before, memorably, in 1970's unfortunately-titled *Frankenstein Must Be Destroyed!*). Keely, a germ warfare expert, has developed for the conspiracy's use a strain of "accelerated" Black Death, capable of wiping out the population of the entire world in a matter of days.

One member of the cabal is unidentified, but is believed to be the mysterious billionaire D. D. Denham. Van Helsing suspects—correctly, of course—that the elusive Mr. Denham is none other than Count Dracula, again operating under an alias. This time we are spared the now-familiar revival of Dracula via blood-soaked ceremony; Van Helsing simply speculates that "a disciple" of Dracula must have discovered his final resting place, at St. Botolph's Church, and done what was necessary to bring him back. The phoenix analogy is again invoked, and the term "reincarnation" is also used, inaccurately, to describe Dracula's return. St. Botolph's has been razed by now, and in its former place there stands a high-rise office building … the home offices of the D. D. Denham Group of Companies.

It is appropriate, from a folkloric standpoint, that vampirism is here associated with plague, since vampires, as has been pointed out elsewhere, were often thought to be the cause of epidemics. Still, in the wake of an apocalyptic, world-decimating super-plague, as Inspector Murray points out, "With only diseased and dead bodies to feed on, surely the vampire himself would perish." Van Helsing speculates that the Count may plan to release the plague because of a death wish; he may want "to end it all," and to "bring down the whole universe with him—the ultimate revenge!" Surely a suicidal Dracula is an odd concept, but as Paul Barber notes, "[The vampire's] condition is intolerable even to him, as is illustrated by the fact that … [a] Serbian word (*ocajnik*) that originally meant 'an undecayed corpse' has come to mean only 'an unhappy, disconsolate person'."

Dracula, meantime, just over half an hour into the story, has made his first appearance at Pelham House: surrounded by a Stokeresque fog, he enters a room where a young woman is being held. The woman, a carjacked office helper of the agency inspecting the cabal, winds up chained to the wall of the cellar, along with four or five other vampire women—human sacrifices of the Satanic rites, who "live" again afterwards. For the first time in a Hammer film, the Count is seen growing a harem or a "cult," only to keep them locked away. Is it he, or scripter Houghton, who is uncertain what to do with them?

Van Helsing gives the government officials the rundown on the characteristics and weaknesses of vampires. They make no image in a mirror or a camera, which is why there is nobody in one of the infiltrator's photos of each of the five plotters. Later in the movie, even a closed-circuit video camera fails to transmit Dracula's image "live," a nice touch. This is the first Hammer Dracula in which photography/videography has been an issue.

The question does not arise in Stoker's novel, either, although it almost did. Stoker's original notes for *Dracula*, preserved in the Rosenbach Museum & Library in Philadelphia, include references to Dracula's non-photographable quality, an aspect which, along with many other ideas (and characters), did not make it into the finished work. But unlike the usual cinematic gimmick, such as in *The Satanic Rites of Dracula*, which has Dracula producing no photographic image at all, Stoker's notes tersely describe how the other characters "Could not Codak [*sic*] him. Come out bluish or like skeleton corpse &c." (Moreover, Dracula's image was to escape the painter's brush as well: Stoker's notes describe the bizarre phenomenon that "Painters cannot paint him—their likenesses always like someone else.")

The folkloric link, as Barber informs us, is certain beliefs in which "a camera is believed to have this [mirror-like] ability to capture one's soul." A vampire is no longer human, and so no longer has a human soul; therefore it does not cast a reflection (or a shadow) or register on film. As we have seen (with Dracula's reflection in water in *Dracula Has Risen from the Grave*, vs. Baron Meinster's non-reflection in Gina's mirror in *The Brides of Dracula*), the Hammer series has not been consistent in its adherence to this aspect of the mythos.

The usual catalog of weapons is

listed: the crucifix, the Bible, sunlight, the stake. Running water is mentioned; the vampire harem in the cellar are later done in *en masse* with a sprinkler system! Hawthorn, the tree from which Christ's crown of thorns is traditionally said to have been made, is listed—an unusual choice in a movie, but folklorically correct. Montague Summers, in *The Vampire, His Kith and Kin*, writes, "the Bohemian peasant never neglects to strew ... his cowsheds and stables with hawthorn, ... so that the witches and vampires will get entangled amid the thorns and can force their way no further."

Finally, silver bullets are included. Again, while silver bullets are more generally thought of as items in an anti-were-wolf arsenal, Barber reports, "One account by a Serbian immigrant states that a silver coin with a cross on it could, if broken into four pieces and loaded into a shotgun shell, be used to kill a vampire." Bunson adds, "Crosses made of pure silver are supposedly much more powerful in providing protection ... against vampires." Accordingly, Van Helsing melts down a silver cross, makes a single bullet, loads his derringer, and heads downtown.

To the astonishment of the security guard at the Denham Building, Van Helsing is allowed straight in to see the mysterious Mr. Denham. In the odd scene that follows, Van Helsing finds himself sitting across a desk from "Denham," who stays in shadow by shining a bright light into

"... a sacred bullet fired into the coffin kill him so that he be true dead..."—Van Helsing

**Peter Cushing as Van Helsing in *The Satanic Rites of Dracula* (1973)
(courtesy Ronald V. Borst of Hollywood Movie Posters)**

the professor's eyes. Speaking in an outlandish, not-quite-Lugosi accent, the shadowy figure explains to Van Helsing that the strain of plague developed by Keely is to be used as a threat to blackmail various national governments into compliance with the cabal's demands. (His use of the phrase "rush and whirl of humanity" is a paraphrase of Stoker.)

Van Helsing isn't buying any of this. He "outs" Dracula with a crucifix and turns the light on him. Dracula stands up, dressed in black as always, but without his cloak—a sight never seen in a Hammer film before. When he speaks, it comes as a relief that he has dropped the phony accent; he was disguising his voice, it turns out. Van Helsing's one shot goes astray when a second member of the conspiracy grabs his arm. A third hands the Count his cloak, so his brief moment onscreen without it is over.

They take Van Helsing back to Pelham House, where he is to take the place of Keely (who "committed suicide") as one of Dracula's "four horsemen" of his own Apocalypse: the men who are to infect the world with the new plague. This plan comes as a nasty shock to the surviving three of the others, who had bought Dracula's lie about the plague's planned use as a deterrent. To complete his triumph, Dracula plans to make Jessica a vampire as Van Helsing watches: "The girl that you love is mine already," he says, in another paraphrase of the novel.

Inspector Murray, meanwhile, has infiltrated the compound. With a little sabotage, the whole place goes up in flames, like the finale of one of Hammer's own Frankensteins—or of a typical Bond film, but with a fraction of the budget. Jessica is rescued, the plague is presumably destroyed, and Dracula, furious, isn't ready to call it quits yet. In a final paraphrase from Stoker, he shouts, "My revenge spreads over centuries, and has just begun!"

As the Count gives chase, Van Helsing leads him into a conveniently-placed hawthorn bush! As Dracula gamely plunges in, one wonders anew how this person originally managed to live for five hundred years. The thorns snag and tear at the Count, and he finally tumbles out with what appears to be a crown of thorns around his brow. Van Helsing grabs a stave from a conveniently-placed picket fence, and you know the rest. After the obligatory crumble to dust, Van Helsing himself retrieves Dracula's ring, which has been such a talisman since *Horror of Dracula*.

If anything sinister was supposed to come of the taking of this souvenir—like, say, another sequel—it was never realized. *The Satanic Rites of Dracula* (84 minutes, cut from 88 in the U.K.; available on video, about which, more later) marks the end of the two-film Dracula mini-series scripted by Don Houghton and directed by Alan Gibson (with music, in this second movie, by John Cacavas). The films have just enough in their favor—Lee and Cushing; some good supporting players like Freddie Jones; some excellent scenery like Caroline Munro; and occasionally strong visual style—to be frustrating that they aren't better. The occasional out-of-context near-quote from the novel is interesting, as is an evident familiarity with the folklore. But neither of these is a substitute for good writing, nor do they make workable these plots in which the Count is gratuitously mixed in with pseudo-James Bond stuff (motorcycle goon squads; snipers with scopes and silencers) or pseudo-hippie stuff that was self-conscious even when it was new and hasn't aged well at all.

(*The Satanic Rites of Dracula* was almost unreleased in the U.S., with only the briefest of theatrical runs under the baffling retitle *Count Dracula and His Vampire Bride*. The second title character, one supposes, must be Jessica Van Helsing.

The U.S. video release is retitled simply *The Rites of Dracula*; apparently, Satanism doesn't sell to the general American public. The retitling of the tape is done in a laughably cheap manner, via a freeze-frame atop which the new title is superimposed in an entirely different lettering style from the rest of the credits!)

Here, too, marks the end of the Christopher Lee Dracula series. After threatening for years to hang up the cape if the scripts didn't improve, Mr. Lee finally made good.

But Peter Cushing's Van Helsing was to return one final time.

The Legend of the Seven Golden Vampires
(1974)

"Vampires, one is tempted to say," writes Leonard Wolf in *A Dream of Dracula*, "have appeared almost everywhere that men have bled." Perhaps, like sharks are supposed to be, they are attracted by the smell of blood, since vampires are traditionally said to haunt battlefields and other blood-soaked human playgrounds. In any case, Van Helsing concurs with Wolf: the vampire, he says, "is known everywhere that men have been. In old Greece, in old Rome; he flourish in Germany all over, in France, in India, even … in China, so far from us in all ways, there even he is, and the peoples fear him at this day." Montague Summers, in *The Vampire: His Kith and Kin*, adds: "Throughout the ancient Empire of China and from the earliest times the belief in vampires is very widely spread, some of which occur in myth and legend and some of which were related as facts, showing us that the Chinese Vampire lacks few, if any of the horrible traits he exhibits in Greek and Slavonic superstition." Summers then relates several colorful stories as examples.

Yes, even in China. And thereby hangs a tale.

Hammer, in this final episode of the Dracula saga—which is, as we shall see, not really an episode of a continuous series

at all, but another thematically-related stand-alone feature, as was *Son of Dracula*—continues to surf the waves of pop culture. First they gave us Dracula in Hippyland; next they gave us Dracula on James Bond's turf. Now, in the early-to-mid-'70s, with Bruce Lee movies and other martial-arts product doing good box office, they team up with Run Run Shaw of Hong Kong to bring us an East-meets-West oddity that can only be described as a kung-fu vampire movie. The result isn't especially good—how could it be?—but it is, at times, perversely enjoyable.

We open with a bizarre variation on Harker's journey to Dracula's castle, taking place, as a title informs us, in TRANSYLVANIA 1804. Right place, wrong time: this is the first time since *The Brides of Dracula* that the setting in a Hammer Dracula film is explicitly referred to as Transylvania, but we are at the opposite end of Stoker's century. The journey this time is undertaken by a Chinese pilgrim, who frightens away a shepherd with his outlandish appearance: yellow silk robe, long hair, fierce eyes. His lameness may contribute to the shepherd's terror, because of a widespread folk belief that when the Devil walked abroad in human form, he could only do so imperfectly, usually with

*"He study new tongues. He learn new social life; new environment
of old ways ... the habit of a new land and a new people..."*—Van Helsing

**Chan Shen (left) as Kah, and John Forbes-Robertson as Dracula in *The Legend of the
Seven Golden Vampires* (1974) (courtesy Ronald V. Borst of Hollywood Movie Posters)**

a limp (cf. Kevin Spacey in 1995's *The
Usual Suspects*). The stranger pauses to
smirk wickedly at a roadside shrine, like
one of those mentioned by Jonathan in
Chapter 1 of the novel, then continues
toward the castle, which is badly matted
into the distance.

At the castle, which he enters unmet
as Jonathan did in *Horror of Dracula*, the
pilgrim finds the crypt and the massive
sarcophagus which bears, not the single
name, but the single initial "D". As he
prostrates himself before the tomb, it
opens, and Count Dracula rises from it.
For the first and only time in the Hammer series, the Count is portrayed by
someone other than Christopher Lee; with
his red lipstick and prissily-sculpted eye-

brows, John Forbes-Robertson plays Dracula as a cartoon drag queen. He hinges up
from the heels as Max Schreck did in *Nosferatu*—and as Christopher Lee never did:
one of the subtle oddities about the Hammer series is that Lee's Dracula is *never*
seen rising from his coffin. (For example,
in *Dracula Has Risen from the Grave*, when
he is staked in his coffin, the camera is on
Paul and the priest when Dracula rises,
struggling with the stake. We then see him
stand up *beyond* the coffin, knocking it
over.) "Who dares to disturb the sanctity
of Dracula?" the Count demands. ("Sanctity"? The word means "holiness." Try
"sanctum" or maybe "sanctuary," and even
then be prepared to tread figuratively.)
The stranger identifies himself as Kah

(Chan Shen), "high priest of the Seven Golden Vampires ... in the province of Szechwan in China." Hard times: "The vampires sleep," so Kah's power over the local village has waned. He begs Count Dracula to "resurrect" them. All this is revealed to us via subtitles; Kah has no interpreter, but the Count evidently understands Mandarin! We are reminded of what Van Helsing said about the Count's "mighty brain," intimidated by "no branch of knowledge." There's no telling how many languages he's mastered, especially in a lifetime spanning centuries ... and with too much time on his hands, as we soon learn.

Dracula testily responds that he doesn't "accede to the requests of minions! Know you not Dracula commands, even from the confines of this miserable place?" He speaks as though he's in prison. "Confines"? Why is he confined? If his confinement has anything to do with the placement of the roadside shrine, then the connection is not made clear to us.

Suddenly an inspiration strikes the Count: "I need your mortal coil," he says to Kah (evidently he's been studying Shakespeare during his confinement as well). "I need to walk this earth again, free from these walls, free from this mausoleum!" In Kah's likeness, he will travel incognito to Szechwan and "recall the Seven Golden Vampires as my own host—tools of my vengeance on mankind!" Again, then, the Count is motivated by revenge, even more ill-defined than usual. It makes sense only in the folkloric light that one of the earliest religious impulses was fear of the dead, who were thought to be the *cause* of death, as envious revenge against the living.

Baring his fangs, Dracula drains off, not Kah's blood, but his very existence, "possessing" and indwelling his body. This metamorphosis may be interpreted as a type of shapeshifting, though not like anything found in either vampire folklore or in Stoker's novel; the magic of expedient screenwriting is what we're witnessing, and not for the first time. We do not know how the Count pulls this trick off, or how it will help him evade his mysterious confinement, but after the transformation, "Kah" has lost the limp, and he speaks English ... in Forbes-Robertson's badly-dubbed voice.

The scene shifts to Chung King, 1904, in another of the hundred-year leaps of which scripter Don Houghton seems to be fond. Professor Van Helsing (Peter Cushing's last hurrah in the role), lecturing the history faculty of Chung King University, tells a legendary tale of a remote village menaced by the Seven Golden Vampires. We see the tale unfold like a flashback: A farmer, attempting to rescue his daughter from the vampires, manages to kill one of them before being killed himself. The vampire is destroyed when he tries to retrieve a large, bat-shaped golden medallion, taken from him by the farmer, who had then placed it on another roadside shrine—this one, of course, adorned by a Buddha instead of a crucifix.

The vampires themselves are utterly unlike anything seen in a Hammer film before. They are a marauding equestrian band, silk-clad and wild-haired, wielding golden swords, wearing golden half-masks over corpse-like faces whose long, needle-like fangs protrude even when their mouths are closed. To Western eyes, they may take a bit of getting used to—even the accounts found in Summers do not prepare us for anything quite so exotic—but the latex false faces in particular are simply laughable.

The bat medallions worn by the vampires deserve comment. In China, the bat traditionally does not have the sinister reputation attached to it by Westerners, but is instead a symbol of good fortune and long life. The "vampirization" of bats

"... even ... in China..."—Van Helsing

Peter Cushing as Van Helsing in *The Legend of the Seven Golden Vampires* **(1974)**
(courtesy Ronald V. Borst of Hollywood Movie Posters)

for the sake of this movie (vampire bats being unknown in the Far East, or indeed anywhere outside of the Americas) may be a self-conscious sign of the plan to market this film abroad. It may also reflect the extent to which Western pop culture, including vampire movies and their mythos, have influenced similar images in the East.

Professor Van Helsing (we never learn his first name; is he Abraham, Lawrence, or someone else?) concludes his lecture by stating his belief that the legend is true. His audience react with skepticism and hostility, notwithstanding Van Helsing's own well-known "confrontation" with Count Dracula in Transylvania.

Now, wait a minute. If Dracula took Kah's identity in 1804 and departed for China immediately (as we are led to believe), how could Van Helsing have encountered him in Transylvania, presumably in the late 19th or early 20th century? Houghton's script, in addition to being incompatible with the "1872" episode in *Dracula A.D. 1972*, now even contradicts itself. There is simply no way to reconcile this difficulty. (Possibly the "1804" title was intended to read "1894", but we can only respond to what finally ended up on the screen.)

Van Helsing is approached that evening by Hsi Ching (David Chiang), an intense young man who sat in at the lecture. Hsi claims to be the grandson of the farmer in the tale Van Helsing told. He adds that the village of Ping Kwei, hunting ground of the vampires, is his own ancestral home, and is still under the vampires' sway. As evidence, he produces the golden bat medallion the vampires had been unable to recover. Hsi asks Van Helsing to join him and his brothers in an expedition to Ping Kwei to rid the village of the remaining vampires. When we learn that Hsi has six brothers, it suddenly becomes clear that we are watching another remake of *The Seven Samurai* (1954). Whereas, in Kurosawa's classic, the village wise man tells the villagers to seek out the warriors, here the village warriors seek out the wise man.

Van Helsing is willing to join such an enterprise, but neither he nor the Hsi brothers have the means to finance it. Fortunately, Van Helsing's adult son Leyland (Robin Stewart) has met a rich young Scandinavian widow named Vanessa Buren (Julie Ege). Adventuresome and independent, she offers to finance the expedition on the condition, of course, that she be included. Van Helsing protests, but to no avail. In any case, since both Vanessa and Leyland have gotten sideways with a local Tong lord who has his eye on the young woman and her wealth, it's a good time for everyone to get out of town.

They are no sooner underway than they are waylaid by the crook and his goon squad outside of town. In a typically frenzied kung-fu battle scene, the seven brothers—and their kid sister—defeat the gang, using a cross-section of the Chinese fighting arts: one brother fights empty-handed; another uses a bow; a third wields a pair of battle axes; a fourth uses a short spear; a fifth fights with a spiked mace, and the remaining two, twins, wield a sword apiece and tend to double-team their opponents. Little sister makes use of two petite, lady-like short swords, while the younger Van Helsing prefers a six-gun. He and kid sister are developing a crush on each other, just as Hsi and Vanessa are experiencing a mutual attraction.

That evening, around a campfire, Van Helsing delivers the usual recitation of the ways of combating what they're up against. Vampires, he tells the others,

"abhor anything that has a holy significance.... In Europe, the vampire walks in dread of the crucifix, but here it will be the image of the Lord Buddha." How to destroy them? A stake through the heart— or better still, a silver shaft. What about fire? "Not in Europe," Van Helsing tells them, although he is uncertain what to expect of the Asian variety of vampire. This statement is not only at odds with folklore, it also contradicts what Van Helsing himself has said before—in *The Brides of Dracula*, for example. (The peculiar notion that vampires are impervious to fire is found in at least one other Hammer film: Tudor Gates makes this same mistake in the screenplay of 1970s *Lust for a Vampire*, one of the Carmilla series.)

On a desolate, windswept plain, Van Helsing, in the grip of precognitive *deja vu*, announces that they are nearing the accursed village and the lair of the vampires. "Well," Vanessa says, "as long as they don't come out to meet us." This line is an odd paraphrase of a title card in the original *Nosferatu*, referring to Jonathan's entrance into the last leg of his journey to Dracula's castle: "And when he had crossed the bridge, the phantoms came to meet him." In the 1922 film, Dracula shortly arrives, driving his carriage; here, the vampires attack the party that night, in a cave where they have taken shelter.

The attack is mounted by three of the remaining six vampires, who arrive in the form of bats and are accompanied by a small army of skull-faced minions. Van Helsing identifies the latter as the vampires' "victims—the undead—their slaves throughout the ages." Since the only victims we've seen (in cutaway scenes to the interior of the temple of Kah/Dracula) are screaming young women, we are led to assume that the shapeless, sack-clad bodies and fleshless faces of the undead horde are those of former women. In any case, all three of the vampires are killed. Two are done in because of Van Helsing's advice to strike at their hearts; the third is destroyed by Van Helsing himself, with a torch. These vampires burn, which makes one wonder why Houghton troubled himself to include the erroneous earlier statement about the alleged fireproof qualities of European vampires.

Soon the expedition arrives at the village of Ping Kwei. One wonders why they're bothering to defend it, since it seems deserted already; a few villagers pitch in to assist with fortifications — trenches for burning oil; barricades of wooden and bamboo stakes — but there's nothing like a triumphal entry for our heroes. When the final attack comes, the vampires and an army of corpses swooping down from their nearby pagoda, it's a disaster for the home team: five of the brothers are killed, along with Vanessa. One of the vampires bites her throat; within minutes, she's sprouting fangs of her own. If vampirism is a disease, then this strain incubates as quickly as the Black Death. However, "In China," Summers continues, "this [i.e., contagion] does not appear to be a feature of the Vampire manifestation." We may infer that it is included here, as is the vampires' association with and transformation into bats, for the sake of audiences familiar with these Western elements. When Hsi Ching learns that Vanessa has become a vampire, he carries out the unpleasant task of impaling her on a bamboo stake — onto which he then throws himself in despair. (Pity, too, since the battle is still raging and the others need him. Bad time to be a fool for a blonde, even if she's the only one in the Far East.)

Several of the villagers join in the fray, joylessly hacking away at the marauders with their farm implements. When two of the vampires have been destroyed, the third grabs kid sister, throws her across his horse's withers, and heads for the pagoda. The two surviving brothers and the Van Helsings pursue them, Leyland in the lead; he frees the girl and is in a grappling match with the vampire when the professor runs a spear through the monster's heart from behind.

Relieved and exhausted, the younger people leave ... but Van Helsing knows there is unfinished business. He comes face to unfamiliar face with Kah, whom he nonetheless somehow recognizes as Dracula. Van Helsing taunts the Count, daring him to show his true face, and the Count does so, metamorphosing back into himself. After a fight which rages for second after second, Dracula lunges at Van Helsing — straight onto another spear. (Five hundred years old! *How?*) The Count decomposes yet again, via special effects which are made no less repellent by their cheesiness. The end credits roll across the pagoda, accompanied by an uptempo arrangement of James Bernard's theme for *Horror of Dracula!*

The Legend of the Seven Golden Vampires (88 minutes; available on video, but beware a cut-to-shreds 72-minute version retitled *The Seven Brothers Meet Dracula*, the form in which this film was finally released in the U.S. in 1979) lingers in memory as a blur of red and gold, of blue and yellow. It is fast-paced, action-packed, colorful junk, and with all its inconsistencies and errors (and its totally unnecessary inclusion of Dracula), it fulfills all the requirements of a retelling of the heroic-quest saga, even if it is a preposterous one. Director Roy Ward Baker has made an enjoyably bad movie, as opposed to the oppressive, wretched badness of *Scars of Dracula*. The film closes the Hammer Dracula series almost as amusingly as *Abbott and Costello Meet Frankenstein* closed the Universal series, though in a different way, and with a much higher body count. (While its blend of martial arts and supernatural horror is unique to the Hammer series, and—prior to *Buffy the Vampire Slayer*—unusual in the West by any standard, Hong Kong's action-oriented cinema is no stranger to outings like this one.)

In commenting on *The Legend of the Seven Golden Vampires*, the words of several other critics come to mind, who may not have been referring to this movie as they wrote, but who might as well have been. "Movies are so rarely great art," Pauline Kael writes, "that if we cannot appreciate great trash we have very little reason to be interested in them." A "flick," Joe Bob Briggs reminds us, can be anything but boring. And *Leonard Maltin's Movie & Video Guide*, referring to Hammer's last Frankenstein movie (1974's delicately-titled *Frankenstein and the Monster from Hell*, also starring Peter Cushing in his final outing in another role he made his own, the Baron Frankenstein), describes it as "amusing if you catch it in the right frame of mind." One can only assume that the reference is to some stage of intoxication. The same recommendation could be applied to *The Legend of the Seven Golden Vampires*.

To recap: The Hammer Dracula series, like the Universal series, can be subdivided into phases. *The Brides of Dracula*, while the immediate sequel to *Horror of Dracula*, features Van Helsing but not the Count, and differs from the original in terms of the supernatural powers available to vampires. The next three sequels (*Dracula, Prince of Darkness*; *Dracula Has Risen from the Grave*; and *Taste the Blood of Dracula*) are Christopher Lee vehicles which continue in the Victorian setting and make ever more tenuous attempts to pick up where the previous entry left off. *Scars of Dracula*, easily the worst of the entire series, is a failed attempt to start all over again with a pseudo-remake of *Horror of Dracula*. The next two (*Dracula A.D. 1972* and *The Satanic Rites of Dracula*) reunite

Lee and Cushing as Dracula and Van Helsing, but in a modern-day setting. And the series ends with *The Legend of the Seven Golden Vampires*, another period-piece saga of the further adventures of Van Helsing, in which Dracula's appearance is gratuitous and could have been dispensed with (*should* have been, in fact, since John Forbes-Robertson's Dracula is no match for Lee's).

Christopher Lee appears as Dracula in every film of the series which includes the character except for the last one. Peter Cushing is the only Professor Van Helsing. Including *Horror of Dracula*, Terence Fisher directed the first three films of the series; the next two were helmed by Freddie Francis and Peter Sasdy; Alan Gibson directed the two modern-day entries; and Roy Ward Baker directed the two films immediately before and after Gibson's. James Bernard's music, mostly variations on the same themes, scores every movie of the series except the two modern-day films. Jimmy Sangster wrote the first three films (though with some rewriting by other hands on *The Brides of Dracula*, and under the pseudonym "John Sansom" on *Dracula, Prince of Darkness*); Anthony Hinds, as "John Elder," wrote the next three; and Don Houghton wrote the final three.

The Legend of the Seven Golden Vampires was one of the very last Hammer films. Another from Hammer's declining years, *To the Devil a Daughter* (1976), attempted to cash in on the rash of *The Exorcist* (1973) rip-offs that were currently popular, but is mainly memorable as the film debut of a 14-year-old Nastassja Kinski. As the Gothics petered out, Christopher Lee went on to appear in a large number of films, ranging in quality from *The Three/Four Musketeers* (1974, 1975) to *The Howling II: Your Sister Is a Werewolf* (1985). He remains active today, the last of the Hammer regulars.

Shortly after the demise of Hammer,

Peter Cushing (laboring under what can be referred to as "the curse of the character actor": major roles in minor films, and minor roles in major) made an important if supporting appearance in the movie that was to change Hollywood forever. In the role for which most "mainstream" audiences are likely to remember him best, he was Grand Moff Tarkin, commander of the Death Star, in *Star Wars* (1977). "And, to our bitter grief," Mina Harker writes of the death of Quincey Morris in what is also a perfect epitaph for Mr. Cushing, "… he died, a gallant gentleman," in 1994.

From the early 1930s to the mid-1970s, then, between the Universal and Hammer series, there always (except for a ten-year gap between 1948 and 1958) was a Dracula franchise at work somewhere. Since Stoker's novel had long since been in the public domain (in fact, because of a paperwork oversight, it never actually was under copyright protection in the U.S.), endless numbers of remakes, rip-offs, and parodies about or including the Count were filmed as well.

For the most part, these movies are beyond the scope of this book. However, in the next section, we'll examine a number of ways in which surprising bits and pieces of Stoker's story still surface on the screen now and then.

IV. Shadows of Stoker

A mentally and emotionally disturbed man, convinced he is becoming a vampire, snatches up and eats a cockroach in his kitchen. Later, he captures a pigeon and devours it raw.

An out-of-control ship, which turns out to be unmanned, slams into the dock of a port city. A canine (or lupine) form leaps to shore … and transforms into a man.

A mortal is invited—or compelled—to lap blood from a cut in the breast of a vampire.

Scenes from one or more adaptations of *Dracula*, right? Depictions of Renfield's mental deterioration, Dracula's arrival in England, and Mina's seduction and assault at the hands of the Count, no?

No.

The first is a description of some of the bizarre behavior of yuppie book editor Peter Loew (Nicolas Cage) in the jet-black comedy *Vampire's Kiss* (1989).

The second describes the grand entrance into New York City made by Maximillian, the Caribbean vampire prince played by Eddie Murphy in *Vampire in Brooklyn* (1994).

The third is an incident in a 1998 flashback episode of the TV series *Buffy the Vampire Slayer* which details how Angel (David Boreanaz) became a vampire two hundred years earlier.

Clearly, in addition to the films either based directly on Stoker's novel, or "based on characters created by Bram Stoker," there are movies and TV shows that borrow more than just their general vampiric themes from *Dracula*, even mining Stoker's story for useful or dramatic details. The following is a further detailing of three of the most striking examples.

Jonathan

(1970)

Also known as *Jonathan Vampire Sterben Nicht* (which means, oddly, *Jonathan the Undying Vampire*), this West German film, written and directed by Hans W. Geissendorfer, is, according to the opening credits, "Zitate ,,DRACULA" von Bram Stoker." While several scenes are lifted from the novel, not enough of Stoker's plot survives for this film to be considered an adaptation.

We start with a protracted introduction in which the cruelties inflicted on the local populace by the vampire Count are detailed: a man leaps to his death rather than allow himself to be captured by the Count's thugs; another man is hunted down and shot; a woman is chased and killed by hounds. The Count (Paul Albert Krumm), wearing a familiar black cape with a stand-up collar and sporting a Hitleresque hairdo, shouts a warning to all who would defy him.

In a nearby town, a group of citizens plot an underground revolt against the vampires' reign of terror. The Count, the leader says, is planning a meeting of vampires at a nearby seaside castle. With all the vampires gathered in one place, the citizens will have the opportunity to attack the castle, kill the servants and the guards, free the prisoners in the dungeon, and drive the vampires into the sea, since "they cannot survive in the water." All the townspeople need is for someone to travel to the castle and reconnoiter the situation. And that's where Jonathan comes in.

Never identified as Harker (or by any other surname), Jonathan (Jurgen Jung) sets out on his journey in a coach. He carries a leather bag containing an assortment of vampire-killing tools: a dagger, a rosary, garlic, the book (of course), and a map to the Count's castle. He leaves behind a girl named Lina (cf. "Mina"), who is promptly attacked by the Count that night in her bedroom. After taking some of her blood, he opens his black raiment to reveal a ready-made gash in his chest, from which Lina then drinks. The Count's face registers obvious but not ecstatic pleasure, as though he's on the receiving end of oral gratification which is merely adequate. (At a viewing of this movie on the big screen, in 1980 or 1981, the audience laughed out loud at this scene. Maybe they were supposed to. This is one of those quirky European productions so different from standard American film fare that it's hard to tell if perceived humor is intentional.) While lifted from the novel, the scene here makes no sense and doesn't amount to anything: nothing has preceded it to set it up, and nothing results from it.

As Jonathan dozes in the coach, which is making its way through the woods, two bandits, operatives of the Count, hop on board. One kills the driver; the other steals Jonathan's bag. Jonathan wakes sometime later to discover that he is stranded, unarmed, alone, and lost. ("*Scheiss!*" he exclaims, as most of us would.) The thief takes Jonathan's bag to a remote hut, home of an idiot hunchback and a young woman, to whom he swaps the bag for some food and a change of clothes. "As we agreed," she says, evidently in on the plot to sabotage Jonathan's mission. Nor is this the first time she's been called upon to fence stolen goods of this nature: the interior of the hut is festooned with inverted crucifixes.

Soon, though, the girl has second

thoughts: she sets out to warn Jonathan, calling his name as she runs down the road. But she is stopped by a troupe of about a dozen little dancing girls, dressed in the palest lavender, who tie her to a tree. We've seen these girls off and on since the early scenes of the movie, striking poses over the bodies of fallen victims. They are apparently incipient members of the vampire cult, or of the Count's harem.

Traveling further into vampire country, Jonathan encounters more and more strange behavior. As he and a traveling companion (the thief, whose face Jonathan never saw, having slept through the highway robbery) try to enter a village, the locals stone them and drive them away. In an isolated house, they discover several mutilated bodies. A dead nun hangs by the neck from a tree as a giggling boy, the church bell-ringer, sets fire to a nearby stable. Jonathan, having killed his untrustworthy companion, arrives in the boy's village to find that all the surviving populace are crammed into a single room, where they watch with passive curiosity a couple copulating in a bed. (Interestingly, de Tournefort, in his account of the panic caused by the revenant on the island of Mykonos, recalls: "One saw entire families abandon their houses and come from the outlying areas of the town into the square, carrying their pallets, to pass the night there.")

Upon finally attaining the castle, it is Jonathan who scales the sheer outer wall, climbing up to break in a window, as opposed to the Count's climbing down the wall head-first. Within, the Count has assembled the red-robed cult and his three white-clad wives. Jonathan is promptly captured, but the Count greets him as a guest with a line from Stoker: "Welcome to my house." He gives Jonathan the run of the place, with certain reservations which are again in keeping with (and paraphrased from) the novel: "You may go anywhere you wish in the castle, except

"... I am noble; I am boyar; the common people know me and I am master."—Count Dracula

The Count (Paul Albert Krumm) in *Jonathan* (1970) (courtesy Ronald V. Borst of Hollywood Movie Posters)

where the doors are locked, where of course you will not wish to go. There is reason that all things are as they are, and did you see with my eyes and know with my knowledge, you would perhaps better understand."

Later, the three vampire women approach Jonathan as he lies in bed. The familiar scene unfolds as Stoker wrote it: the women observe Jonathan's youth and strength; they hanker for his kisses; the Count suddenly intervenes, rebuking them for daring to touch him, and claiming Jonathan is his; they accuse the Count of being unloving; he gives them a baby to feed on and shoos them away. The next morning, a woman appears outside the castle, screaming for the return of her child. The Count's black-clad goons drag her away, binding and gagging her as they go.

Meanwhile, the revolt of the townspeople is underway. They take to the roads and start streaming toward the castle, accompanied by the same inappropriately peppy music that scored the earlier rob-

*"... all that die from the preying of the Un-Dead become themselves Un-Dead,
and prey on their kind. And so the circle goes on ever-widening,
like the ripples from a stone thrown in the water."*—Van Helsing

Ritual gathering in *Jonathan* (1970) (courtesy Ronald V. Borst of Hollywood Movie Posters)

bery of Jonathan's coach. If Jonathan has somehow relayed intelligence to them, we haven't seen it happen.

Jonathan, in the castle, has troubles of his own. Infiltrating the dungeon, he tries to rally the prisoners, telling them the townspeople are on the way. But the Count catches him in the act. Furious that Jonathan has disobeyed his order about staying out of locked rooms (but evidently indifferent as to *why* Jonathan has done so), the Count has him beaten, imprisoned, and tortured. (One of the torturers stomps a dungeon rat to death in a scene that cannot possibly have been faked. The typical disclaimer about how no animals were harmed, etc., does not appear at the end of this film.)

The revolt soon arrives. The townspeople defeat the Count's black-clad thugs in a pitched gun battle; the sight lingers in memory of a weeping woman, sitting astride the chest of one of the downed enemy, repeatedly slapping his bloodied face. Some rebels enter the castle, freeing and arming the prisoners; others raid the hut, kill the hunchback, and grab all the crucifixes. With these, the people successfully complete the plan, driving the vampires along the shoreline and into the (uncinematically placid) sea, where they quickly and painfully die. The people, with Jonathan bringing up the rear, slowly walk away along the beach, leaving the vampires' half-submerged bodies behind like flotsam after a shipwreck.

Jonathan (97 minutes; difficult to find on video, but available) is often interpreted as an allegory about fascism. In fact, there seems very little allegorical about it. These vampires are organized, powerful, and oppressive; the people tire of them and overthrow them. The Count could be any oppressor from Hitler to Batista to Ceausescu to George III. The sight of the mob, crosses and crucifixes in hand, driving the vampires to their death, brings to mind, if anything, the triumph of Solidarity, a Catholic workers' party, over Communism. What is of interest to us here is the inclusion of several scenes from Stoker, as they suit Geissendorfer's purposes, and much removed from their original context.

The film itself is, overall, fairly standard Eurofare, with its unhurried pace, its enigmatic characters, its brooding atmosphere, its odd music (by Roland Kovac, plus bits by Edvard Grieg), its plot sometimes just shy of coherence ... and its occasionally striking images, served up by Robert Muller's fluid camera work. The choreographed little girls, the hunchback cackling and rocking back and forth as he taps a suspended (and inverted) crucifix with a spoon, the unfortunate rat, the color scheme for the Count and his entourage (black for him, white for his three wives, red for the rest of the cult)—images that stay in the mind's eye.

━━━━━◆━━━━━

Count Yorga, Vampire

(1970)

Count Yorga, Vampire would have gotten its makers sued had it been filmed while Stoker's novel was under copyright protection. The basic plot is familiar: a vampire nobleman from Eastern Europe leaves his ancient homeland, infiltrates a modern city of the West, sets up housekeeping in a large old home, mingles socially with the locals (be it ever so non-Stoker), vampirizes one young woman, and sets his sights on a second before being destroyed by a group of reluctant vampire hunters.

The particulars grafted onto this general framework vary from the original to greater or lesser extents: Count Yorga is from Bulgaria, a Balkan neighbor of Romania; the city he chooses is Los Angeles. Jonathan's trip to the Count's castle is omitted this time, as we see Count Yorga arriving, as Dracula does, by ship. There are no blood-and-thunder theatrics: no

storm, no shipwreck, no panicked seamen as are found in the novel (and at the beginning of the later Langella version, which also starts with the Count's arrival). A dock worker uses a fork lift to load Count Yorga's coffin (with the Count presumably inside, since it is daylight) into the bed of a red pickup truck, which matter-of-factly plies the heavily-trafficked freeways en route to the Count's new home. Evil has arrived, in plain sight, unheralded and unannounced, and right under our noses ... but nobody notices.

A sinister voice-over immediately clues us in to the powers and problems of vampirism, ironically speaking in the past tense, even as we see a vampire arriving in the present day. Vampires could see in the dark; their powers of hypnosis were formidable; they were immortal. They "could not die by the mere passing of time"; therefore, their "cunning was the growth of ages." These quotes from the intro are paraphrased from Stoker's novel, so once again there is no mistaking the original source of inspiration. The stake and sunlight are the only two means listed to kill a vampire.

Strangely, we first see Count Yorga (Robert Quarry) making the acquaintance of his neighbors, not by a trip to the symphony, but at a seance he is conducting! While there may be some question as to whether the Count would make use of such a capability at a dinner party, Stoker tells us, in Van Helsing's words, that "he have still all the aids of necromancy, which is, as his etymology imply, the divination by the dead...." The ostensible aim of this seance is to contact the spirit of the recently-deceased mother of Donna, one of the young women present. As we later learn, Donna's mother, who *dated* Count Yorga, died three weeks earlier of pernicious anemia!

Despite the giggling self-consciousness of some of the participants, enough of a contact with the spirit world is made to throw Donna into a fit of hysteria. The Count calms her down with a dose of hypnotism blended with telepathy, giving her a post-hypnotic command only she can hear: "You will do everything I say, whenever and from wherever I say it." He is inside her head now, as Dracula is when he says to Mina in the novel: "When my brain says 'Come!' to you, you shall cross land or sea to do my bidding." Not until later does one of the men present remark how odd it was that the Count was able to hypnotize a hysterical person.

For the time being, Erica (Judith-Lang) simply observes Count Yorga's apparent difficulty to please as a dinner guest: he hasn't eaten or drunk anything. Van Helsing again: "Even friend Jonathan, who lived with him for weeks, did never see him to eat, never!"

Oddly, Donna (Donna Anders) does

"... the eyes fell full upon me, with all their blaze of basilisk horror ... and ... a grin of malice that would have held its own in the nethermost hell."—Jonathan Harker

Robert Quarry played the vampire in both *Count Yorga, Vampire* (1970) and *The Return of Count Yorga* (1971); this shot is from the latter (courtesy Ronald V. Borst of Hollywood Movie Posters)

not become the "Lucy" of the story. That fate is reserved for Erica, who, along with her boyfriend Paul (Michael Murphy), gives the Count a ride home from the dinner party. Count Yorga "lives" in a huge, Carfax-like estate, where he is attended by Brudah, a servant who can only unkindly be compared to Renfield; facially deformed, brutally strong, and evidently retarded, Brudah (Edward Walsh) lacks both Renfield's intellect and his tortured, conflicted soul.

As Paul and Erica leave via the only driveway, their van gets stuck in a huge mudhole that wasn't there only a few minutes earlier. The howling of coyotes, the New World substitute for the all-but-vanished wolf, gives the couple the willies. After the obligatory sex scene (what are vans for?), Count Yorga attacks: he knocks Paul unconscious, then victimizes Erica with a mouthful of "disappearing" fangs, a sharklike double row similar to those sported by Lon Chaney in *London After Midnight*.

In the morning, the mudhole is gone, a minor manifestation of the vampire's ability, per Van Helsing, "within his range, [to] direct the elements; the storm, the fog, the thunder...." Paul didn't get a look at his assailant, but remembers that "his grip was like a steel vise," echoing Jonathan's use of the words "grip of steel," and consistent with Van Helsing's warning that the Count "is of himself so strong in person as twenty men." Erica, who remembers nothing, has lost a lot of blood. Under the care of Dr. James Hayes (Roger Perry), she enters into the "Lucy syndrome": the symptoms of anemia; the marks on her throat; the transfusions. Left alone at home, she partially eats her kitten! Renfield, in the novel, asks Dr. Seward for a kitten. If there was ever any doubt as to what he had in mind for the animal, Erica clears the matter up.

Dr. Hayes is the equivalent of Dr. Seward assuming the mantle of Van Helsing with great reluctance and inadequate preparedness. His own mentor, this film's Van Helsing surrogate, is an unseen character named Dr. Steingart. Dr. Hayes tells Paul that Dr. Steingart, having run tests on a sample of Erica's blood, is convinced she was attacked by a vampire, but that he unfortunately had to leave for a two-month trip to Europe immediately after rendering this diagnosis. It sounds almost as if he has fled.

Meanwhile, Count Yorga relaxes at home with his expanding harem. On marble slabs next to a basement fireplace are stretched out two undead women: a red-head, who is a stranger to us, and a blonde —Donna's mother, it turns out. Count Yorga evidently wants to complete his collection—his version of Dracula's three wives—with raven-haired Erica.

He somehow turns up on the balcony of her bedroom. Since it is a night of the full moon, we are again reminded of Van Helsing's words: "He come on moonlight rays as elemental dust...." But there is no dust, no fog—and no bats. The makers of this film wisely follow Hammer's *Horror of Dracula* example by avoiding the use of special effects beyond the reach of their modest budget. Instead, Yorga simply and matter-of-factly appears, walking in out of the night at the upstairs French doors. After smothering Erica with messy, bloody kisses, he abducts her.

Paul sets out alone to Yorga's home to try to rescue Erica. Dr. Hayes and Michael, Donna's boyfriend, are unable to dissuade him. They agree that the police would be no help; once again, *a la* Stoker, the vampire finds strength in the advantage of modern unbelief. More than once, Dr. Hayes makes the call anyway, only to be told by the police that he is the "forty-seventh nut" to report a vampire on the loose in the city.

Many of the calls are prompted, evidently, by a newspaper story (described to Dr. Hayes by his bimbo girlfriend) which reports that the body of a baby has been discovered, totally drained of blood, its throat savaged. Here is another parallel with Stoker: Lucy's attacks on children are first made known to us in a newspaper story. (A still exists showing Donna's undead mother callously tossing the dead baby's body aside, as Lucy does in the novel with the child she brings to her tomb, but the scene is not in the final cut of the movie. It may have been deleted because of its excessive cold-bloodedness, but more likely the real reason for its deletion is that the "baby" is too obviously a doll.)

Dr. Hayes, Michael, and Donna go to Count Yorga's in the wee hours of the morning, hoping to keep him distracted with small talk while one of them slips away to look for Paul and Erica. The Count, surprised (but not *too* surprised) to see them, is nonetheless a gracious host, plying them with brandy which he does not drink himself. ("Do you drink at all?" Dr. Hayes asks. "No," the Count replies. It's a familiar situation.) The plan not only fails, but backfires: Dr. Hayes' questions—about the occult, about folklore, about werewolves and vampires—tip the Count off that these people know, or at least suspect, too much.

Dr. Hayes and Michael decide to return to Yorga's during the day to seek out Paul and Erica and to destroy Yorga. As Michael gets some sleep, Dr. Hayes goes about doing some research: this film's version of the all-important book of lore is titled *Vampire Ancestry*. Count Yorga, from inside his coffin, plays the ace up his sleeve, sending out a psychic call to Donna. She now manifests herself as this version's Mina: embodying Mina's fears, expressed in the novel, that the Count could force her to work in league with him, she rises, turns off Michael's alarm clock, and drives to Yorga's place. (Upon her arrival, Brudah further distances himself from Renfield: far from being the underling who rebels against the Count in an effort to save the girl, he sexually assaults her.)

Michael, of course, oversleeps, and Dr. Hayes nods off during his research; they both wake up in the late afternoon, too late to get to Count Yorga's place before dark. Like the Universal films of 1931, this movie lacks the budget for a chase all the way back to Eastern Europe (nor, this time, is the vampire in enough trouble to make such a flight necessary), so the vampire hunters only pursue him as far as his home. This being New-Age, post-Christian California, the sort of milieu where

necromancy is looked upon as a party game, they have to *make* improvised crosses out of broken sticks and twine. Upon arrival, they split up: as Michael searches the house, Dr. Hayes, stake in hand, makes increasingly awkward small talk with the Count. Dr. Hayes suffers the same fate as Jonathan Harker in the Jack Palance version of *Dracula* (filmed several years *after* this movie): the three vampire women, now including Erica, get him.

Michael, on his own, finds Donna and encounters the vampires. He stakes Donna's mother with a length of broken broomstick, of which he snaps off a piece for later use. It shortly comes in handy: Count Yorga, who attacks in a full-tilt run like a charging predator, runs onto the stake and is destroyed. ("They don't live that long by being fools," Dr. Hayes had earlier warned. Again, one wonders.) Michael and Donna evade Erica and the red-headed stranger, but—in an ending almost identical to that of *The Fearless Vampire Killers* of just a few years earlier—Michael learns too late that there are still *three* vampire women afoot in Yorga's home.

Count Yorga, Vampire (91 minutes; available on video) is a striking example of what can (or could, in 1970) be done on a small budget, even with such a familiar plot. The movie benefits from the presence of Robert Quarry as Count Yorga, who smoothly blends Lugosi's menacing urbanity with Stoker's original vision of the Count as an arrogant nobleman *and* a take-no-prisoners predator.

Most of the other performances are simply adequate, but none are embarrassingly bad. This comes as surprising good news, considering the film's apparent "family" origins: Michael is played by Michael Macready, who also produced; the voice-over at the beginning (and, briefly, the end) is provided by George Macready; and Erica Macready has a tiny part as a nurse. (In addition, there is the more significant role named Erica, and the film was made by Erica Productions.) The eponymous nature of the roles of Michael and Donna add to the "vanity piece" appearance of the movie. These backyard projects often yield dreadful results (1959's *The Giant Gila Monster* and *The Killer Shrews*, financed by Gordon McLendon of Texas, who owned a chain of radio stations and—surprise!—drive-in theaters, come to mind). This time we got lucky.

Credit must go to Bob Kelljan, who wrote and directed, for reworking selected elements of Stoker's plot intelligently, and for directing in a low-key manner, in such a way as not to struggle with or strain the film's low budget (a problem Jess Franco was having with *El Conde Dracula* at about this same time). The film's atmosphere is greatly enhanced by William Marx's moody, violin-laden score.

Kelljan also co-scripted and directed the 1971 sequel, *The Return of Count Yorga* (an obvious title choice, but at least it's a title and not a number). Robert Quarry reprises the role of Count Yorga in the follow-up (97 minutes; available on video); no explanation is given for his return, which is as inexplicable as that of John Carradine's Dracula in the Universal series. Edward Walsh returns as Brudah, also despite his apparent death in the first movie.

In contrast to Dracula's having taken up residence next door to an asylum, Count Yorga moves in near a San Francisco orphanage. In a nod to earlier adaptations of the novel, if not directly to Stoker, Yorga laps the blood from the cut finger of Mariette Hartley (most of whose career has been in TV roles): "An old Bulgarian cure," he calls it. Whereas Hammer's Dracula belatedly mastered Mandarin, Count Yorga demonstrates a knowledge of sign language! "When you've lived as long as I," he explains, "you

gather a bit of knowledge along the way." His comings and goings are still a mystery: when Hartley asks him how he managed to make it to the orphanage's fundraiser despite the collapse of the area's only bridge, his laconic reply is, "I flew." Count Yorga commands a harem of, not three, but at least a half-dozen women, frightwigged and cheap-fanged, who attack as a pack; they carry out a home-invasion massacre which must have been especially harrowing to audiences at the time of this film's release, just a few years after the Manson killings.

Roger Perry, who played the ill-fated Dr. Hayes in the first film, returns as a "different" (in name only) character. A young(ish) Craig T. Nelson (billed without the middle initial) appears as a cop, as does Rudy De Luca, Mel Brooks' co-scripter for *Dracula: Dead and Loving It*. Once again, there are Macreadys on both sides of the camera: Michael Macready co-produces, and George Macready is a useless, one-scene Van Helsing surrogate, Professor Reichstat (played as a Timothy Leary-esque '60s burnout case!). "Bill" Marx (as he is listed this time) again provides the musical score.

Robert Quarry played a similar vampiric role, Khorda, in *The Deathmaster* (1972), which suffers from the look of low-budget cheapness avoided by the *Count Yorga* films. It also makes the same mistake Hammer was making at the same time with *Dracula A.D. 1972*: the vampire is injected into trendy "youth culture," becoming a guru to a hippie commune! Bob Kelljan had nothing to do with this turkey, but he directed something else as awkwardly timely: *Scream, Blacula, Scream!* (1973), the second and last installment of a series blending vampirism with the blaxploitation movies of the early '70s. At the time *Count Yorga, Vampire* and its sequel were released, Hammer was starting to remake (and spoof) its own remakes. (The

"If ever a face meant death—if looks could kill—
we saw it at that moment."—John Seward

Robert Quarry as Count Yorga in *The Return of Count Yorga* (1971)
(courtesy Ronald V. Borst of Hollywood Movie Posters)

*"I knew ... the bright hard eyes, the
white teeth, the ruddy colour, the
voluptuous lips."*—Van Helsing

**Donna's belated mother in *Count Yorga,
Vampire* (1970) (courtesy Ronald V. Borst
of Hollywood Movie Posters)**

makers of the *Count Yorga* films indicate
their awareness of, if not their exact attitude toward, the Hammer films of the pe-

riod by showing the Count, in the sequel,
watching a late-night TV screening of the
1970 Hammer effort, *The Vampire Lovers*—
dubbed into Spanish!) George Romero's
Night of the Living Dead (1968) had already begun to transform the modern horror film into something more visceral, and
much less romantic, than what had gone
before. (Herschell Gordon Lewis' "gore"
movies of the '60s—which, like Romero's
film, had played almost exclusively at
drive-in theaters—had generated legendary notoriety, but had not attracted the
critical attention and acclaim Romero's
opus did.) Tobe Hooper's *The Texas
Chainsaw Massacre* (1974) was lurking just
around the corner to continue that transformation, which would bypass the stylish
minimalism of John Carpenter's *Halloween* (1978) in favor of the splatter-punk
approach of the *Friday the 13th* series, beginning in 1980. In the midst of changes
made, changes in the making, and changes
soon to come, Kelljan and the Macready
clan demonstrated that, with a return to
the basics of Bram Stoker's plot, and of
simple, straightforward, no-nonsense sto-
rytelling and filmmaking, an elegant
Gothic jewel of a movie could still be cut
and polished.

Nadja

(1994)

Nadja is a remake of *Dracula's Daughter* on acid. Its overall plot generally follows that of the 1936 film, so there is
enough detectable Stoker here to invite
comment ... slightly more Stoker than in
the earlier movie, what with the presence,
not only of Van Helsing, but of Renfield
and an imperiled young Lucy as well.

Nadja (Elina Löwensohn) is, in fact,

Dracula's daughter, reimagined this time
as a twentyish Goth chick, haunting
Manhattan's all-night bars and java huts,
cruising for victims while doing things the
undead don't usually do: chain-smoking,
swilling coffee and booze, and talking
endlessly and rather tiresomely about herself. She tells her latest pickup that her father is "a real bastard," but that "he looks

*"Here was my own pet lunatic—the most pronounced of his type
I had ever met with—talking elemental philosophy, and with the
manner of a polished gentleman."*—John Seward

Elina Löwensohn as Nadja and Karl Geary as Renfield in *Nadja* (1994) (Photofest)

after me"—i.e., he sends her money, "family money. From Romania." A short while later, in the midst of her bloody attack on the man, she has a premonitory flash: "My father is dead."

Jim (Martin Donovan) soon receives word from his wife Lucy (the improbably-named Galaxy Craze) that his eccentric uncle is in trouble again, this time arrested for murder. Jim's uncle is none other than Van Helsing, played (by Peter Fonda, of all people!) as a babbling, wild-haired, suited-and-tied, bicycle-riding, homeless conspiracy nut whose nutty theories happen to be true (if not in every particular). The murder rap, to which Van Helsing has confessed, arises, of course, from his having staked Count Dracula—about a hundred years later than Stoker tells it, and thousands of miles away. "It didn't make sense," Lucy says of the news, "but it didn't sound too surprising either. You know how he gets." Jim bails Van Helsing out of jail and subsequently has his ear bent by him for awhile. One gets the impression this sort of thing has been going on for years.

Nadja, accompanied by her taciturn young manservant—whose name, we later learn, is Renfield (Karl Geary); she refers to him matter-of-factly as her "slave"—turns up at the morgue, wearing a hooded cape reminiscent of Gloria Holden's. She announces to the startled officer at the desk (David Lynch, who executive produced), "We have come for the body of Count Voivoda Arminius Ceausescu Drakula."

What *is* in a name? First, there is politics: a voivode, as noted earlier, is a warrior prince, ruler of an entire principality (e.g., Wallachia), and therefore of considerably greater rank than a count, ruler of a mere county, the basic unit of local government that survives to this day. It's not inconceivable—not uncommon, in fact—for a single ruler to have held more than one position at a time in this manner;

whether he would be announced by more than just the highest-ranking one was a matter of variable custom. Arminius (Latin for "Herman") is a reference to Stoker's Hungarian correspondent Arminius Vambery, alluded to by Van Helsing in the novel as "my friend Arminius, of Buda-Pesth University." Finally, what an interesting touch to link Dracula explicitly to Nicolae Ceausescu, Romania's last Communist dictator! Nadja earlier says of the Dracula family's fortune that "it comes from the suffering and exploitation of the poor," a succinct description of Ceausescu's brutal domestic economic policies.

We see the policeman's eyes glazing over with the onset of an hypnotic spell as Nadja informs him that she has not come to identify the body, but to take it. Meanwhile, Van Helsing warns Jim that, since Dracula is undead, "If they don't destroy his body correctly, he'll be back." Nadja's burning of the Count's body is handled symbolically this time, with a shot of one of those firework pellets that sends out a snaky rope of black ashes when ignited; in this context, this common pyrotechnic toy takes on an eerie beauty. We learn that the actual cremation has been accomplished when Nadja turns up later with an urn which she says contains Dracula's ashes. (Happily, nobody named Alucard shows up to bleed into them.)

In a scene strongly reminiscent of the comparable one in *Dracula's Daughter*, Nadja sits chatting with Renfield while absently playing a piano. Now that the Count has been destroyed, she sees new possibilities for herself: "I want to change my life," she says. "It's not that easy," Renfield replies. "Shut up. Things *will* be different. He's gone. I'm free," she says. "Sure you are," Renfield says, unconvinced. "I'll find someone," Nadja answers defiantly.

Find someone she does. At a bar, she meets Lucy. As they strike up a conversation, Nadja explains she is on her way to

Brooklyn to meet her brother Edgar, and is worried about the encounter because she knows Edgar hates her. Nadja ends up going home with Lucy, seducing her in a scene that is far more explicit in its lesbian content than the one involving the Countess and Lili in *Dracula's Daughter*. Both women come away with problems: Lucy is subject to trancelike states and massive menstrual hemorrhaging, and Nadja fancies herself to be in love. "Why do you say that?" Renfield asks. "I feel terrible," she moans.

Van Helsing, meanwhile, tells Jim that over the last four hundred years, Dracula has spawned "countless bastard children," almost all of them "idiots—insane—monsters—deformed—the walking dead!" These creatures, he says, have infiltrated every major city, where they blend in with the population. But, he continues, two hundred years ago, the Count fell in love with a simple peasant girl who inspired him to try to change his evil ways. She died giving birth to twins, a son and a daughter, and the embittered Count returned to his destructive habits.

In the flashback scenes that illustrate this narrative (and in briefly-seen glimpses of Dracula being staked), the Count is also played, mostly in silhouette, by Peter Fonda. But in brief close-ups of his face, he is none other than Bela Lugosi, still typecast nearly forty years after his death! The image is not from *Dracula*, but from *White Zombie*, in which Lugosi's character, Murder Legendre, has a mustache, in keeping with Stoker's description of the Count.

Van Helsing lists for Jim the supernatural powers of vampires. They can see in the dark, they can "exert their will on weaker minds," they can "penetrate solid matter, pass through any window, any door, cracks in the wall, mirrors...." The vampire's ability to walk through walls and slip through cracks is in keeping both with Stoker and with certain folklores. The idea of a mirror as a "dimension doorway," as in Lewis Carroll's *Through the Looking-Glass*, lends itself occasionally to effective cinematic use, e.g. in *Vampire Circus* (1971). This concept may have its roots in ambiguous feelings toward mirrors and our own mirror images. One of the reasons it was thought to be bad luck to break a mirror is that a mirror was believed to "remember" everything it had "seen," and that breaking it would release all these images onto the world—including our own, in the form of a doppelganger. Lucy's haunting glimpse of Nadja's image in a bathroom mirror is a beloved horror-movie cliche. Oddly, though Nadja evidently doesn't cast a reflection, she can be photographed ... as can the phenomenon of her non-reflection.

"The door was open," Nadja tells Cassandra, Edgar's nurse, who knows better, and who is startled by the sudden appearance of Nadja and Renfield in Edgar's home. Edgar is dying. Nadja says she can cure him with special "plasma supplements" (made from Mexican shark embryos!) of which she has a large supply in her own home, and which she herself takes. She is apparently lying, either about the existence of these supplements, or about their efficacy: we've not only seen her prey on a man for blood, but as soon as Cassandra leaves the room, Nadja perks up Edgar (Jared Harris) with a taste of her own. Edgar, who is in love with Cassandra (Suzy Amis), clearly hates and fears Nadja, but she uses her stronger mental power to rob Edgar temporarily of the ability to speak English in Cassandra's presence. She then tells him the news of the death of their father, whom Edgar also hated.

Everyone in the story, in fact, has family issues centered around his or her father. Lucy and her father were alienated over a religious matter (her brother also committed suicide). Jim's father, as it happens, wasn't really his father; he learns this belated bit of news from Van Helsing, who was in a position to know. When Nadja tells Cassandra that her father was a "cruel and distant man," Cassandra says that her father was the same. (In view of the rueful fatherlessness that hovers over everyone in the film, it's ironic that in the end credits, the director thanks David Edelstein for "additional dialogue" from something called "Blaming Mom.") At the same time, Nadja tells Edgar that she has come to realize that "family is all that really matters. What else is there?" What, indeed? Fatherless or not, almost everybody in the story is somehow related, by blood (one way or another), by marriage, or simply by choice.

Cassandra, in turns out, is Jim's sister, although Van Helsing ("Uncle Ben"), who makes this revelation as well, then claims she is not who she seems: vampires are "shapeshifters," he explains, who can "take on the form of the people you love." (He has, by this time, also killed a tarantula in Jim and Lucy's apartment, convinced it was sent by the "forces" out to get him. In fact, it was Lucy's pet.)

As Nadja and Renfield relocate Edgar and Cassandra to Nadja's place, Nadja explains why she keeps it so gloomy: "My father was a night bird. I am the same. I find comfort in the shadows. I'm no good in the day. We have an allergy to sunlight—my whole family." While there is a hint of paraphrased Stoker in her use of the words "comfort in the shadows," there is a more direct allusion here to the words of Count von Krolock (Ferdy Mayne) in *The Fearless Vampire Killers*, who says, "I'm a night bird. I am not much good in the daytime."

Lucy, in one of her trances, goes to Nadja's home. "She's an apprentice in the realm of shadows," Van Helsing announces, as he and Jim follow her. Imme-

diately upon their arrival, Van Helsing tries to stake Renfield, who vanishes. It is unclear whether Renfield is a vampire or another "apprentice," but this is one of several times we see him defy time and space. Nadja describes him as "the last one [prior to Lucy] that I decided to keep," at which point the situation starts to remind one of the Catherine Deneuve/David Bowie/ Susan Sarandon triangle in *The Hunger* (1983).

The subsequent effort of Jim and Van Helsing to secure Lucy's release from Nadja's power results in a dreamlike chase through the streets; Cassandra, at Edgar's urging, also flees, hiding in a garage. After attacking a pair of mechanics, Nadja is shot and wounded by police. She nonetheless manages to abduct Cassandra and flee via plane to Transylvania. Cassandra thus, in addition to paralleling abductee Janet in *Dracula's Daughter*, also becomes the story's "Mina" figure (the second woman imperiled), as Lucy is, of course, this film's "Lucy" (never fully vampirized, but under Nadja's lingering influence nonetheless). Edgar, now recovered, learns Nadja's whereabouts from Nadja herself via "psychic fax." This means of remotely tracking the vampire parallels Mina's psychic link to the Count in the novel. Nadja, Edgar reveals, has lost a lot of blood and is "dying ... for a cigarette."

Van Helsing, Edgar, Jim, and Lucy set out for Transylvania in the usual manner of low-budget movies: a map that fills the screen tells us of both their destination and their arrival. The old country isn't as isolated from the West as it used to be: a roadside fire is no longer a pile of timbers, but blazes in a 55-gallon oil drum (petroleum is Romania's chief mineral resource); a child frolics past wearing Mickey Mouse ears, as if to welcome the expedition to the *real* Magic Kingdom.

As the vampire-hunting party close in on the castle, Renfield prepares to hold them off, not with a bow and arrow as Sandor tried, but with a rifle. Nadja arranges for a blood transfusion between herself and Cassandra, evidently to compensate for her lost blood. Cassandra, resisting, knocks off Nadja's wig, revealing her to be as shaven-headed as Count Orlok. (Or as Sinead O'Connor, annoying pop thrush, who is afforded "respects" in the film's closing credits. So is Sheridan LeFanu, for obviously more substantial reasons.)

When the vampire-hunting party arrive, Jim and Lucy take on Renfield, while Edgar and Van Helsing stake Nadja. Afterward, Renfield commits suicide, throwing himself onto a spike as Hsi Ching did in *The Legend of the Seven Golden Vampires*.

"They cut off my head—burned my body," Nadja herself says in a voice-over. Cassandra and Edgar are married—a pairing Nadja refers to as "we." Apparently the transfusion was of Nadja's blood into Cassandra, not the other way around, and it means that she isn't totally dead yet. By the incestuous act of marrying her own brother, she keeps what Edgar has referred to as "the curse of this fucked-up family" within the family itself … that is, the family resulting from the merger, in this wedding, of the Dracula and Van Helsing clans, a union prefigured by Fonda's having played both the loopy Professor and the shadowy Count.

Nadja (92 minutes; available on video) demonstrates how the basics of a well-known mythology can be workably woven into a contemporary story. The film's otherworldly atmosphere is reinforced by Simon Fisher Turner's music, which is complemented by songs from such bands as My Bloody Valentine and Space Hog. (The soundtrack CD is from Gyroscope, GYR 6617-2.) Beautifully (and appropriately) shot in black and white, with lengthy scenes shot with a toy Pixel-Vision camera adding to its low-budget surreal-

ism, the film will seem too self-consciously "arty" for many audience members. But even on those terms, *Nadja* works, mainly because writer-director Michael Almereyda doesn't make the mistake of taking things too seriously. While hardly a comedy, the film is marked by deadpan absurdist humor, most of it in the dialogue. At one point, Lucy, in a trance, says, "Today I had a bag of M&M's. But I didn't eat the yellow ones." "Face it, Jim," Van Helsing comments, "she's a zombie."

Peter Fonda's casting as Van Helsing comes as a surprise; given the budget restraints of the film, he must have done it as a labor of love. But he doesn't overwhelm the rest of the cast, especially not Elina Löwensohn, who, in the title role, owns the movie. Löwensohn's dark, soulful eyes successfully hint at the great age, the tremendous sadness, *and* the dangerous narcissism lurking behind Nadja's youthful appearance.

By now it has been established that Stoker's novel, as a popular literary entertainment, has staying power. A century in print is no mean feat, especially for a work that, until rather recently, had little or no academic backing, no "respectability" of the sort afforded to any number of other 19th-century novels. The people who still read *Dracula*, in the numerous paperback editions made possible by the novel's public-domain status, do so because they want to, not because some college prof has assigned it. There wasn't a Cliff's Notes edition available until 1983. Even today, more often than not, when colleges and universities discuss *Dracula*, the focus is less likely to be on its limited literary merits than on various psychological or sociological readings of it: what it reveals about Victorian sexual attitudes, or about Bram Stoker's relationship to Henry Irving, or what-have-you. The novel is also often examined in terms of its persistence as a

"… though you and I have seen some strange things together, you may at the first think that I, Van Helsing, am mad…"—Van Helsing

Peter Fonda as Dr. Van Helsing in *Nadja* (1994) (Photofest)

pop-culture phenomenon, and its effects on other aspects of popular culture. Like the movies.

As we have seen, Stoker's novel, in whole or in part, continues to inspire both straightforward adaptations to film, and filmic borrowings of bits and pieces. To be sure, after more than seventy-five years, these bits and pieces of Stoker are often filtered through earlier adaptations. Jonathan Harker, for example, cuts himself in the novel while shaving, and the blood excites the Count. This incident becomes Harker/Hutter's cut thumb in *Nosferatu* and Renfield's pricked finger in Lugosi's *Dracula*, surfacing as a young woman's glass-cut finger in *The Return of Count Yorga*. Van Helsing's assertion that the Count's "power ceases, as does that of all evil things, at the coming of the day," be-

comes death-by-daylight in the 1922 *Nosferatu*, after which it is axiomatic that (in the formulaic words of Universal's *House of* films) "a single ray of sunlight falling upon a vampire would destroy him."

But, despite the inevitable distortions wrought by years of retelling, Stoker's novel continues to be the ultimate source —the "fountainhead," to use Hammer's term—of these borrowings, which have even started to spill over into non-vampire films. (Two 1997 releases—*The Relic* and *The Lost World: Jurassic Park*—used the motif of the unmanned ship arriving in port bringing a monstrously dangerous cargo.) As is the case with adaptations of the whole of Stoker's novel, there is little reason to believe that these cinematic cribbings of bits and pieces will be ending anytime soon. Like its title character, *Dracula* is a shapeshifter, capable of slipping through narrow cracks, and is likely to surprise us by turning up anywhere, in almost any movie. To put it another way, Stoker's most famous novel, unlike his most famous character, casts a long shadow indeed.

That shadow forms in the flickering light of the modern storyteller's campfire: the movies. The 1998 feature film *The X Files* contains a sequence in which Mulder descends below the Antarctic ice to rescue Scully from the alien stronghold, similar to the rescue of Newt by Ripley in *Aliens* (1986). The derivation actually was much older: it is yet another variation on the myth of Orpheus and Eurydice. The movies are the campfire where we gather in the dark to hear the same tales retold again and again, because the stories reflect on the same themes repeatedly: the mysteries of life and death, good and evil, order and chaos, sex and blood. The story of Bram Stoker's undead prince addresses all these themes, and so is sure to be with us as long as audiences wonder about these matters—not only in its printed form, but translated into whatever fantastic images the movies can conjure up.

And a darkened movie theater will remain a perfect home for Dracula, since, as we have seen, he is more powerful in the dark.

Appendix:
Sources for Video and Audio

Most of the videos described as available for rental can be found at a well-stocked Blockbuster, though bear in mind that the Universal horrors may wind up in the "Classics" section instead of "Horror." For the later, more obscure Hammers, a larger, more comprehensive video store, likely a locally-owned operation, would be a better bet.

For the truly obscure entries, the Internet may be the place to go to find a mail-order house. Rare copies of *Nosferatu in Venice* and *Jonathan*, for example, can be found on the Web. Try these outlets. (Given the ever-changing face of site and e-mail addresses, should the information given be outdated, try a search on http://www.yahoo.com.)

Video Wasteland
214 Fair Street
Berea, OH 44017
1 (440) 891-1920
wasteland@slaughter.net
http://slaughter.net/wasteland

Video Search of Miami
P.O. Box 16-1917
Miami, FL 33116
1 (888) 279-9773
email@vsom.com
http://www.vsom.com

Trash Palace
P.O. Box 2565
Silver Spring, MD 20915
1 (301) 681-4625
trashpal@erols.com
http://trashpalace.com

As for the soundtrack CDs, again, the more common releases (*Bram Stoker's Dracula*, Frank Langella's version, etc.) are pretty easy to come by. Start (and probably finish) by looking in the music section of a large bookstore. For the more obscure or imported items (e.g. the 1979 *Nosferatu*), try CD Now (www.cdnow.com), or the CD section of Amazon, the on-line bookstore (www.amazon.com). The Hammer selections, the 1922 *Nosferatu*, and some of the others referred to as being on Silva Screen CDs can be obtained from this U.S. outlet:

Silva Screen Records America Inc.
Suite 910, 1600 Broadway
New York City, NY 10019
1 (212) 757-1616
1 (206) 943-4427 (catalog information)

Bibliography

Anonymous. "The Mysterious Stranger." In *A Feast of Blood*, Charles Collins, ed. New York: Avon Books, 1967.

Barber, Paul. *Vampires, Burial, and Death: Folklore and Reality*. New Haven and London: Yale University Press, 1988.

Bloch, Robert. "The Clown at Midnite." In *Famous Monsters of Filmland Strike Back!*, Forrest J Ackerman, ed. New York: Paperback Library, 1965.

Briggs, Joe Bob (aka John Bloom). *Joe Bob Goes to the Drive-In*. New York: Delacorte Press, 1987.

Bunson, Matthew. *The Vampire Encyclopedia*. New York: Crown Publishers, Inc., 1993.

Cushing, Peter. *Peter Cushing: An Autobiography*. London: Weidenfeld and Nicolson, 1986.

Deane, Hamilton, and John L. Balderston. *Dracula, the Vampire Play*. 1927. Garden City, NY: Nelson Doubleday, 1971.

Durrell, Lawrence. "Vampire in Venice," excerpted from *Balthazar*. In *A Clutch of Vampires*, Raymond T. McNally, ed. Greenwich, Conn.: New York Graphic Society, 1974.

Florescu, Radu, and Raymond T. McNally. *Dracula: A Biography of Vlad the Impaler, 1431-1476*. New York: Hawthorn Books, Inc., 1973.

_____. *Dracula, Prince of Many Faces: His Life and Times*. Boston: Little, Brown and Company, 1989.

Halliwell, Leslie. *The Dead That Walk: Dracula, Frankenstein, the Mummy, and Other Movie Monsters*. New York: Continuum Publishing Co., 1988.

Hauge, Michael. *Writing Screenplays That Sell*. New York: McGraw-Hill, 1988.

Hogan, David J. *Dark Romance: Sex and Death in the Horror Film*. Wellingborough, England: Equation Books, 1988.

Hurwood, Bernhardt J. *The Monstrous Undead*. New York: Lancer Books, 1969.

Jones, Stephen. *The Illustrated Vampire Movie Guide*. London: Titan Books, 1993.

Kaye, Marvin, ed. *Dracula, the Definitive Edition*, by Bram Stoker. New York: Barnes and Noble Books, 1996.

Kish, Ken. *Video Wasteland Video Review and Reference Guide #5*. Berea, OH: Video Wasteland, 1997.

Kuttner, Henry. "The Graveyard Rats." In *The Unspeakable People*, Peter Haining, ed. New York: Popular Library, 1969.

Landau, Diana, ed. *Bram Stoker's Dracula: The Film and the Legend*. New York City: Newmarket Press, 1992.

LeFanu, J. Sheridan. *Carmilla*. 1872. In *Vampires: Two Centuries of Great Vampire Stories*, Alan Ryan, ed. Garden City, NY: Doubleday & Company, Inc., 1987.

Lucas, Tim. "The Black Stare of Soledad Miranda," *European Trash Cinema*, reproduced in the FrancoFile on the Web. http://members.aol.com/timothyp2/francofolder/francofile.html.

Maltin, Leonard, ed. *Leonard Maltin's 1996 Movie and Video Guide*. New York: Penguin Books, 1996.

McNally, Raymond T., ed. *A Clutch of Vampires*. Greenwich, Conn.: New York Graphic Society, 1974.

_____. *Dracula Was a Woman: In Search of the Blood Countess of Transylvania*. New York: McGraw-Hill, 1983.

Moore, Darrell. *The Best, Worst, and Most Unusual: Horror Films*. New York: Beekman House, 1983.

Noll, Richard, ed. *Vampires, Werewolves, and Demons: Twentieth Century Reports in the Psychiatric Literature*. New York: Brunner/Mazel, 1992.

Ozkaracalar, Kaya. "*Drakula Istanbul'da*: Little-Known Aspects of a Forgotten Movie." From http://www.dark-waters.com.

Parish, James Robert, and Michael R. Pitts. "Christopher Lee," *Cinefantastique*, Fall 1973, 4-23.

Pirie, David. *The Vampire Cinema*. New York: Crescent Books, 1977.

Prawer, S. S. *Caligari's Children: The Film as Tale of Terror*. Oxford: Oxford University Press, 1980.

Rigby, Jonathan, ed. "Re: Lee Classic Quotes," *Shivers*, February 1998, 23.

Riley, Philip J., ed. *Dracula: The Original 1931 Shooting Script*. Atlantic City and Hollywood: Magic Image Filmbooks, 1990.

Silver, Alain, and James Ursini. *The Vampire Film: From Nosferatu to Bram Stoker's Dracula*. 2nd ed. New York: Limelight Editions, 1994.

Skal, David J. *Hollywood Gothic: The Tangled Web of Dracula from Novel to Stage to Screen*. New York: W. W. Norton & Co., 1990.

_____. *The Monster Show: A Cultural History of Horror*. New York: Penguin Books, 1993.

Stoker, Bram. *Dracula*. 1897. New York: Modern Library, 1932.

Summers, Montague. *The Vampire: His Kith and Kin*. 1928. New Hyde Park, NY: University Books, 1960.

_____. *The Vampire in Europe*. 1929. New Hyde Park, NY: University Books, 1961.

_____. *The Werewolf*. 1933. New York: Bell Publishing Co., 1966.

Wolf, Leonard. *The Annotated Dracula*. New York: Clarkson N. Potter, 1975.

_____. *A Dream of Dracula: In Search of the Living Dead*. Boston and Toronto: Little, Brown and Company, 1972.

Wright, Bruce Lanier. *Nightwalkers: Gothic Horror Movies: The Modern Era*. Dallas: Taylor Publishing Co., 1995.

Wright, Dudley. *The Book of Vampires*. 1924. New York: Causeway Books, 1973.

Ziegler, Philip. *The Black Death*. New York: Harper & Row, 1969.

Index

Bold numbers refer to illustrations, including captions.